USE OF LIBRARY MATERIALS

BOOKS IN

LIBRARY AND INFORMATION SCIENCE

A Series of Monographs and Textbooks

EDITOR

ALLEN KENT

Director, Office of Communications Programs
University of Pittsburgh
Pittsburgh, Pennsylvania

Vol. 1 Classified Library of Congress Subject Headings, Volume 1—Classified List, *edited by James G. Williams, Martha L. Manheimer, and Jay E. Daily, (out of print)*

Vol. 2 Classified Library of Congress Subject Headings, Volume 2—Alphabetic List, *edited by James G. Williams, Martha L. Manheimer, and Jay E. Daily*

Vol. 3 Organizing Nonprint Materials, *by Jay E. Daily*

Vol. 4 Computer-Based Chemical Information, *edited by Edward McC. Arnett and Allen Kent*

Vol. 5 Style Manual: A Guide for the Preparation of Reports and Dissertations, *by Martha L. Manheimer*

Vol. 6 The Anatomy of Censorship, *by Jay E. Daily*

Vol. 7 Information Science: Search for Identity, *edited by Anthony Debons*

Vol. 8 Resource Sharing in Libraries: Why • How • When • Next Action Steps, *edited by Allen Kent*

Vol. 9 Reading the Russian Language: A Guide for Librarians and Other Professionals, *by Rosalind Kent*

Vol. 10 Statewide Computing Systems: Coordinating Academic Computer Planning, *edited by Charles Mosmann*

Vol. 11 Using the Chemical Literature: A Practical Guide, *by Henry M. Woodburn*

Vol. 12 Cataloging and Classification: A Workbook, *by Martha L. Manheimer*

Vol. 13 Multi-media Indexes, Lists, and Review Sources: A Bibliographic Guide, *by Thomas L. Hart, Mary Alice Hunt, and Blanche Woolls*

Vol. 14 Document Retrieval Systems: Factors Affecting Search Time, *by K. Leon Montgomery*

Vol. 15 Library Automation Systems, *by Stephen R. Salmon*

Vol. 16 Black Literature Resources: Analysis and Organization, *by Doris H. Clack*

Vol. 17 Copyright—Information Technology—Public Policy: Part I—Copyright—Public Policies, Part II—Public Policies—Information Technology, *by Nicholas Henry*

Vol. 18 Crisis in Copyright, *by William Z. Nasri*

Vol. 19 Mental Health Information Systems: Design and Implementation, *by David J. Kupfer, Michael S. Levine, and John A. Nelson*

Vol. 20 Handbook of Library Regulations, *by Marcy Murphy and Claude J. Johns, Jr.*

Vol. 21 Library Resource Sharing, *by Allen Kent and Thomas J. Galvin*

Vol. 22 Computers in Newspaper Publishing: User-Oriented Systems, *by Dineh Moghdam*

Vol. 23 The On-Line Revolution in Libraries, *edited by Allen Kent and Thomas J. Galvin*

Vol. 24 The Library as a Learning Service Center, *by Patrick R. Penland and Aleyamma Mathai*

Vol. 25 Using the Mathematical Literature: A Practical Guide, *by Barbara Kirsch Schaefer*

Vol. 26 Use of Library Materials: The University of Pittsburgh Study, *by Allen Kent et al.*

Additional volumes in preparation

USE OF LIBRARY MATERIALS

The University of Pittsburgh Study

Allen Kent
Jacob Cohen
K. Leon Montgomery
James G. Williams
Stephen Bulick
Roger R. Flynn
William N. Sabor
Una Mansfield

MARCEL DEKKER, INC. New York • Basel

Library of Congress Cataloging in Publication Data
Main entry under title:

Use of library materials.

(Books in library and information science ; v. 26)
Includes index.
1. Libraries, University and college--Administration.
2. Libraries, University and college--Use studies.
3. Library cooperation. I. Kent, Allen. II. Pittsburgh. University. III. Series.
Z675.U5U83 025.1 79-11513
ISBN 0-8247-6807-8

Based on research on "A Cost Benefit Model of Some Critical Library Operations in Terms of Use of Materials," supported in part by the National Science Foundation, Grant DSI-75-11840.

MARCEL DEKKER, INC.
270 Madison Avenue, New York, New York 10016

Current printing (last digit):
10 9 8 7 6 5 4 3 2 1

PRINTED IN THE UNITED STATES OF AMERICA

CONTRIBUTORS*

Principal Investigator

ALLEN KENT, Distinguished Service Professor of Information Science; author of Chapter I, co-author of Chapters VI and VII.

Director of Economic Studies

JACOB COHEN, Ph. D., Professor of Economics and Finance; author of Chapters IV and V, co-author of Chapter VI.

Project Manager

K. LEON MONTGOMERY, Ph. D., Interdisciplinary Department of Information Science; co-author of Chapter VII.

Consultants

JAMES G. WILLIAMS, Ph. D., Interdisciplinary Department of Information Science; co-author of Chapters VI and VII.

DONALD L. SHIREY, Ph. D., Department of Educational Research; statistical consultant.

Research Associates

STEPHEN BULICK (currently with Bell Telephone Laboratories, Murray Hill, New Jersey); co-author of Chapter II.

ROGER R. FLYNN, Ph. D., Interdisciplinary Department of Information Science; author of Chapter III and Appendix; co-author of Chapter II.

WILLIAM N. SABOR (currently coordinator of Information Systems Planning); co-author of Chapter II.

UNA MANSFIELD, report editor.

Research Assistants

JAMES R. KERN, Graduate Assistant, Department of Economics; co-author of a section of Chapter IV.

LIGIGAYA J. ANGELES, Graduate Assistant, Department of Economics.

MICHAEL MILLER, Graduate Assistant, Department of Economics.

*All participants are from The University of Pittsburgh, Pittsburgh, Pennsylvania

PREFACE

The plan of this study is to deal with an intractable problem—"the library problem"—one that may turn out to be unsolvable but which nevertheless must be confronted.

Let me start with an observation that colleges and universities are not terribly successful in preparing their students for the future. This is simply because they do not know the future, and predict it only by extrapolating from trends. This approach is fraught with risks and we are currently living with the consequences of this way of predicting the future. But perhaps higher education is faced with an unsolvable problem—in attempting to find a better way to predict futures.

The topic of this study is a derivative of the intractable, or unsolvable, problems of higher education. Libraries buy mostly for future needs. But the judgments of librarians as to those future needs are no better than those of the presidents. Let us examine why librarians have such a difficult time in guessing what future requirements will be.

Their task is to select from the world's information store those materials that will be useful and <u>used</u>. These must be selected from great quantities of materials that are available. Thus:

- There have been 30 million unique titles published since Gutenberg —how many libraries have anything more than 5% of these? I guess some have less than 1/2%.
- There are 50 - 100 thousand journals published worldwide—how many libraries subscribe to more than 10 - 15%? Some subscribe to less than 1/2%.
- About 500 thousand books will be published worldwide in 1978—how many libraries will buy more than 10 - 15%? Some will buy less than 1/2%.

Given this situation, it is like finding a needle in a haystack to pick the "right" materials that will be <u>both useful and used</u>. Since the needle is not frequently found, presidents, chancellors, provosts, deans and librarians sometimes are confronted by students and faculty who demand a better acquisitions budget to try to relieve their frustrations.

The question that arises is whether more money for materials alone can relieve these frustrations. It has been my hypothesis that the answer is "No" and that more money may lead to the acquisition of materials that are seldom if ever used.

And so a study was designed to develop measures for determining the extent to which library materials are used and the full cost of such use. It was our expectation that much of the material purchased for a research library was little or never used, and that the costs entailed are beyond ordinary expectations. This expectation has been substantially supported by the study's findings. But the results are not useful in planning future purchases unless some decision rules are provided in this regard. And so a first step toward a decision model has been made in this study. As results of the study may be tested in various environments, it is hoped that "the library problem" may be better understood, and may become more tractable.

The academic research library has many functions, including symbolic, inspirational and museum functions; this study has been concerned with only one aspect of the library's function, the provision of book use. This makes it less of a cost-benefit study than one emphasizing, simply, the cost of materials' use. The ultimate purpose of the study can be stated in terms of a simple equation: $X - Y = Z$, where X represents the in-house costs of furnishing library services (book use), Y the comparative costs of resource sharing, and Z the difference, which is expected to be positive and will thus measure the saving from resource sharing. Whether or not this saving is worth the sacrifice of on-shelf convenience is a matter for each departmental faculty to decide. The interest of this study is solely in measurement. The study represents one step in this direction—the measurement of X. In future work we hope to get a better idea of the value of Y.

As is typical with projects which require the collection and analysis of enormous quantities of data, difficult choices had to be made in deciding what to include and what to omit in a final report. It is expected that omissions will be covered in reports and papers long after the project is completed. Two examples are the dissertations of Stephen Bulick and Alexander Strasser. In the latter dissertation an attempt is made to distinguish between "the use of library materials" and "the total use of published materials by the University population" (in Physics). Also, this study stimulates further data collection projects; some attempt has been made to consider these new data to check our results, but could only be referenced in footnotes as the deadline for publication of this book approached.

There was a continuing problem of obtaining agreement as to precise baseline data. For example, our original figures for acquisition of books and monographs led to "official" figures being issued, which suggested a slightly lower number acquired, to take into account books that had disappeared since acquisition. So, late in the game, in order to present a conservative picture, we re-analyzed our data painstakingly. But as the results of the journal study emerged, it became clear that quarrels about baseline data would be un-ending, so we retained our original figures and merely noted the disagreements in footnotes. These disagreements (coming from the same library system but from different sources) highlight the need for a library to use single, agreed-upon sources of data. This indeed became the policy in the library system under study.

It is perhaps for this reason—the study's concern with the "use" function—that certain tensions arose as the early results of the study were disseminated. One example is the statement by an articulate faculty member that the study should not be done. When questioned whether he found the methodology unsound, he replied "No"—he only feared that the results would be used to cut library budgets. As is obvious from the results presented herein, the study proceeded, with the hope that the objective data would be used appropriately with no emotions interfering with good decision processes.

As this report was being "put to bed" many excellent suggestions emerged for further analyses of data; but most of these were cut off mercilessly, lest the report never emerge. And so, this report must be considered as only a "first edition".

It should be noted that all of our original objectives were not met. An attempt has been made to note these cases in the appropriate sections of the report. On the other hand, new objectives emerged during the study, which have been addressed.

ALLEN KENT
Principal Investigator

Pittsburgh, Pennsylvania
January, 1979

ACKNOWLEDGMENTS

The authors wish to acknowledge the contributions of the following University of Pittsburgh personnel:

Glenora Rossell, Director of Libraries, and her staff—including Oxanna Kaufmann, Sally Rowley, Florence McKenna, Frank Slater, James Moon, Homer Bernhardt, Paul Kobulnicky, Drynda Johnston and Ronald Schuetz—whose assistance in facilitating data collection and in reviewing this report is much appreciated;

Robert Neumann, Assistant to the Director of Libraries, who contributed in a special way by furnishing the underlying data for the analysis of cost;

Graduate students Nina Mills, Alex Strasser, Boaz Lazinger, John Griffiths, Thomas Kutz, A. Bogage and L. Picciano, who collected the data;

Priscilla Mercier, whose assistance in the administrative area kept the project smoothly on course;

Una Mansfield, for the compilation, editing and production of the final report which led to this book;

Karen Schirra, for the composition of this book.

We wish to acknowledge the help of the following reviewers whose comments on the draft of this report were most helpful and have been incorporated in the final document:

Yale M. Braunstein, Richard De Gennaro, Glyn T. Evans, Miriam A. Drake, Robert W. Frase, Donald W. King, James E. Rush and Alice Wilcox.

Finally, we wish to acknowledge the support of the National Science Foundation, Division of Science Information (now Division of Information Science and Technology) which made this study possible, and the encouragement of Helene Ebenfield, Project Officer.

CONTENTS

Contributors iii

Preface v

Acknowledgments ix

Chapter I BACKGROUND OF THE STUDY 1

Allen Kent

A. Objective of the Study 1
B. Rationale for the Study 1
C. Locus of the Study 5
D. Dimensions of the Study 5
E. The Study as Part of an Ongoing Research Program 7

Chapter II CIRCULATION AND IN-HOUSE USE OF BOOKS 9

Stephen Bulick, William N. Sabor, and Roger R. Flynn

A. Summary of Findings 9
B. Data Collection -- Books and Monographs 11
C. Discussion of Findings 12
  1. Use of Unique Items 12
  2. Frequency of Use 38
  3. Alternative Classifications of Use 42
  4. Sampling Algorithms 43
D. Some Practical Applications of Findings 48
  1. Weeding 48
  2. Storage 51

Chapter III USE OF JOURNALS 57

Roger R. Flynn

A. Summary of Findings 57
B. Purpose of and Approach to Journals Study 59
  1. The Purpose of the Study 59
  2. The Approach to the Study 60

C. Discussion of Findings 65
1. Number of Uses 65
2. Usage by Title 67
3. Usage by Age 77
4. Usage by Alert Method 78
5. Photocopying of Journals 82
6. Usage by Academic Status 86
7. Alert Method as a Function of Status 93
8. Usage by Department 95
9. Observations Missed When Recording Data on Forms 99
10. Sampling of Engineering Library During Summer Months 100

Chapter IV THE ECONOMICS OF MATERIALS' USE 105

Jacob Cohen

A. On Measuring Costs 105
B. Measuring the Cost of Book Use 107
1. Combining Cost and Book Use Data 107
2. Inter-Year Comparisons 115
3. Allowing for Inflation 115
C. Measuring the Cost of Journal Use 116
1. Subscription Costs 116
2. Other Costs 123
D. Towards a Library Decision Model for Book Purchase 126
1. Introduction 126
2. The Underlying Data 126
3. Decision Variables 127
4. Risk in Ordering Books on the Basis of Their LC Classification 134
5. Risk in Ordering Books on a Cost Center Basis 136
6. Analysis by LC Subclasses 137

Chapter V A COST BENEFIT MODEL OF LIBRARY OPERATIONS 161

Jacob Cohen

A. The Ubiquitous Economist 161
B. The Economic Model 162
C. Optimality of Library Operations Over Time 166

D. Benefits from Book Use 170
1. Measuring Benefits 170
2. The Question of Substitutability 171
E. The Economies of Increasing Book Use 172
F. Measuring Cost-Benefit Over Time 173
1. Description of Data in Matrices A and AA 174
2. Matrices B and BB 177
3. Matrices C and CC 179
4. Matrices D and DD 180
5. Analysis of Results 182
6. Standardizing the Data for Student Enrollment 185

Chapter VI ALTERNATIVES TO LOCAL QUESTIONS 189

Allen Kent, James G. Williams, and Jacob Cohen

A. The Move Towards Resource Sharing 189
B. The Goals of Resource Sharing 193
C. Classification of Resource Sharing 194
D. Unanswered Questions 195
E. Minimizing Book Cost by Resource Sharing 196

Chapter VII THE PATH AHEAD 199

Allen Kent, K. Leon Montgomery and James G. Williams

A. The Implications of the Present Study 199
1. Implications for the University of Pittsburgh 199
2. Implications for the Library and Information Science Field 200
3. Implications for Publishers 202
4. Implications for Further Research 203

APPENDIX 207

Roger Flynn

Part 1 Technical Data-Journals Study 209
Part 2 Applying the Methodology to Journal Use Studies Elsewhere 247
Part 3 The Management and "Marketing" of the Journal Collection 265

Index 269

Chapter I

BACKGROUND OF THE STUDY

Allen Kent

A. Objective of the Study

Initiated in 1975 under a grant from the National Science Foundation, Division of Science Information, the overall objective—as stated in the proposal for the study—was

> "to develop measures for determining the extent to which library materials (books/monographs and journals) are used, and the full cost of such use"

This was to be achieved through an intensive longitudinal study of the use of materials in one large, multipurpose university library. In this way a foundation would be provided for: (1) the improvement of acquisitions decisions; (2) determination of the point when materials should be purged from the collection or placed in low-cost, remote storage facilities; and (3) assessment of the critical points at which alternatives to local ownership are economically feasible. The aim, in short, was to develop a cost benefit model of some critical library operations in terms of use of materials.

B. Rationale for the Study

University research libraries, as we have come to know them over the past 100 years, may face revolutionary changes. A revolution in the scope, nature and structure of these organizations may be necessary if they are to serve as reasonably effective instruments of scholarship. The areas of knowledge pursued in universities, and the universities themselves, are subject to constant change. Their survival may hinge, in part, upon their ability to achieve and maintain some sort of sensitive and flexible balance among the ever-shifting academic interests which characterize their campuses. To the service-oriented library administrator, the library needs of these pluralistic interests frequently appear to exert conflicting pressures upon library operation; but while the conflicts are readily apparent, a rational solution to these conflicts is much less obvious.

Many factors are currently contributing to a need for change, for example:

- insights resulting from a century of attention to specialized knowledge are demanding the development of a more interdisciplinary intelligence;
- university libraries are facing increasing demands to add to the services they contribute to the ever-growing educated community outside their campuses, at a time when the financial resources of the universities are more limited than they have been for decades;
- budgets for libraries are generally being kept level or are decreasing, therefore improvements in service must come from increases in productivity;
- the increase in cost of library materials continues to reduce the "real" purchasing power of the budget;
- declining enrollments in colleges and universities and consequent loss of funds aggravate the effect of inflation;
- the increase in cost of new library buildings discourages the use of prime space for materials storage;
- advances in technology heighten the probability that alternatives exist to the purchasing and possession of library materials.

For some time now, those responsible for the development of research library collections and the management of research library funds have understood in a general sense that a minority of titles accounts for a majority of uses, and that books and journals are subject to rapid rates of aging and obsolescence. In this period of growing demand for library services, of steady-state or declining acquisitions budgets, and of diminishing buying power, it becomes necessary to restate these understandings of pattern use of large library collections in a more forthright manner. The hard facts are that research libraries invest very substantial funds to purchase books and journals that are rarely, or never, called for, as well as equally large sums to construct and maintain buildings designed to make accessible quickly titles some substantial portion of which are no longer either useful to or sought by their clientele.

There is no objective way to forecast future needs, and consequently there is no objective way to make acquisition decisions with the certain knowledge that what is acquired will be used. Furthermore, there are no objective means for measuring benefit from materials use. The problem is exacerbated by the increasing quantity of materials available for acquisition which makes the selection process even more difficult. The librarian's problem leads to an inclination

- to increase continuously the quantity of material that is acquired;
- to have the materials close at hand; and
- to have complete "runs" of materials, particularly journals.

The tacit assumption is frequently made that these actions result in greater library quality and therefore greater benefit to patrons. The consequences of these actions have been: (1) increasing pressure for larger library budgets for augmentation of local collections, supported by extensive and growing unfulfilled "desiderata" files which are fed by requests from faculty, bibliographers and acquisitions librarians; (2) construction of new and larger library facilities as existing buildings become full; and (3) lack of emphasis on programs for retirement ("deacquisition") of older materials. It is difficult to deal with these inclinations, both because of insufficient funds and because of insufficient objective evidence of need. Measures of use or of collection "quality" frequently consist of counting of numbers of volumes held locally.

Responsible library management would seem to demand a major revision of library acquisitions policies in response to findings such as those by a number of investigators who have provided corroborating evidence to support and strengthen the conclusions of Fussler and Simon in 1969[1] regarding patterns of use of research library collections. Yet major shifts in philosophies of collection development have not occurred. In part, as De Gennaro observes in the February 1977 issue of _American Libraries_,[2] this is because old habits die hard:

> "Librarians have a weakness for journals and numbered series of all kinds. Once they get volume 1, number 1 of a series they are hooked until the end."

The question that frequently is not faced by librarians is whether books bought are _used_. Certainly books and other library materials acquired

---

1 Herman H. Fussler and Julian L. Simon, _Patterns in the Use of Books in Large Research Libraries_, The University of Chicago Press, Chicago, 1969.

2 Richard De Gennaro, "Escalating Journal Prices: Time to Fight Back," _American Libraries_, published by the American Library Association, February, 1977.

must have a use. Otherwise the arguments for bigger and better acquisitions budgets are suspect. This was the point of departure for the initial proposal for this study.[3]

> "As library funds become scarcer, and as opportunities for consortium and network relationships among libraries increase, it becomes increasingly important to develop and apply cost-effectiveness analysis techniques to library operations. One such area requiring special attention is acquisition of materials, particularly the more expensive science/technology materials. The chief measure of effectiveness of an acquisition program is use of the materials purchased; the same measure must be employed for storage as well, since the high cost of space must be justified in terms other than providing a permanent location to park materials.... As the attempt is made to improve management of the library, it becomes necessary to have better predictors of the use-outcome of purchases. Such predictors would have an effect on local as well as resource-sharing decisions."

In part, the failure up to now to modify acquisitions practices results from the fact that:

- only recently have networking and resource-sharing developed technologically to the point where they may offer a viable alternative to exclusive ownership;
- there has been a collective reluctance to accept the hard fact that the new depression in higher education is not a temporary fiscal indisposition but may be a long-term malady;
- the gross data available up to this point have been too global in character and too imprecise in nature to serve as an adequate basis for the reformulation of acquisitions policies.

In relation to the last point, it is not particularly useful for a bibliographer to know that 10% of all the titles (s)he selects will satisfy 90% of client demand for materials in a given discipline, unless (s)he can also be

---

3 Proposal to the National Science Foundation entitled "A Cost Benefit Model of Some Critical Library Operations in Terms of Use of Materials," submitted by the University of Pittsburgh, February 4, 1975.

told which 10%. It is useless to tell the acquisitions librarian that half the monographs ordered will never be used, unless you are also in a position to say which 50% to avoid buying. The simple fact is that the available data lack sufficient predictive power to enable the librarian to modify selection practices with assurance that the results will be more responsive to future needs of clients.

It is hoped that the results of this study will prove useful in the search for a solution to this problem.

C. Locus of the Study

The study centers on an examination of the use and cost of books/monographs and journals in the libraries of the University of Pittsburgh—a large, research-oriented, urban multiversity, with a student population on its main (Oakland) campus of 22,385 and a faculty of 2,153. The annual operating budget in 1976/77 exceeded \$188,000,000, of which approximately \$5,300,000 went to support its libraries: the Hillman Library, a central research library emphasizing the Humanities and Social Sciences; and a collection of some twenty school, departmental and divisional libraries, ranging in size from the 180,000-volume Falk Library of the Health Professions to the 4,500-volume Computer Science Library. Holdings university-wide in 1977 were estimated at 2,900,000 volumes, and current acquisitions for 1974/75 stood at 78,762 books and monographs (excluding microforms) and 16,740 serial subscriptions.

In 1968 a new research library was completed at a cost of \$12 million, with the prediction that in ten years it would be filled with some 1.5 million volumes. The author estimated that an investment in bookstock would reach \$45 million (hypothesized to be \$30 per volume, counting purchase price, processing cost, and proportionate cost of storage space), at which time another new building would have to be constructed. But the assumption was that another building would not be needed if it were possible to "turn over" the collection by retiring materials that are little or never used; or if correlation of collections with resource-sharing partners in a consortium or networking environment could be accomplished effectively. To make this possible, it is necessary to be able to measure the use of the collections and to develop a weeding/trading methodology based on quantitative use data.

D. Dimensions of the Study

This present study incorporates the complete record of substantially all book and monograph acquisitions and transactions made by the Hillman Library from October 1968 through the end of the calendar year 1975. In 1969 approximately 88% of the external patron charges were recorded through the automated circulation system. The remainder were charged manually. The percentage of automated circulation system charges increased so that by 1975 more than 95% were recorded via the automated circulation system. The existence of this file of transactions made possible a longitudinal study of collection use of unusual scope and dimension, as well as enabling the investigators to chart very precisely the effects of aging of materials on borrowing practices. The records of external loans have been supplemented by a study of in-house use (on a sampling basis). In-house use of journals has been studied on a sampling basis in the Physics Library, Langley Library for the Life Sciences (including Psychology), Bevier Engineering Library, the Chemistry Library, the Mathematics Library and the Computer Science Library.

Algorithms for using smaller samples have been investigated, so that similar measurements can be taken at other libraries and compared with the results of this investigation.

Several hypotheses were developed for the purpose of <u>initiating</u> the study:

(1) There exists a high positive correlation between the class areas of book titles that circulate and the class areas that are used in-house. This correlation approaches a 1 to 1 correspondence.

(2) A very small portion (perhaps 10%) of the library collection of book titles accounts for the major portion (80% or more) of the circulation and in-house use.

(3) There is a positive correlation between patron characteristics and the utilization of library materials and the various academic programs.

(4) At the 50,000 title level (the recommended size of an undergraduate collection), the collection would be used much more frequently than for the remainder of the collection.

(5) Approximately one-quarter of the collection would not be used in 10 years, and one-half of the collection would be used only once or not at all in a 10-year period.

As the study progressed, it became apparent that some of these hypotheses could not be tested in the way we had anticipated. This will become clear in the detailed report which follows.

The methodology used to collect, organize and analyze data is detailed throughout the report, in the sections describing the various elements of the study.

E. The Study as Part of an Ongoing Research Program

This study is one of several being conducted at the University of Pittsburgh that are related to library problems. One of these is the development of an experimental library resource-sharing network which attempts to take into account all functions which assure "full service." This study has spawned the development of a computer simulation which is expected to permit computation of equilibrium points between local and network functions in various library environments. WEBNET, the acronym for this activity, has been funded in part by a grant from the Buhl Foundation.

Chapter II

CIRCULATION AND IN-HOUSE USE OF BOOKS

Stephen Bulick, William N. Sabor and Roger Flynn

A. Summary of Findings

The following is a brief summary of the findings of the study dealing with the collection of books and monographs at Hillman Library; a more detailed description and explanation of each point is given in subsection "C" below.

External Circulations: When the complete circulation history of the 36,892 books and monographs acquired [1] by the Hillman Library in the calendar year 1969 was traced through the end of calendar year 1975, it was found that 39.8% or 14,697 of these 36,892 books and monographs had never circulated during the first six years on the library's shelves. Of the 22,172 items that did circulate one or more times during this period, 16,132—or 72.76%—were borrowed one or more times during the year of initial acquisition or the year immediately following. The six-year circulation history of all books and monographs added to the collection in the calendar year 1970 exhibited a similar pattern.

On the basis of these data, and by means of the standard statistical technique of asymptotic regression analysis, it was possible to begin developing a mathematical model to enable us to predict the number of previously uncirculated items which would circulate for the first time after five or six years of ownership, and to demonstrate the dramatic effect of "aging" on the patterns of use of books and monographs in a general university research library.

Frequency of Use: The full circulation history of every item was traced over the entire 86-month time span for which data were available. The study

---

[1] More than this number were actually acquired; the figure given here is the number that could be accounted for at the time of the study. In order to take a conservative approach in our calculations, we used the latter figure.

showed that a small portion of the collection contributes most of the use. An interesting by-product was the discovery that circulation for a given calendar year exhibits a log-normal distribution when graphed on a semi-log scale.

In-House and Interlibrary Loan: The study addressed the browsing function on the basis of 30-day samples of in-library use, and examination of the reserve book and interlibrary loan use over a maximum period of 86 months. The study showed that, by the end of the sample period, 75% of the titles used in-house had also circulated externally, and that an additional 4% circulated in the year following. Similarly, it was found that 99.6% of books loaned to other libraries by the Hillman Library also circulated to its own users during the study period, as did 98.1% of the titles housed in the reserve book room. This suggests that external circulation data can be utilized with a high level of confidence to measure total book use in terms of books used at least once, since the books that were used in-house, placed on reserve, or requested by other libraries on interlibrary loan were predominantly the same books that were circulated to Hillman Library users.

Sampling Algorithms: The study included the development and testing of sampling algorithms which could be applied to more limited data files in other research libraries. Preliminary results of book use within each Library of Congress class indicate that for the study period there is relatively little significant short-term variation in book use.

In order to determine the value for other libraries of data gathered through use studies of shorter duration, samplings of data selected ex post were analyzed in comparison with complete circulation data. It appears that random samples of loan records representing as few as three days produce correlations as high as .95 with the total population in regard to percent of circulation use by LC class. This means that for libraries that do not have complete retrospective circulation data available in machine-readable form, or do not choose to engage in a study of this magnitude, much smaller samples of manipulable size can be used to identify aggregate usage patterns within the LC classes.

Thus, when book use in the University of Pittsburgh central research library was studied over a seven-year-and-two-month period, it was found that any given book purchased had only slightly better than one chance in two of ever being borrowed. When a book had not circulated within the first two years of ownership, the chances of its ever being borrowed were reduced to only one in four. And when a book did not circulate within the first six years of ownership, the prospects of its ever being borrowed were reduced to one chance in fifty. If a minimum of two uses were arbitrarily established ex post facto as a criterion for a cost-effective acquisition program, 54.2% of the titles purchased in 1969 would not have been ordered; if three uses, then 62.5% would not have been ordered.

B. Data Collection—Books and Monographs

When a patron checks out a book from Hillman Library, information from three sources is combined to create a book transaction. From the machine-readable card in the book itself comes bibliographic information unique to the book; from the patron identification card comes information unique to that patron; and from the data collection device comes the date, time, and a number identifying the device. Such transactions have been created and preserved since October 1968 when the automated circulation system came into being. Although the system itself has been improved over the years, the format for a transaction has remained essentially the same.

The possibilities for exploiting such a large volume of data were considered carefully. It was decided that, since the study was to focus primarily on use of library materials, a book-oriented approach to creating a usable data base from the collected transactions would be the most appropriate, but that the integrity of individual transactions should be preserved. The book control number—a unique identifier assigned to each item during processing (and which, incidentally, gives a rough chronology of acquisitions)—was used as a key in organizing the file. A typical record contains the control number, bibliographic information unique to the book, a transaction count, and the unique data for each transaction; in effect, a complete circulation history for the book. Such a format was well suited to the longitudinal approach used to study the behavior of the collection.

By a series of successive sorts and merges, a file containing virtually complete circulation history for the period 1969 through 1975 was created. The product, a variable-length-record, fixed-block-size, ASCII file residing on two standard reels of magnetic tape labelled and recorded at 1600 bpi, forms the basis for much of the work concerning use of the books and monographs collection.

Another important file contains images of the machine-readable cards in the books. This file was created by transferring the card files to magnetic tape and then sorting the tape records by control number. The result was an almost complete shelflist of items acquired since 1968 and such items acquired before then as have passed through the automated system since then, or were prepared for the automated system before it became operational. Most of the circulating collection is represented in this two-reel ASCII file.

In support of the effort to develop cost data for collection use, machine-readable output from the semi-automated processing system was exploited. In order to tie cost data to use data it was necessary to match accounting files with processing files, then match the result with the circulation history file. The resulting single-reel ASCII file contains cost, processing and circulation data for a sample of about 8,000 items.

C. Discussion of Findings

The two primary indicators of use of books and monographs that have been studied are: (1) unique items that have circulated externally or been used in-house; and (2) the frequency of use of unique items circulated (transactions).[2] The first indicator should be helpful in evaluating the basic decision to purchase the items; the second indicator should provide evidence useful in making decisions regarding resource-sharing. The total population of use has been studied for external circulation;[3] data on in-house usage were collected on a sampling basis (over an eight-month period). Interlibrary loans and reserve book room use were also analyzed.

1. Use of Unique Items[4]

a. Circulation: Our results support the major hypothesis of the study, that a very small portion of the library collection of book titles accounts for the major portion of the circulation use. In fact, 285,373 items of the entire collection of 552,674 items—or 51.63%—actually circulated externally

---

2 The external patron circulation data file contains an estimated 95%-97% of the Hillman Library charges. That is, 3%-5% of the external patron circulations involve books without machine-readable book cards. These books are manually charged out and machine-readable book cards are prepared when the books are returned to the library. In addition, it is estimated that the circulation records contain 2%-3% miscellaneous errors (misread characters, unreadable tape records, etc.). Thus, it is estimated that the data discussed in this report probably contain about 92% of the external patron records.

3 This includes charges to: undergraduates, staff, graduate students, Pittsburgh Regional Library Center undergraduates, reserve book room, library carrels, interlibrary loan, internal loan (to another Pitt library), lockers, and faculty study. Charges specifically excluded are: system test, bindery, storage and mending.

4 As used in this context, there is a difference between "items" and "titles." There is some "error" which results from our use of "item." It has been estimated that there are fewer than 5% of the titles for which duplicate copies are available. Our figures do not coalesce the items into titles.

during the seven years and two months of the study period. In other words, 48.37% of the collection as a whole (all books) did not circulate at all via external patron circulation during the period between October 1968 and the end of the calendar year 1975. These figures include a loss rate of 5% per year through 1974. (Full details of these findings are given under the heading "Frequency of Use" in subsection 2 below.)

b. "Aging": Initial results dealt with the use of the collection as a whole; but it appeared important to study use in terms of newly acquired materials to discover the relationship between use and time. Development of such a relationship would provide an indication of the aging of a collection of books. Some of the questions to be asked about acquisitions concern what happen to materials once they are available for circulation. Are they used at all? If so, in what time frame? How does use change over time? For materials that have never been used after a certain period, can probabilities be assigned for their ever being used?

Others had probed these questions in various ways. Fussler and Simon[5] chose to take a cross-sectional look at use, largely for methodological and practical reasons. Trueswell used a cross-sectional approach for similar reasons.[6,7,8] Morse took a historical approach but noted the difficulty of collecting accurate data.[9] We were in the position of being able to examine some entire populations of materials, since we had virtually complete historical data for circulation use of our collection by patrons over the past seven years. Thus, we chose to take a historical approach initially, with a view to developing a sampling methodology for future studies.

---

5 H. H. Fussler and J. L. Simon, Patterns in the Use of Books in Large Research Libraries, University of Chicago, 1969, p. 7.

6 R. W. Trueswell, "Quantitative Measure of User Circulation Requirements and its Possible Effect on Stock Thinning and Multiple Copy Determination," American Documentation, 16; 20-25, January 1965.

7 R. W. Trueswell, "Determining the Optimal Number of Volumes of a Library's Core Collection," Libri, 16(1); 49-60, 1966.

8 R. W. Trueswell, "User Circulation Satisfaction vs. Size of Holdings at Three Academic Libraries," College & Research Libraries, 30; 204-213, 1969.

9 P. M. Morse, Library Effectiveness: A Systems Approach, MIT Press, Cambridge and London, 1968, pp. 84-110.

Our results are presented in two parts: first, the use of groups of materials acquired in successive years is examined; and second, predictions are developed for use following the years for which actual use data are available.

Table 1 presents first time use of acquired items in years succeeding acquisition. Table 2 shows the same data as percentage of acquired items first being used in years succeeding acquisition. As can readily be seen from these two tables, a definite "aging" pattern emerges; that is, similar percentages of items enter the collection of circulating items in each year succeeding acquisitions. (Further analysis of these data will be found in Chapter V of this book.)

Taking 1969 as a representative year (and the year for which we have the most historical data), we can show the aging pattern quite well. Later we will develop a model using data for all years.

Figure 1 shows the number of 1969 items circulating for the first time in each year. "Items" mean physical volumes; only about 5% of the "items" in the library represent multiple copies of the same title.

Table 1
First-Time Use of Acquisitions

Base Acquisitions	Base Year # first circulated	Base Year+1 # first circulated	Base Year+2 # first circulated	Base Year+3 # first circulated	Base Year+4 # first circulated	Base Year+5 # first circulated	Base Year+6 # first circulated
1969	1969	1970	1971	1972	1973	1974	1975
36,869	9708	6424	2449	1452	915	644	580
1970	1970	1971	1972	1973	1974	1975	
35,997	9876	5342	2185	1358	930	648	
1971	1971	1972	1973	1974	1975		
27,311	8687	4577	1745	1095	796		
1972	1972	1973	1974	1975			
30,199	9170	5757	2209	1258			
1973	1973	1974	1975				
28,438	8373	5395	2013				
1974	1974	1975					
35,097	8593	4344					
1975	1975						
30,894	8532						

Table 2
First-Time Use as Percent of Acquisitions*

YEAR	Year 0		Year 1		Year 2		Year 3		Year 4		Year 5		Year 6	
	col. 1	col. 2	col. 1	col. 2	col. 1	col. 2	col. 1	col. 2	col. 1	col. 2	col. 1	col. 2	col. 1	col. 2
1969	.2633	.2633	.1742	.4375	.0664	.5039	.0394	.5433	.0248	.5681	.0175	.5856	.0157	.6013
1970	.2744	.2744	.1484	.4228	.0607	.4835	.0377	.5212	.0258	.5470	.0180	.5650		
1971	.3181	.3181	.1676	.4857	.0639	.5496	.040	.5896	.0291	.6187				
1972	.3037	.3037	.1906	.4943	.0731	.5674	.0417	.6091						
1973	.2944	.2944	.1897	.4841	.0708	.5549								
1974	.2448	.2448	.1238	.3686										
1975	.2762	.2762												

* Col. 1 is % acquired items circulated
Col. 2 is cumulative % of acquired items circulated

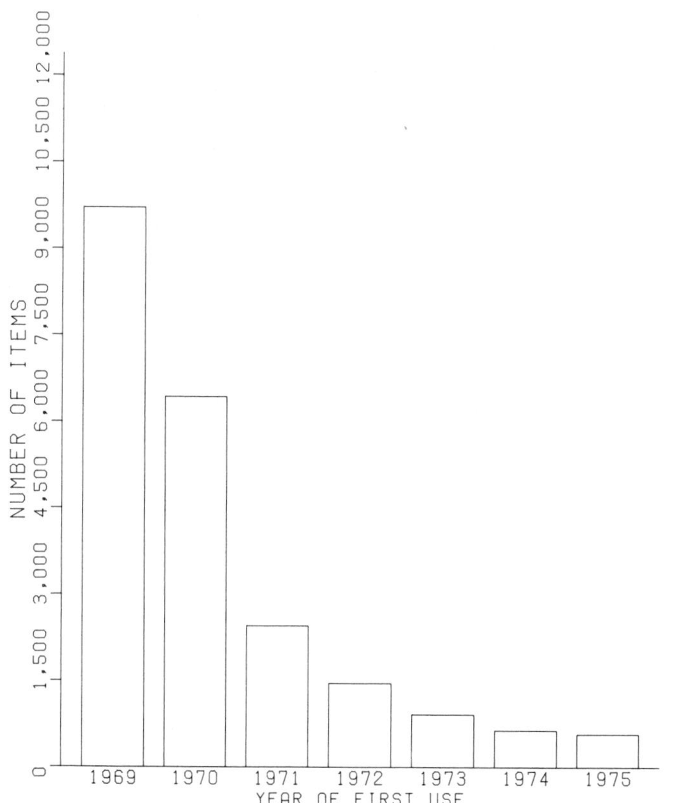

Figure 1. Year of first circulation of 1969 items.

Figure 2 shows the growth in cumulative use of items acquired during 1969. In this graph, for each successive year the data for newly circulated items (Fig. 1) are added to the residual data for the years before. Thus, by the end of 1975, 9708 + 6424 + 2449 + 1452 + 915 + 644 + 580 = 22,172 of the 36,869 items acquired in 1969 had been used at least once. (See Table 1 for numbers.) This total represents about 60% of acquisitions. As might be expected, the greatest increases take place in the first two years.

The total items used, however, presents only a part of the picture; it is interesting to know how many transactions there are for the items used, since in any given year only a fraction of the items available for use are actually used. With the exception of a kernel of constantly used items, the

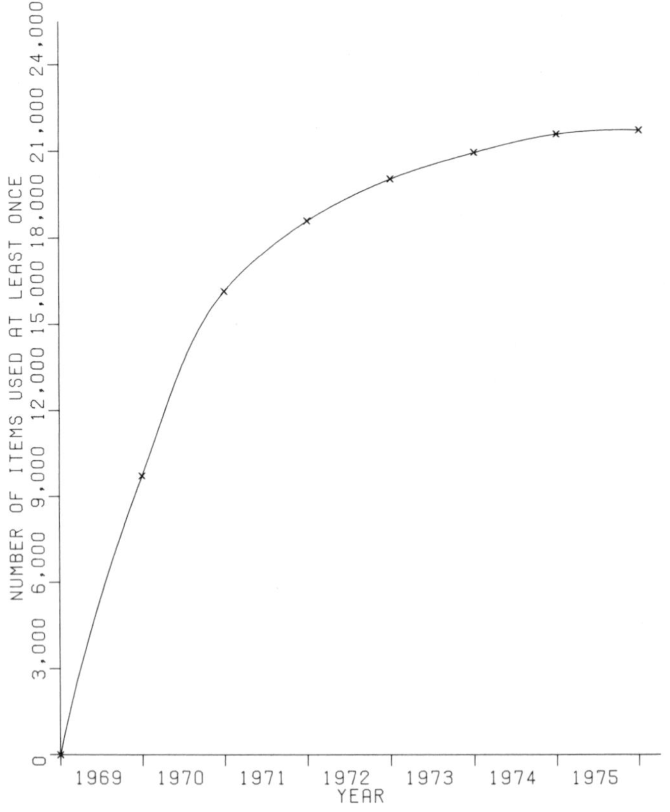

Figure 2. Cumulative use of items acquired in 1969.

population tends to turn over from year to year. Table 3 presents circulation activity for 1969 through 1975 by number of items used, i.e., transactions. One item then may account for zero or more transactions over a given period of time.

Table 3
Circulation of 1969 Acquisitions: 1969-1975

Times Used	Number of Items	% of Items Acquired	% of Items Circulated
0	14,697	39.838	-
1	5,291	14.342	28.869
2	3,065	8.308	13.827
3	2,214	6.001	9.988
4	1,711	4.638	7.719
5	1,330	3.605	6.000
6	1,100	2.982	4.962
7	913	2.475	4.119
8	764	2.071	3.447
9	696	1.886	3.140
10	600	1.626	2.707
11	553	1.499	2.495
12	473	1.282	2.134
13	393	1.065	1.773
14	397	1.076	1.791
15	314	0.851	1.417
16	296	0.802	1.335
17	250	0.678	1.128
18	215	0.583	0.970
19	185	0.501	0.835
20	170	0.461	0.767
21	167	0.453	0.753
22	143	0.388	0.645
23	122	0.331	0.550
24	107	0.290	0.483
25	97	0.263	0.438
26+	601	1.629	2.711
error records	28	0.076	-
	36,892	100.000	100.003

Figure 3 is a graphic representation of Column 1 of Table 1, plotted against Column 3 of Table 3, i.e., "times used" against "percentage." Figure 4 then shows the growth in percentage of items used various numbers of times over the period studied. Note that all percentages represented in Figures 3 and 4 are percentages of total acquisitions in items.

The data are suggestive of the point at which further use may be negligible (statistically). It is interesting to compare the decay in usage for one-time, two-time, three-time, etc. circulations. This comparison may be useful in assessing collection-building policies, and in developing resource-sharing models which would aim at distributing collections over a number of cooperating libraries.

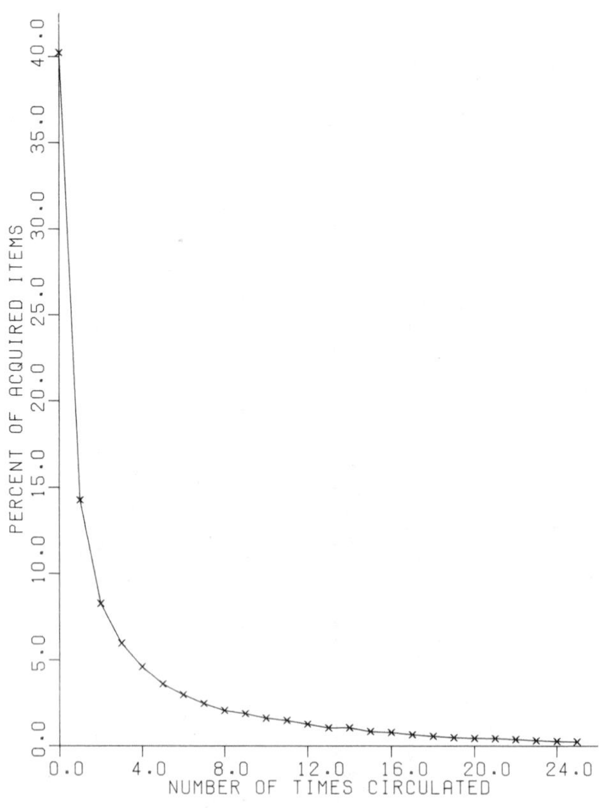

Figure 3. Circulation of 1969 acquisitions from 1969 to 1975.

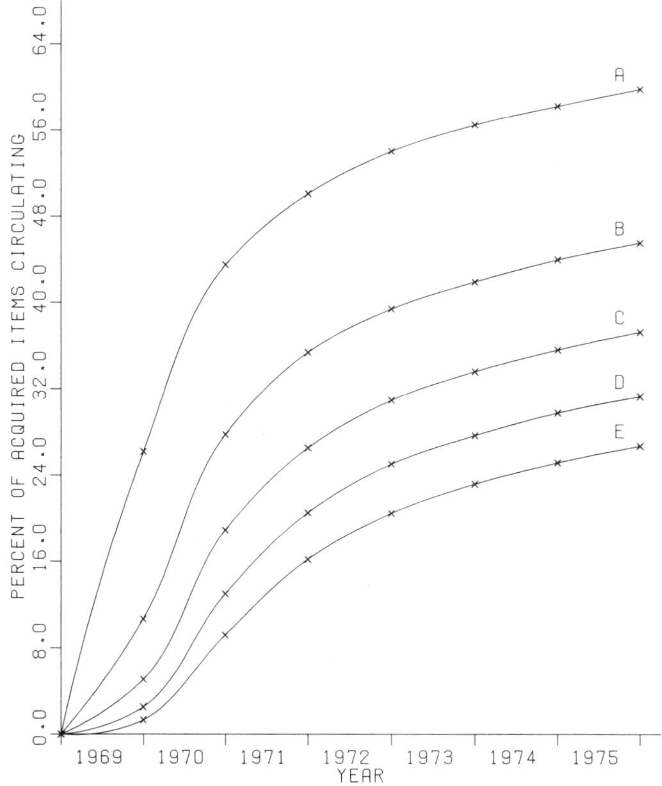

Figure 4. Percentage of items used by frequency of circulation. A: circulated at least once; B: circulated twice; C: circulated 3 times; D: circulated 4 times; E: circulated 5 times.

c. Predicting the Future Use of the Collection: As the data in Table 2 show, each year's acquisitions behave much like any other year. Given such consistent behavior, it is possible to use these data to construct and test predictive models.

As a first attempt, polynomial regression was used to fit a curve to the data in Table 2. The result was a six-degree equation that acceptably fits the data but is not a good predictor because it produces Y values which, after reaching a low, begin to rise again (not to mention the unwieldiness of a six-degree polynomial). Figure 5 shows the portion of this curve which fits our data well. (Note also the similarity between Figure 5 and Figure 1.) It is true that data for more years will produce a better and better polynomial but it is also true that the polynomial will get more and more complex and increase in degree. While a useful start, this approach appears to lead down such a complicated path that we began looking for a simpler one.

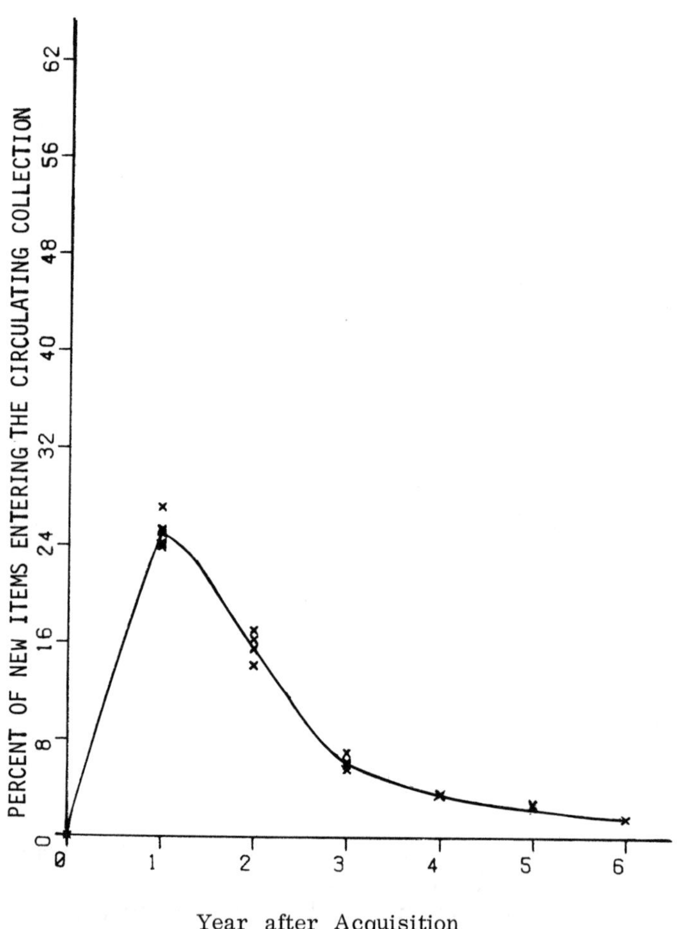

Figure 5. Predicting percentage of first-time use of acquisitions.

It can be seen from Figure 5 that the percentage of new items entering the circulating collection peaks in the first year and then rapidly declines. In addition, the data from Table 1 indicate that the decline is roughly 50% from one year to the next. At such a rate of decline it does not take long before new contributions are negligible. This suggests that the distribution is some sort of exponential function that approaches a ceiling and that the technique of asymptotic regression may be appropriate. Accordingly, data were fitted to a modified exponential asymptotic function with time as the independent variable. Data for years 1969 thru 1974 were used to develop a model which is represented in Table 4. The mean difference between predicted and observed percentages is 0.9529% with a standard deviation of

Table 4
Predicting Use of Acquisitions*[10]

(1)	(2)	(3)	(4)
1	29.8049	30.1601	29.3508
2	44.6799	14.8750	14.4758
3	52.0162	7.3363	7.1395
4	55.6345	3.6183	3.5212
5	57.4191	1.7845	1.7366
6	58.2992	0.8801	0.8565
7	58.7333	0.4341	0.4224
8	58.9474	0.2141	0.2083
9	59.0529	0.1056	0.1028
10	59.1050	0.0521	0.0507
11	59.1307	0.0257	0.0250
12	59.1434	0.0127	0.0123
13	59.1496	0.0062	0.0061
14	59.1527	0.0031	0.0030
15	59.1542	0.0015	0.0015
16	59.1550	0.0007	0.0007
17	59.1553	0.0004	0.0004
18	59.1555	0.0002	0.0002
19	59.1556	0.0001	0.0001
20	59.1557	0.0000	0.0000
21	50.1557	0.0000	0.0000
22	59.1557	0.0000	0.0000
23	59.1557	0.0000	0.0000
24	59.1557	0.0000	0.0000

Columns: (1) Year
(2) Cumulative % of a given year's circulation
(3) % of previously uncirculated items entering the circulating collection
(4) % of non-circulating items that will ever circulate

* Based on the exponential relation $y = A + B \times R^x$ where:

A = 59.1557
B = -59.5109
R = 0.4932
x = Col. 1
y = Col. 2

[10] Take a typical row (2), read—by end of second year after acquisition, 44.6799% of items will have circulated; 14.875% will have circulated in Year 2; 14.4758% will ever circulate in the rest of years. In row 1, Cols. 3 and 2 should be the same. The differences are an artifact of the model; other differences are due to "rounding."

0.597%. Even allowing for the variance given up by using mean Y values for the comparison, this is an acceptable fit.

In order to test the model's predictive ability, its predictions of percent of previously uncirculated items entering the circulating collection were compared with actual 1975 performance. Table 5 shows this comparison for each year; Table 6 shows it for cumulations for each year. The model appears to predict more accurately for the years earlier in the life of a year of acquistions than it does for later years. This is understandable since we have more data for the early years; not enough of the collection has "aged" sufficiently for the later years.

Table 5
Comparison of Model Predictions
with Actual Performance—Yearly Values

Year of Acquisition	'69-'74 Model Prediction	Actual 1975 Performance	New Model Figures
1975	29,8049	27,6170	29,1797
1974	14,8750	12,3371	15,1796
1973	7,3363	7,0786	7,8205
1972	3,6183	4,1657	4,0291
1971	1,7845	2,9146	2,0758
1970	0,8801	1,8002	1,0695
1969	0,4341	1,5732	0,5510

Table 6
Comparison of Model Predictions
with Actual Performance—Cumulative Values

Year of Acquisition	Predicted Cumulation	Actual 1975 Performance	New Model Cumulation
1975	29,8049	27,6170	29,1797
1974	44,6799	36,8607	44,3593
1973	52,0162	55,4927	52,1798
1972	55,6345	60,9092	56,2089
1971	57,4191	61,8799	58,2847
1970	58,2992	56,5019	59,3542
1969	58,7333	60,1373	59,9052

The additional year of data was next added to the model and a new function was produced. It is shown in tabular form in Table 7 and graphically in Figure 6. Data from the new model, which includes 1975, are also presented in Tables 5 and 6.

Table 7
Predicting the Use of Acquisitions Over Time*

(1)	(2)	(3)	(4)
1	29.1799	29.4632	31.3108
2	44.3594	15.1795	16.1313
3	52.1799	7.8205	8.3108
4	56.2090	4.0291	4.2817
5	58.2847	2.0758	2.2059
6	59.3542	1.0694	1.1365
7	59.9052	0.5510	0.5855
8	60.1890	0.2839	0.3017
9	60.3353	0.1462	0.1554
10	60.4106	0.0753	0.0801
11	60.4494	0.0388	0.0412
12	60.4694	0.0200	0.0212
13	60.4798	0.0103	0.0109
14	60.4851	0.0053	0.0056
15	60.4878	0.0027	0.0029
16	60.4892	0.0014	0.0015
17	60.4899	0.0007	0.0008
18	60.4903	0.0004	0.0004
19	60.4905	0.0002	0.0002
20	60.4906	0.0001	0.0001
21	60.4906	0.0001	0.0000
22	60.4907	0.0000	0.0000
23	60.4907	0.0000	0.0000
24	60.4907	0.0000	0.0000

Columns: (1) Year
(2) Cumulative % of a given year's circulation
(3) % of previously uncirculated items entering the circulating collection
(4) % of non-circulating items that will ever circulate

* Based on the exponential relation $y = A + B \times R^x$ where:

$A = 60.4907$
$B = -60.7740$
$R = 0.5152$
$x =$ Col. 1
$y =$ Col. 2

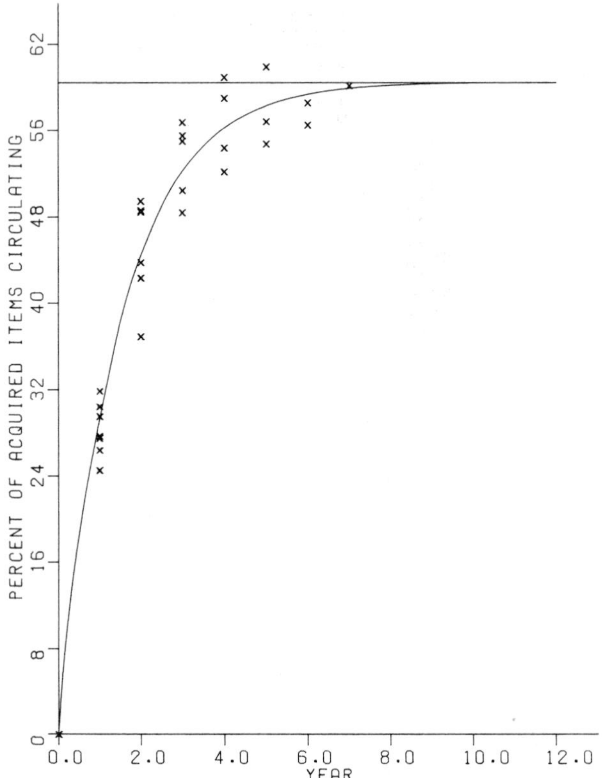

Figure 6. Predicting cumulative use of acquisitions.

The mean difference between predicted and observed percentages for the new model is 0.719% with a standard deviation of .540%, again an acceptable error. It appears to predict somewhat better than the older model although it is still more accurate for the earlier years in the life of a year's acquisitions.

Theoretically, we know that the percentage of items circulating can reach 100% maximum. However, from data collected we know that 100% is above the actual level. There is a sharp turn down in the rate of books being brought into the circulating collection from about the third or fourth year. We expect that the level of the potential circulating collection that will ever be used will settle somewhere between 60% and 70% of acquisitions for any single year. We also expect the predictive power of the model to improve as more data are added to it.

d. External Versus In-House Circulation: A second hypothesis of this study has been that books which circulate externally are also those used internally. Accordingly, a study was undertaken to test this point.

We decided to sample internal use of the collection during two terms. Days were selected—one per week—for each of the fifteen weeks of the Fall 1975 and Winter 1976 terms. The particular day of the week was drawn randomly for each week. Figure 7 shows a breakdown of sample days by day of week and term.

Week beginning:			SUN	MON	TUE	WED	THU	FRI	SAT
1975	AUG	31					x		
	SEP	7			x				
		14				x			
		21			x				
		28					x		
	OCT	5							x
		12						x	
		19				x			
		26						x	
	NOV	2	x						
		9		x					
		16					x		
		23		x					
		30				x			
	DEC	7							x
1976	JAN	4						x	
		11	x						
		18					x		
		25			x				
	FEB	1			x				
		8							x
		15			x				
		22	x						
		29							x
	MAR	7		x					
		14	x						
		21						x	
		28		x					
	APR	4					x		
		11				x			

Figure 7. Sampling at Hillman Library (days sampled marked "x").

The policy of the Hillman Library is to request that patrons not reshelve material but instead place it in special areas in the stacks or leave it on the table where it was used. Signs are place prominently throughout the stack area to indicate this policy. We have assumed that patrons obey this rule. Given the long standing of this policy, the special stack areas, a systematic collection method, and our more formal notion of "use," we think that we have faced most of the objections raised by Fussler and Simon to the collection method for studying internal use.[11]

On each of the 30 sample days materials left on tables and designated areas were collected. A transaction was recorded for each item. Since items were not reshelved until the next day, no items could be used more than once on a given sample day. Items were collected at 10 a.m., 2 p.m., 7 p.m. and 10 p.m. on weekdays, and at 10 a.m., 2 p.m. and 7 p.m. on Saturdays and 2 p.m., 7 p.m. and 10 p.m. on Sundays, to fit into the service hours of the library. (In-house circulation data was captured by the automated circulation system of the Hillman Library.) During the 30 sample days, a total of 29,098 unique items were used, accounting for 32,373 transactions. Table 8 shows this by number of times used.

Table 8
In-House Use Sample by Number of Times Used

Times Used	Number of Items	Transactions
1	26282	26282
2	2445	4890
3	314	942
4	39	156
5	12	60
6	1	6
7	3	21
8	2	16
TOTALS:	29098	32373

[11] H. H. Fussler and J. L. Simon, Patterns in the Use of Books in Large Research Libraries, University of Chicago, 1969, p. 108.

Discussion: A problem in comparing internal and external use is that the categories are mutually exclusive during the same time, i.e., items are equally available for both types of use but as soon as something is used in one way it becomes impossible for it to be used in the other way. This inherent problem does not, however, totally defeat investigation because we have chosen to examine the external "track record" of items in the internal file. The question which most interests us is: What items are being used in-house that have not circulated externally? Or, put another way: What are we excluding if we study only external circulation and allow it to stand for all use? Collecting in-house use data is more difficult and more expensive; we would like not to have to do it. We would also like to tighten what many have considered a methodological loophole in all studies which rely on external use data.

Analysis: Of the 29,098 items which were used in-house in the 30 sample days, 19,144 had circulated at least once before the study was begun. If we include the time period during which the 30 sample days fall, we find that an additional 2,729 items circulate, for a total of 21,873 items. This represents .75 of the total in-house sample, i.e., 75% of the in-house sample had been externally circulated by the end of the sample period. Table 9 shows a breakdown of the 29,092 in-house items by year acquired; Table 10 shows the same breakdown for the 21,873 items falling in the intersection of the in-house and external use files.

Table 9
In-House Sample by Year Acquired

Year Acquired	Items	Transactions
pre-1968	12818	13959
1968	787	863
1969	1603	1781
1970	1544	1698
1971	1622	1837
1972	2166	2441
1973	2349	2707
1974	2875	3318
1975	2954	3371
1976	376	392
UNKNOWN	6	6
TOTALS:	29098	32373

Table 10
In-House Items Circulating Externally at Least Once
From 1968 Thru the End of the Study Period

Year Acquired	Items	Transactions
pre-1968	9498	96694
1968	684	8058
1969	1410	16661
1970	1308	14539
1971	1372	13606
1972	1766	14034
1973	1877	12818
1974	2037	9569
1975	1784	5715
1976	125	198
UNKNOWN	12	115
TOTALS:	21873	191987

Table 11
In-House Items Not Previously Circulated Externally

Year Acquired	A In-House		B In-House & External		C In-House Not External	D C/A as Percent
pre-1968	12818	-	9498	=	3320	25.9
1968	787	-	684	=	103	13.09
1969	1603	-	1410	=	193	12.04
1970	1544	-	1308	=	236	15.29
1971	1622	-	1372	=	250	15.41
1972	2166	-	1766	=	400	18.47
1973	2349	-	1877	=	472	20.09
1974	2875	-	2037	=	838	29.15
1975	2954	-	1784	=	1170	39.61
1976	376	-	125	=	251	66.76
UNKNOWN	6	-	12	=	-	
TOTALS:	29098	-	21873	=	7233	24.86

Of interest to us is Table 11 which shows the in-house items which are being newly used and the percentage of the sample they account for. The single largest group is that consisting of items acquired before 1968, which accounts for 45.9% (3,320/7,233) of the newly used items. One must bear in mind, however, that this group contains items ranging from 10 to more than 50 years old. If it were possible to separate this group by year acquired, we may assume that these 3,320 items would spread over many years with the percentage for any individual year quite small. Column 'D' of Table 11 shows the in-house items never circulated externally as percentages of the total in-house use for a given year's acquisitions. Except for the pre-1968 group, the largest percentages occur in the most recent years of acquisitions. Given that the first two to three years after a group of items is acquired is the heaviest use period of those items, and that the most recently acquired groups still contain many unused items that will eventually be used (as opposed to unused items that have only small potential for ever being used, as in the older groups), this is to be expected.

In answer to our earlier question we find that, at least for our sample, three-quarters of the books used in-house have also circulated externally sometime between 1968 and the end of the sample period. If we extend the period of comparison an extra year (thru June 1977), an additional 899 items are circulated for a total of 22,772 or 78%.

It was also discovered that 12,178 items, or 42% of the sample of in-house items, also circulated externally during the sample period. If we extend that comparison an extra year (i.e., the total period is September 1975 thru June 1977, the sample period plus one year), we find that 16,711 items, or 57% of the sample circulate externally. That is, 57% of the items used in-house circulate either during the sample time period or within one year.

In-house items which circulate externally show greater external circulation than the circulating collection as a whole. For all items circulating externally during the period 1969-1975, the average was 5.024 transactions per item; for items used in-house the external track record for 1969-1975 was 8.186 transactions per item.

In summary, these data show that 75-78% of those books and monographs that circulate in-house also have circulated externally. Further, based on this analysis, this percentage is increasing with time. Thus we conclude that in terms of whether or not a book or monograph is ever used, it is sufficient to examine the external patron circulation data.

Based on our earlier statement about most recently acquired items having the highest probability of still being used, we would expect that the additional year of data would contain more recent items than older ones. This turns out to be the case, as Table 12 shows. Of course, we would not expect 1976 to be well represented since, when the sample was taken, most 1976 items had not yet entered the collection. Note also that the pre-1968 items range from 10 to more than 50 years old, which tends to make this category seem large by comparison with the other one-year categories.

We have chosen to study the items which are used in-house and to compare them with the items which circulate externally. We have found a substantial overlap which, over time, promises to increase. But there is another question that can fairly be raised and it is this: How much will in-house use inflate the figures for total use? Here we are talking about transaction counts. Recall that our transactions for the 30 sample days totalled 32,373 and that out external transactions during a seven-year period total 1,433,727 or about 204,818 per year. If we simply extrapolate the 30-day sample to 365 days we get 393,871. However, the sample days were drawn from the busiest two-thirds of the year so that figure is somewhat inflated. If we assume that the "summer slowdown" affects use in-house in about the same way as it affects external circulation, then in-house use accounts for about 351,067 transactions per year and increases total use by about 2.75 times. This is worked out as follows: Approximately 75% of transactions occur during the Fall and Winter trimesters, about 244 days. Extrapolating in-house use to 244 days yields 363,300 transactions. This latter figure is .75 of 351,067 and so we say that this should approximate the number of in-house transactions for a year. The total transactions for a year, then, is about 550,000.

Table 12
In-House Items Circulating Externally
During Year After Sample Period

Year Acquired	Items
pre-1968	222
1968	8
1969	12
1970	15
1971	16
1972	44
1973	56
1974	154
1975	292
1976	80
TOTAL:	899

The question of whether the kind of use which takes place in the library should be equated with the use made of a book when it is checked out remains open.

Based on our comparisons, therefore, we speculate that the number of items used in-house which have circulated or will circulate externally will increase with time, approaching but not reaching 100%. Accordingly, we must agree with Fussler and Simon that

> "the recorded circulation use of books is a reasonably reliable index of all use, including the unrecorded, consultative, or browsing use within the library."[12]

e. Interlibrary Loan and Reserve Book Room Item Use: These two factors must also be taken into account, particularly in a university library.

(1) Interlibrary Loan Usage:

One aspect of book and monograph usage concerns books lent by Hillman Library on interlibrary loan. Such loans are captured by the automated circulation system. Data have been collected throughout the time period October 1968 through July 1977, but files containing comprehensive circulation histories for each item are available only through July 1976. Since all discussion and tables refer to calendar years, the time period under consideration is from January 1969 through December 1975.

The question that interests us is the same as that of other aspects of the study: What are we excluding if we study only external circulation and allow it to represent all use? Before directly answering the question, let us look at the overall interlibrary loan circulation patterns. Table 13 indicates that the overwhelming majority of items having interlibrary loan use have only one such transaction. The figure is almost 90%. Overall each item that circulated averaged 1.17 interlibrary loan transactions. It can be shown from Table 14 that this phenomenon is constant (±.12) for items acquired in different years.

By comparing Tables 14 and 15 we see that 3,246 of the 4,250 items that had interlibrary loan transactions also had external circulations. Thus, with respect to individual items we find 76.4% would be included in a study of only external circulations. Table 15 also indicates that these items are

---

[12] H. H. Fussler and J. L. Simon, Patterns in the Use of Books in Large Research Libraries, University of Chicago, 1969, p. 3.

high-use items in their own right—these interlibrary loan materials averaged 6.75 external circulations per item in addition to their interlibrary loan circulation.

Table 13
Interlibrary Loan Use by Number of Times Circulated

Times Circulated	Number of Items	Number of Interlibrary Loan Transactions
1	3,798	3,798
2	313	626
3	76	228
4	31	124
5	16	80
6	6	36
7	3	21
8	4	32
9	1	9
10	1	10
11+over	1	13
Totals:	4,250	4,977

Table 14
Interlibrary Loan Breakdown by Year Acquired

Year Acquired	Items	ILL Transactions
Pre-1968	2,693	3,308
1968	201	211
1969	305	324
1970	288	318
1971	200	224
1972	167	176
1973	197	206
1974	120	127
1975	79	83
Totals:	4,250	4,977

Table 15
Interlibrary Loan Items Circulating Externally at Least Once From 1969 Through 1975

Year Acquired	Items	ILL Transactions	External Transactions
Pre- 1968	2,052	2,464	13,445
1968	167	177	1,374
1969	258	273	2,564
1970	221	242	1,599
1971	150	168	1,012
1972	141	146	871
1973	137	144	665
1974	85	91	295
1975	35	37	83
Totals:	3,246	3,742	21,908

Again, as a general rule, the majority of items used in a type of circulation different from external circulation—in this case, interlibrary loan—re-emphasizes the pre-eminence of the highly used items in external circulation; the exceptions to this general rule are difficult to predict. It is this very difficulty of identification that would make these "marginal" items candidates for alternative means of access. If we cannot be assured of external circulation or internal usage, the relatively rare interlibrary loan request might best be handled through means such as resource-sharing.

Table 16 introduces a new variable—items acquired that circulated—which provides a guage of interlibrary loan activity with respect to total circulation activity. The response to our initial question is this: only 1.44% of all items have interlibrary loan use; more significant still is that only 0.34% of all items that circulate would be ignored if only external circulations were counted. For most purposes, this seems an acceptably small error.

(2) Reserve Book Room Usage:

Another aspect of book and monograph usage is reserve book room usage, which is partially captured by the Hillman Library automated circulation system. We say "partially" because:

Table 16
Comparison of Various Partitions of Items Circulated Through Interlibrary Loan: 1969/1975

Year Acquired	A Items acquired that circulated	B ILL	C ILL External	D ILL Not external	E B/A as %	F D/B as %	G D/A as %
Pre-1968	152,491	2,693	2,052	641	1.77	23.80	.42
1968	15,063	201	167	34	1.33	16.92	.23
1969	22,472	305	258	47	1.36	15.41	.21
1970	20,879	288	221	67	1.38	23.26	.32
1971	17,606	200	150	50	1.14	25.00	.28
1972	20,607	167	141	26	0.81	15.57	.13
1973	17,475	197	137	60	1.13	30.46	.34
1974	16,280	120	85	35	0.74	29.17	.21
1975	11,894	79	35	44	0.66	55.70	.37
Totals:	294,767	4,250	3,246	1,004	1.44	23.62	.34

- Only charges from the collection to the Reserve Book Room are recorded in the automated circulation file—charges from the Reserve Book Room to patrons are not recorded in the automated circulation file.[13]

- Personal copies are placed in the Reserve Book Room and are not in any way recorded in the automated circulation file; the number of these non-library-owned materials varies from trimester to trimester and comprises between 20% and 40% of the materials in the Reserve Book Room.

- Renewal transactions to the Reserve Book Room from the general collection are not assigned a unique renewal code; therefore renewals to the Reserve Book Room are excluded from this study.

The period under consideration in this report is from January 1969 through December 1975. Reserve Book Room (RBR) transactions are charged to the Reserve Book Room from the collection; renewals are excluded.

The same question is addressed here as in the In-House Use and Interlibrary Loan Studies: What would we exclude if we study only external circulation and allow it to represent all use?

---

13 A reserve book room attempts to make frequently requested material available on short-term loan. Frequency of use data would have been helpful but was not available in machine-processible form.

Before directly answering the question, let us examine the overall RBR circulation patterns. Table 17 indicates that the majority of items (57%) that have RBR use have only one transaction. Eighty-nine percent of RBR items have three or fewer charges. Overall, each RBR item averaged 1.83 charges. It can be shown from Table 18 that overall the largest deviation from the mean for individual years is .81. But further analysis indicates that two partitions of this data might yield better understanding. By grouping the first five categories together and the second three together, we can show that the mean circulation for the groups is $1.92 \pm .09$ and $1.29 \pm .35$ respectively. This suggests that it takes five years before the transaction per item ratio stablizes.

By comparing Tables 18 and 19, we see that 27,854 of the 33,277 items that had RBR transactions[14] also had external circulations. Thus, with respect to individual items we find that 84% would be included in a study of only external circulations. Table 19 also indicates that these items are high-use items in their own right—these RBR materials averaged 7.72 external circulations per item in addition to their RBR circulation.

Table 17
Reserve Book Room Use by Number of Times Circulated

Times Circulated	Number of Items	Number of RBR Transactions
1	19,043	19,043
2	7,126	14,252
3	3,444	10,332
4	2,033	8,132
5	946	4,730
6	416	2,496
7	168	1,176
8	74	592
9	20	180
10	4	40
11+over	3	34
Totals:	33,277	61,007

[14] A transaction (i.e., item checked out to RBR) does not mean that the item was indeed used; nor, of course, does it reveal how many times it was used, if indeed it was used.

Table 18
Reserve Book Room Breakdown by Year Acquired

Year Acquired	Items	RBR-Transactions
Pre-1968	18,315	35,121
1968	2,576	5,054
1969	3,223	6,446
1970	1,890	3,450
1971	1,801	3,396
1972	2,243	3,646
1973	1,371	1,894
1974	1,130	1,259
1975	728	741
Totals:	33,277	61,007

Table 19
Reserve Book Room Items Circulated Externally
at Least Once From 1969 Through 1975

Year Acquired	Items	RBR Transactions	External Transactions
Pre-1968	15,935	30,868	128,346
1968	2,267	4,531	16,784
1969	2,894	5,669	27,201
1970	1,722	3,160	15,048
1971	1,492	2,629	11,017
1972	1,804	2,803	10,134
1973	1,068	1,387	4,650
1974	543	575	1,509
1975	129	132	224
Totals:	27,854	51,754	214,913

Table 20 introduces a new variable—items acquired that circulated—which provides a guage of RBR activity with respect to total circulation activity. The response to our initial question is this: a significant amount of library material has RBR use—11.29%. Yet only 1.84% of all items that circulate would be ignored if only external circulation were studied. For many purposes this would seem an acceptably small error.

Table 20
Comparison of Various Partitions of Items Used in the Reserve Book Room: 1969-1975

	A	B	C	D	E	F	G
Year Acquired	Items acquired that circulated	RBR	RBR External	RBR but Not external	B/A as %	D/B as %	D/A as %
Pre-1968	152,491	18,315	15,935	2,380	12.01	12.99	1.56
1968	15,063	2,576	2,267	309	17.10	12.00	2.05
1969	22,472	3,223	2,894	329	14.34	10.21	1.46
1970	20,879	1,890	1,722	168	9.05	8.89	0.80
1971	17,606	1,801	1,492	309	10.23	17.16	1.76
1972	20,607	2,243	1,804	439	10.88	19.57	2.13
1973	17,475	1,371	1,068	303	7.85	22.10	1.73
1974	16,280	1,130	543	587	6.94	51.95	3.61
1975	11,894	728	129	599	6.12	82.28	5.04
Totals:	294,767	33,277	27,854	5,423	11.29	16.30	1.84

Table 21
External Circulation: 1969-1975

# Times Used	Items	Cumulative Items	Transactions	Cumulative Transactions
26+	3805	3805	121804	121804
25	649	4454	16225	138029
24	682	5136	16368	154397
23	803	5939	18469	172866
22	955	6894	21010	193876
21	1145	8039	24045	217921
20	1291	9330	25820	243741
19	1527	10857	29013	272754
18	1713	12570	30834	303588
17	2011	14581	34187	337775
16	2333	16914	37328	375103
15	2716	19630	40740	415843
14	3142	22772	43988	459831
13	3742	26514	48646	508477
12	4374	30888	52488	560965
11	5183	36071	57013	617978
10	6268	42339	62680	680658
9	7430	49769	66870	747528
8	9004	58773	72032	819560
7	11088	69861	77616	897176
6	13653	83514	81918	979094
5	17874	101388	89370	1068464
4	23478	124866	93912	1162376
3	31867	156733	95601	1257977
2	47110	203843	94220	1352197
1	81530	285373	81530	1433727

2. Frequency of Use

Data on external transactions analyzed for a period of 86 months support the hypothesis that a small portion of the book collection accounts for a major portion of total use. Table 21 shows external circulation for the period 1969-1975 ranked by frequency of use. The transaction total for the entire period is 1,433,727, accounted for by 285,373 unique items. From this table, using interpolation, various percentages of the total transactions and the items which account for them can be calculated. Table 22 shows these data for a range of percentages. Note that 42.41 percent of the items yield 80 percent of the transactions.

An interesting by-product of this investigation was the discovery that external circulation for a one-year period shows a log normal distribution[15] and is, in fact, an almost straight line when graphed on a semi-log scale. Figure 8 shows such a graph of circulation data for the typical calendar year 1974. Table 23 shows the data and reveals another phenomenon: the number of items that circulated twice is approximately half the number that circulated once; the number that circulated three times is approximately half the number that circulated twice; and so on for a fairly regular progression. It appears that circulating books form a Bradford set and that the distribution of circulation over a population of items is a Bradford-Zipf distribution.[16]

Table 22
Percent Items Yielding Percent Transactions

% Transactions	# Transactions	% Items	# Items
20.0	286745	4.06	11593
40.0	573491	11.59	33081
60.0	860236	22.63	64584
80.0	1146982	42.41	121018
100.0	1433727	100.00	285373

[15] Other distributions may also fit these data. See R. E. Quandt, "On the Size Distribution of Firms," American Economic Review, June 1966.

[16] S. Bulick, "Book Use as a Bradford-Zipf Phenomenon," College and Research Libraries, in press.

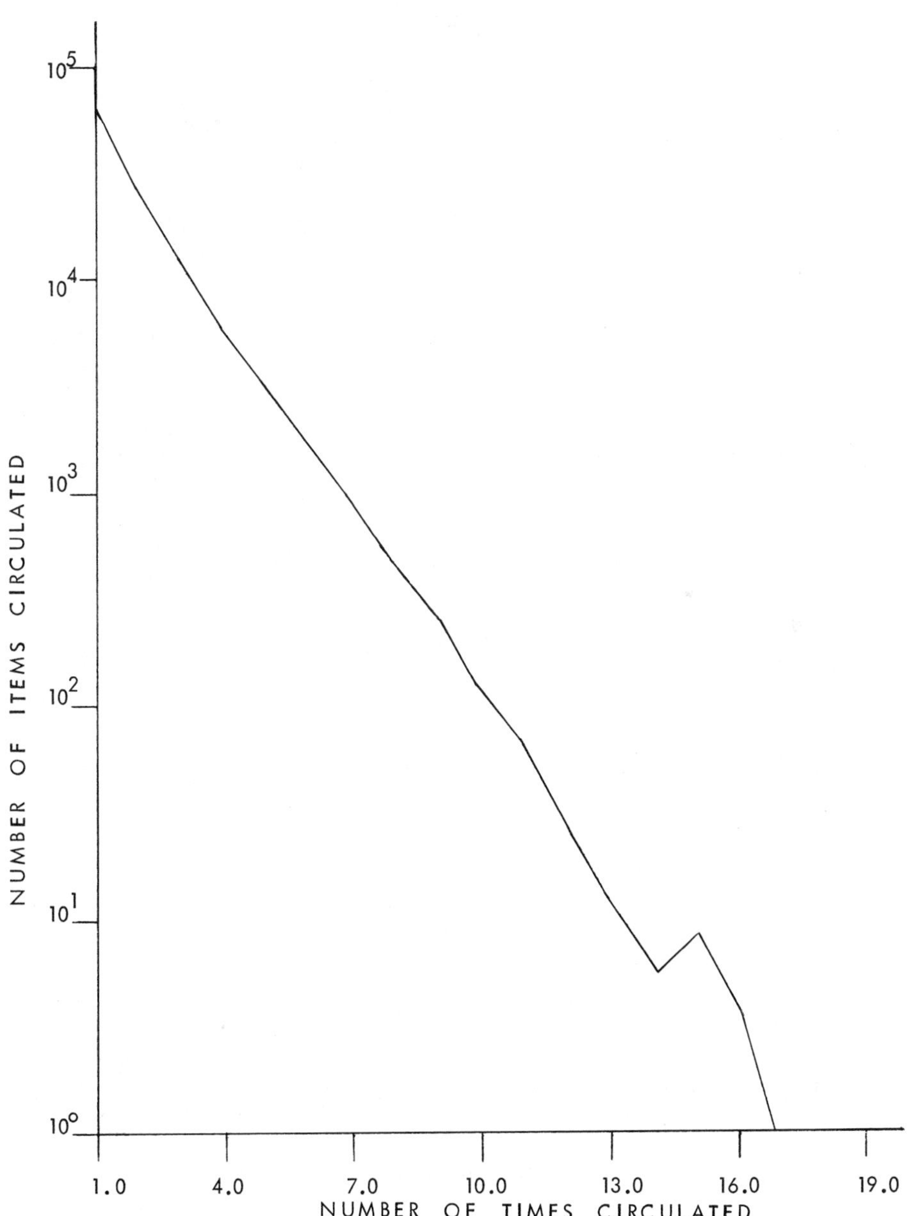

Figure 8. Circulation data for calendar year 1974.

Table 23
Circulation Data for Calendar Year 1974

Circulated	Items	Transactions
1	63526	63526
2	25653	51306
3	11855	35565
4	6055	24220
5	3264	16320
6	1727	10362
7	931	6517
8	497	3976
9	275	2475
10	124	1240
11	68	748
12	28	336
13	13	169
14	6	84
15	9	135
16	4	64
17	1	17
18	1	18
19	0	0
20	1	20
21	1	21
22	0	0
23	0	0
24	0	0
25	0	0
26+	0	0
TOTALS	114039	217119

A natural question concerns the aging of this distribution. Figure 9 shows successive cumulations of circulation data for a 7-year period. Counts for successive years include previously uncirculated items as well as previously circulated ones. We also note that the 285,373 items which circulated over the 7-year period represent about 51% of the approximately 550,000 items available for circulation by the end of 1975.

We next focus on the frequency of use over time of items acquired in the same year—1969. The time period represented is 1969-1975.

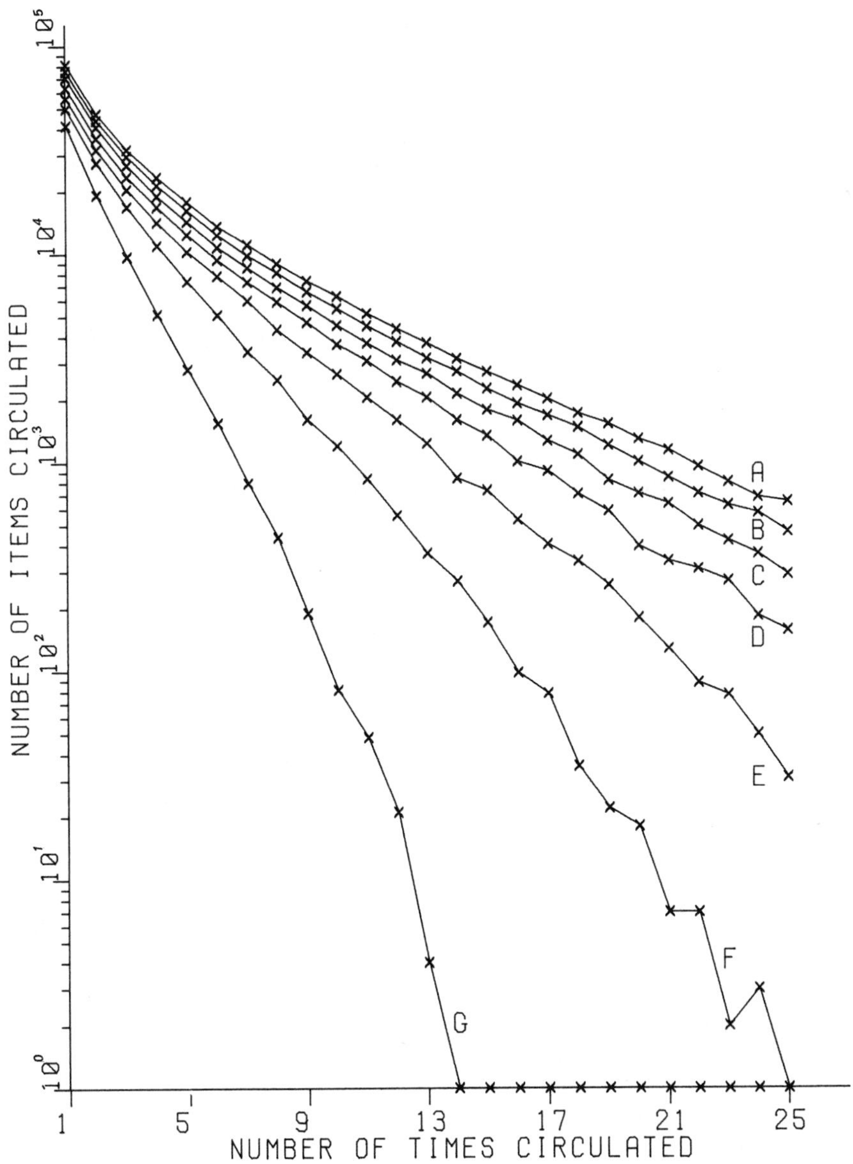

Figure 9. Seven-year circulation study 1969-1975. A: 1969-75; B: 1969-74; C: 1969-73; D: 1969-72; E: 1969-71; F: 1969-70; G: 1969.

The portion of the collection acquired in 1969 which would have been a candidate for non-acquisition according to frequency-of-use criteria is given in Table 24. For example, if a minimum of two uses is set as the criterion, ex post, 54.22% of the collection would not have been ordered; 62.5% would not have been ordered if three uses were set as the criterion; and so on. The same figures can be used as a foundation for resource-sharing, secondary storage, retirement and/or weeding decisions at the zero- and low-use frequencies.

3. Alternative Classifications of Use

Until this point, we have considered use of books and monographs in aggregated terms. Use can be disaggregated from many points of view, to permit more detailed analysis of use patterns. Examples are given here of disaggregation by "type of user" and by "type of subject matter."

a. User Types: Table 25 shows the distribution of user types (for external circulations) over the time period 1969-1975. The composition of the user population appears to be relatively stable over time.

NOTE: Items comparisons with totals for any given year are meaningless since more than one user type may use the same item. Transactions comparisons, however, are meaningful.

Table 24
Criteria for Not Buying Books

Number of Uses	% of Items Acquired	Cumulative % of Items
0	39.863	39.863
1	14.350	54.213
2	8.313	62.526
3	6.005	68.531
4	4.641	72.572
5	3.607	76.179
6	2.984	79.163
7	2.476	81.639
8	2.072	83.711
9	1.888	85.599
10	1.627	87.226
11 and over	12.774	100.00

Table 25
User Types by Year

Year	Undergrad		Graduate		Faculty		Staff		All others	Totals	
	Items	Trans	Items	Trans	Items	Trans	Items	Trans	Trans	Items	Trans
1969	45393	72650 .4387*	34923	54917 .3316	10045	10626 .0642	4035	4322 .0261	23103 .1395	81623	165618 1.0001
1970	57122	92115 .4526	41533	63640 .3127	13601	15446 .0759	5560	6041 .0297	26281 .1291	99677	203523 1.0000
1971	58611	93725 .4225	44224	69102 .3115	14795	16739 .0755	7504	8254 .0372	34018 .1533	108207	221838 1.0000
1972	56555	86704 .3967	44442	68372 .3128	16909	18682 .0855	7146	7852 .0359	36949 .1691	112587	218559 1.0000
1973	54040	79269 .3880	44464	67425 .3300	14095	15876 .0777	9643	10443 .0511	30942 .1514	108675	204315 .9982
1974	54174	80557 .3710	44296	68591 .3159	15570	18029 .0830	11836	13190 .0608	36752 .1693	114039	217119 1.0000
1975	51773	74418 .3671	46119	71365 .3520	15689	19400 .0957	7929	8941 .0441	28577 .1410	108971	202701 .9999

* Represents fraction of total use for a given year.

b. Use in Relation to Coursework: On an experimental basis, courses within the University of Pittsburgh were classified according to the LC classification scheme. The purpose was to determine whether students in a particular course class used books in the same LC class. For example, Class 'P' was studied for one four-month academic term. It was discovered that 14% of the students enrolled in 'P' courses used books in LC Class 'P'; they accounted for 23% of the total transactions during this period in the 'P' category.

c. Use (External Circulation) Based on Language: The period 1969-1974 was studied in order to discern relative use of materials in various languages. Findings are given in Table 26.

4. Sampling Algorithms

In order to provide guidance to libraries which do not have complete circulation data, samplings of data selected *ex post* were analyzed in relation to our complete data. Correlating items circulated externally on given sample days with the items circulated externally in the entire population for various time periods, it was found that random samples of as few as three days produced correlations as high as 0.95-0.98 with the total population in regard to percent of usage by LC class (Table 27).

The implication is that samples of a manipulable size can be used to identify the aggregate usage patterns within the LC classes; for example, in order to estimate whether the budget for each class is allocated in a fashion commensurate with its "benefit," defining benefit as use.

Table 26
Relative Use of Materials in Various Languages

LANGUAGE	Use (1969-1973)			
	Items		Transactions	
	No. of Items	% of Items Used	No. of Transactions	% of Transactions
English	209,991	84.22	1,068,575	91.16
Spanish	10,297	4.13	29,483	2.52
French	7,694	3.09	23,122	1.97
German	7,545	3.03	19,228	1.64
Russian	2,687	1.08	6,030	0.51
Chinese *	3,054	1.22	6,057	0.52
Italian	1,256	0.50	3,593	0.31
Others	6,826	2.74	16,111	1.37

* The East Asian Collection was not keypunched until late 1971; therefore the usage data for the Chinese language may be underestimated.

Table 27
Reliability of Sampling Data

Sample Size		Period of Time							
		1969-1974 (277,734 items)		1973-74 (100,090 items)		1974-75 (98,366 items)		1975-76 (99,348 items)	
Days	Items Used during sample period	Sample, %	Correlation	Sample, %	Correlation	Sample, %	Correlation	Sample, %	Correlation
3	1,900	0.7	.96	1.9	.98	1.9	.99	1.9	.98
5	3,693	1.3	.93	3.7	.96	3.8	.97	3.7	.97
10	7,049	2.5	.95	7.0	.98	7.2	.98	7.1	.98
15	10,596	3.8	.95	10.6	.98	10.8	.98	10.7	.99
30	20,672	7.4	.96	21.6	.98	21.0	.99	20.8	.99

In examining usage within each LC class, there seems to be almost no change in the relative usage, indicated by ranking the LC classes according to percent of usage, over the short-term. For example, considering the data for external circulation from 1974-75 with the comparable data from 1975-76, on an item basis, only two of the 21 LC classes have switched positions. In 1974-75, LC Class C ranked 12th, and LC Class N ranked 13th; in 1975-76 these two rankings were reversed, that is, Class C was 13th and Class N was 12th. The difference in percent of usage between the two classes was 0.1%, or about 100 items out of 100,000. The ranking of the first eleven classes was: P, H, B, D, L, E, Q, J, G, F and R. The last eight classes were: T, M, K, U, A, S, Z, V.

There seems to be more of a shift over a longer period of time. For example, 15 of the 21 LC classes shift positions when we compare the data from 1969-74 with the data for 1975-76. However, the change in percent of use is seldom greater than 2%, and often is less than 1%. The fact that the shift is slight is indicated by the fact that the data for 1969-74 correlated with the data for 1975-76 at 0.92. Furthermore, if we consider aggregating the data, we see that the grouping of the classes by percent of usage results in no shift in the members of a particular group over time (Table 28).

Table 28
Stability in Use Patterns by LC Classes[17]

Category of Usage, by %	LC Classes in Category	
	1975-76 only[18]	1969-1974
over 25%	P	same
15 - 24%	H	same
6 - 14%	B,D,L	same
3.6 - 5.9%	E,J,Q	same
1.0 - 3.5%	C,F,G,N,R,T	same
under 1%	A,K,M,S,U,V,Z	same

[17] For an interesting example of School/Departmental usage data, see Miriam A. Drake, "Circulation of Materials from the General and Krannert Libraries—Purdue University," January 1978. Unpublished.

[18] The data for 1975-76 was based on "items," not "transactions." Data provided by the Hillman Library for transactions included the category "unclassified," whereas the data used here did not. Adjusting the Hillman data to omit the category of "unclassified," this table remains substantially the same. The only adjustment needed would be that categories J and Q show usages of 3.4 and 3.3% respectively, which is .3 of 1% off the lower limit of the 3.6 - 5.9% category shown in this table.

In considering the change in percent of usage within each class, no LC class changed as much as 2% when comparing the 1969-74 data with that for 1975-76. Rounding to the nearest 0.5%, the categories showing the greatest change in percent of usage are given in Table 29. Thus, it would seem that the percent of usage by LC class is not a highly variable item.

If we consider the percentages obtained in the various samples as individual scores on the samples, there is very little variation in the scores. Computing a standard deviation for each LC class, only three classes (H, L, P) have a standard deviation greater than one percentage point. Furthermore, if we restrict the scores to those obtained in the 30 days of sampling, the deviations in the sample are either smaller or the same in all but one case.

In considering restricted groups of years, the wider deviation is among newer items, with the entire collection showing more stability.

We have calculated the standard deviations for several categories of data. They are:

a. all samples—that is, 3-day, 5-day, etc.; as well as totals for 1969-74, 1973-74, 1974-75, 1975-76, etc.
   This resulted in 18 scores.

Table 29
LC Classes with Increasing and Decreasing Usage[19]

L.C. CLASS	% Usage 1969-74	% Usage 1975-76	Difference (rounded to nearest 0.5%)
Classes increasing in usage:			
H	17.0	18.7	+ 1.5
L	6.5	8.1	+ 1.5
B	9.8	10.7	+ 1.0
R	1.6	2.1	+ 0.5
Classes decreasing in usage:			
P	27.9	26.2	- 1.5
D	9.9	8.6	- 1.5
T	2.2	1.3	- 1.0
Q	4.4	3.7	- 0.5
F	3.2	2.7	- 0.5
C	2.3	1.8	- 0.5

19 The transaction data supplied by Hillman Library for fiscal 1975-76 are slightly different in percentage than those reported in this "item" data. However, in all cases the direction of movement is the same and is within 2.5% of the figures reported here. However, similar transaction data for 1969-74 were not supplied by Hillman, so no comparison could be made.

b. only the sample days—that is, 3-day, 5-day, 7-day, 10-day, 15-day and 30-day samples
   This resulted in 11 scores.

c. yearly circulation in 1973-76 considering the entire collection
   This resulted in only 3 scores.

d. yearly circulation from 1973-1976 only, considering only the newly-acquired items (acquired in the fiscal year whose circulation we are examining)
   This resulted in only 3 scores.

The deviations for these groups are:

Table 30
Standard Deviation of Scores Based on % of Use by LC Class

LC CLASS	SAMPLE TYPE			
	Sample 1 (18 scores)	Sample 2 (11 scores)	Sample 3 (3 scores)	Sample 4 (3 scores)
A	0.2	0.1	0.0	0.1
B	0.8	0.5	0.2	0.9
C	0.5	0.1	0.1	0.1
D	0.8	0.5	0.2	0.2
E	0.5	0.6	0.1	0.6
F	0.5	0.3	0.1	0.6
G	0.5	0.3	0.1	0.6
H	2.2	1.3	0.3	0.7
J	0.5	0.3	0.2	0.2
K	0.3	0.4	0.1	0.2
L	1.0	0.4	0.3	1.6
M	0.2	0.1	0.1	0.1
N	0.3	0.3	0.1	0.2
P	1.6	1.0	0.4	2.1
Q	0.6	0.4	0.3	0.5
R	0.6	0.6	0.0	0.5
S	0.1	0.1	0.1	0.1
T	0.3	0.1	0.1	0.1
U	0.2	0.1	0.1	0.2
V	0.1	0.04	0.0	0.1
Z	0.1	0.1	0.1	0.2

As Morse has indicated,[20] there is an "aging" factor in the book usage. For example, when comparing the items circulated in the total collection with circulation of new items only, LC Classes A, D, G, K, L, Q and Z consistently show higher circulation among new items than among old. Classes C, M, R show less circulation of new items.

D. Some Practical Applications of Findings[21]

1. Weeding

One of the practical applications for libraries that results from this study is a specific plan for weeding the collection. Books and monographs that can be moved to low-cost storage facilities without disrupting service to library users have been identified individually as well as in categories.

Weeding has been classified into two main types—scientific and non-scientific. The "non-scientific" methods are subjective, i.e., they require expert(s) to decide what will (should) be read in the future by retaining those books in primary storage. By applying scientific (usually statistical) techniques, usage models can be developed by examining certain tangible evidence—for example, publication date or the past circulation history. In order to implement the model all that is necessary is to examine the data for a particular item, from which the decision to retain or weed is automatic. No "expert" decisions are required.

Some early investigators such as Fussler and Simon advocated a mixed strategy for weeding the external circulating collection.[23] More recent investigators such as Jain, Trueswell and Morse[24] lean primarily, if not solely, on the scientific approach to weeding. We place ourselves in the latter camp and would consider only objective techniques.

---

[20] P. M. Morse, Library Effectiveness: A Systems Approach, MIT Press, Cambridge and London, 1968.

[21] See also Chapter VI, "Alternatives to Local Acquisitions."

[22] H. H. Fussler and J. L. Simon, Patterns in the Use of Books in Large Research Libraries, University of Chicago Press, 1969, p. 144. While primary selection would be done by "scientific" prediction, they recommend that one or more scholars review the titles recommended for storage.

[23] A. K. Jain, "A Statistical Model of Book Use and Its Application to the Book Storage Problem," Journal of the American Statistical Association, December 1969, pp. 1211-1224.

When viewed broadly there is surprisingly little variation in the scientific approach. All such methods propose to examine the collection and form some decision rule. While investigators would like to examine the entire collection,[24] they have not been able to do so for lack of time, money, and/or manpower in the rare—if existent—occasions when complete data are available. As a result, the studies vary in sample size, sampling methodology and time duration. No studies of which the authors are aware overcome the assumptions that the investigators make to the investigators' own satisfaction. We are in a position to confirm or refute some of their assumptions by examining the entire collection for which we have complete data in machine readable form.

With the exception of Jain,[25] researchers agree that past use is the best indicator of the future use of material. We utilized this fact by concentrating our efforts on this indicator through the concept of "core collection." While there are different meanings[26] attached to the concept of "core collection," we will define an item as being in the core collection if it has circulated externally one or more times, thus being in the active circulating collection. Similarly, the potential circulating collection is defined to contain the core collection (active circulating collection) and those items that have never circulated. In this simple model, once an item enters the core collection it will always remain in that category.[27] By examining the relationships between these categories, we hope to provide rules that will allow decisions as to which items to remove to secondary storage as having an acceptably low probability of ever being used. The results can be used by librarians and administrators to prolong the useful life of the library. In addition, when

---

[24] R. W. Trueswell, "Determining the Optimal Number of Volumes for a Library's Core Collection," Libri, 16(1); 50, April 1966.

[25] A. K. Jain, et. al., A Statistical Study of Book Use, Ph.D. Dissertation, Purdue University, 1967. Jain asserts that his method is superior to one of usage histories. However, Slote points out that "...no evidence was found in his (Jain's) report that usage history was in fact studied by him and found wanting." Stanley J. Slote, "Identifying Useful Core Collection: A Study of Weeding Fiction in Public Libraries," Library Quarterly, 41(1); 27, January 1971.

[26] See, for example, American Library Association, Books for College Libraries: A Core Collection of 40,000 Titles, 2nd ed., Vol. 1 (Chicago: American Library Association, 1975), p. vii; and Stanley J. Slote, op. cit., pp. 25-34.

[27] A similar model was developed by Trueswell using the concept of last time circulated. Trueswell, op. cit.

weeding is done objectively, the probability of eliminating or removing books that should be retained and keeping books that should be discarded is much less than otherwise,[28] thus contributing to maintaining the patron satisfaction level.

Care should be taken when implementing this or any other weeding model. While it may be necessary to discard some materials, the user community should be assured of access to the information contained in the weeded materials in some manner. When the material is not available elsewhere and it is impossible to store materials in secondary storage or a regional depository, less conventional storage media can be considered, such as microform or other yet to be developed techniques.

However, a more complex model would have a dynamic core collection. It would contain items which have circulated as well as relatively new (<5 years old) items which have never circulated. Circulation records carried trigger the weeding automatically.[29]

The discussion on "Predicting the Future Use of the Collection" (see section C. 1. c. above) now gives us our

> Proposed Weeding Rule: In order to satisfy the requirement that less than one-half of one percent of yearly acquisitions be returned to the actual circulating collection, do not weed any materials that are less than seven years old, irrespective of whether they have circulated or not; and weed only those books seven years old or older that have not circulated.[30]

In actual numbers our current acquisitions are roughly 35,000 items per year. If this technique were implemented at the correct time after the library opened and acquisitions were constant, this requirement would predict a maximum of 175 items recalled from secondary storage a year or an

---

28 In fields where information becomes obsolete very quickly, such as economics and chemistry, the subjective method was found equivalent to the objective measure, while history may remain a "probable exception." Fussler and Simon, p. 128.

29 Miriam A. Drake, personal conversation.

30 This is in agreement with Trueswell's decision rule: "Remove all books that have not circulated during the previous eight-year period. After doing this, it would be expected that no more than 1% of the users would be unable to find the books they required." Richard Trueswell, "A Quantitative Measure...," pp. 22-23.

average of just one book in two days. Of course, knowing yearly acquisitions, one could work the other way and determine from what year one should start weeding in order to retrieve an average of, for example, fifty books a day from storage.

2. Storage

Most librarians have the desire to keep all books in primary storage. Yet this is not always possible in the real situation. Decisions on how best to weed should be based upon at least the following factors: present book stock, rate of acquiring new stock, maximum shelf space for the circulating collection, and the user satisfaction created by having desired items in primary storage.[31] Librarians who wish to avoid "management weeding by crisis" may adopt a similar strategy to the one presented. Use of our model requires that the following major points or their estimates be ascertained:

a. the percent of shelving available as a function of time;

b. the percent of shelving being vacated by weeding as a function of time;

c. the asymptotic regression coefficients (as explained previously and as found in Table 2 above).

The following equation may be used to determine the percentage of shelving used at a future time T + ΔT:

$$\%U_{T+\Delta T} = \frac{B_T + BA_{\Delta T} - BL_{\Delta T} - BW_{\Delta T} + BRS_{\Delta T}}{B_{max}} \times 100\%$$

where $\%U_{T+\Delta T}$ = percent of shelf space used at time T+ΔT

when given B_T = books held by the library at time T

$BA_{\Delta T}$ = number of books acquired during time ΔT

$BL_{\Delta T}$ = number of books lost, stolen, etc. during time ΔT

$BW_{\Delta T}$ = number of books weeded during time ΔT

[31] The costs associated with weeding must also be estimated in any decision making. At this juncture it is assumed that secondary storage is always cheaper than primary storage.

$BRS_{\Delta T}$ = number of books returned from storage during time ΔT

B_{max} = maximum number of books the library can shelve in the area under investigation

Of the 2,900,000 volumes available in the University system, an inventory in the last half of August 1974 showed 538,000 books and monographs were held in the Hillman Library. We used data presented in a study internal to Hillman Library[32] to calculate the maximum number of books the circulating collection can hold—790,000. Loss through theft and deterioration[33] was approximately 5% per year until the installation of a tattle tape system in 1974 reduced losses to 1% per year. Knowing the exact number of books purchased since 1969, we were able to calculate shelf space used at the beginning of 1970 through the present. Since there had been only insignificant weeding, the factors having to do with weeding were effectively zero. Using

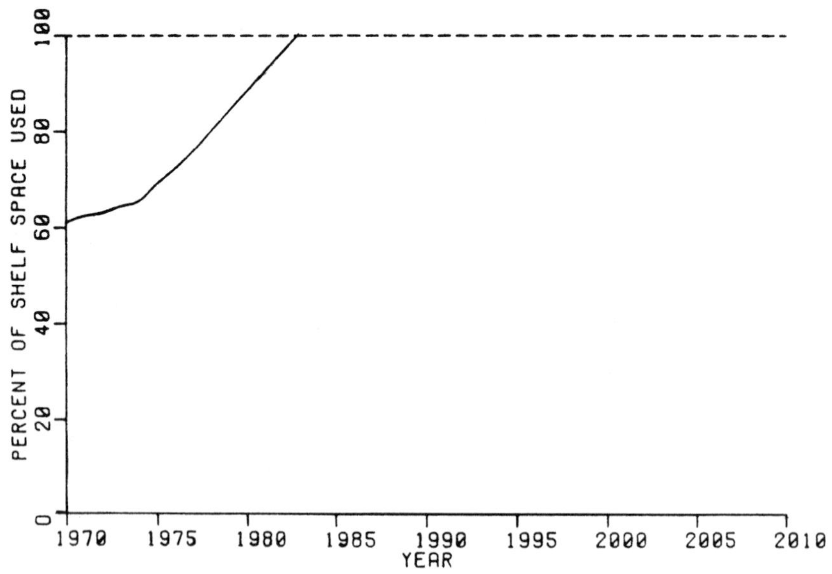

Figure 10. Future shelf space availability without pruning.

---

[32] Margaret L. Zenk, "Shelf Space Availability Before Full Capacity is Reached in the University Libraries," Internal Report, January 30, 1976. The East Asian Collection is also excluded from this figure.

[33] We used these as the best available "guesstimates."

projected acquisition figures, we then calculated shelf space availability while maintaining a 99.5% user satisfaction level from the present until shelf space capacity exceeded 100%. This is projected to occur in 1982.[34] (See Figure 10.)

By using the model to annually prune the roughly 45% of the items that have not circulated during the last seven years, the library will recover roughly 18,000 spaces annually (which is approximately 2.25% of the circulating collection shelving space). The initial pruning should release about 200,000 books, freeing more than 20% of the circulating collection shelf space. The total effect would be to extend the time before the library runs out of shelf space by 21 years[35] (from 1977; see Table 31, Figure 11).

Table 31
Predicted Collection Behavior—Shelf Space and Returned from Storage

Year	No. Books at Year start	No. Books acquired	No. Books lost	No. Books weeded	No. Books from storage	No. Books at year's end	% of shelf space filled
1969	467903	36869	25238	0	0	479534	60.70
1970	479534	35997	25776	0	0	489755	61.99
1971	489755	27311	25853	0	0	491213	62.18
1972	491213	30199	26070	0	0	495342	62.70
1973	495342	28438	26189	0	0	497591	62.99
1974	497591	35097	5326	0	0	527362	66.75
1975	527362	30894	5582	0	0	552674	69.96
1976	552674	35000	5876	0	0	581798	73.65
1977	581798	40000	6217	208694	1052	407939	51.64
1978	407939	40000	4479	14882	595	429173	54.33
1979	429173	40000	4691	11291	352	453543	57.41
1980	453543	40000	4935	12485	235	476358	60.30
1981	476358	40000	5163	11757	175	499613	63.24
1982	499613	40000	5396	14510	161	519868	65.81
1983	519868	40000	5598	12772	144	541642	68.56
1984	541642	40000	5816	14470	142	561498	71.08
1985	561498	40000	6014	16537	153	579100	73.30
1986	579100	40000	6191	16537	158	596530	75.51
1987	596530	40000	6365	16537	160	613788	77.69
1988	613788	40000	6537	16537	163	630877	79.86
1989	630877	40000	6708	16537	164	647796	82.00
1990	647796	40000	6877	16537	165	664547	84.12
1991	664547	40000	7045	16537	165	681130	86.22
1992	681130	40000	7211	16537	165	697547	88.30
1993	697547	40000	7375	16537	165	713800	90.35
1994	713800	40000	7538	16537	165	729890	92.39
1995	729890	40000	7698	16537	165	745820	94.41
1996	745820	40000	7858	16537	165	761590	96.40
1997	761590	40000	8015	16537	165	777203	98.38
1998	777203	40000	8172	16537	165	792659	100.34

[34] Note that this is for the entire circulating collection—some sections of the collection will run out sooner and others later.

[35] We intend to continue data collection in order (among other things) to validate the model and make modifications if necessary.

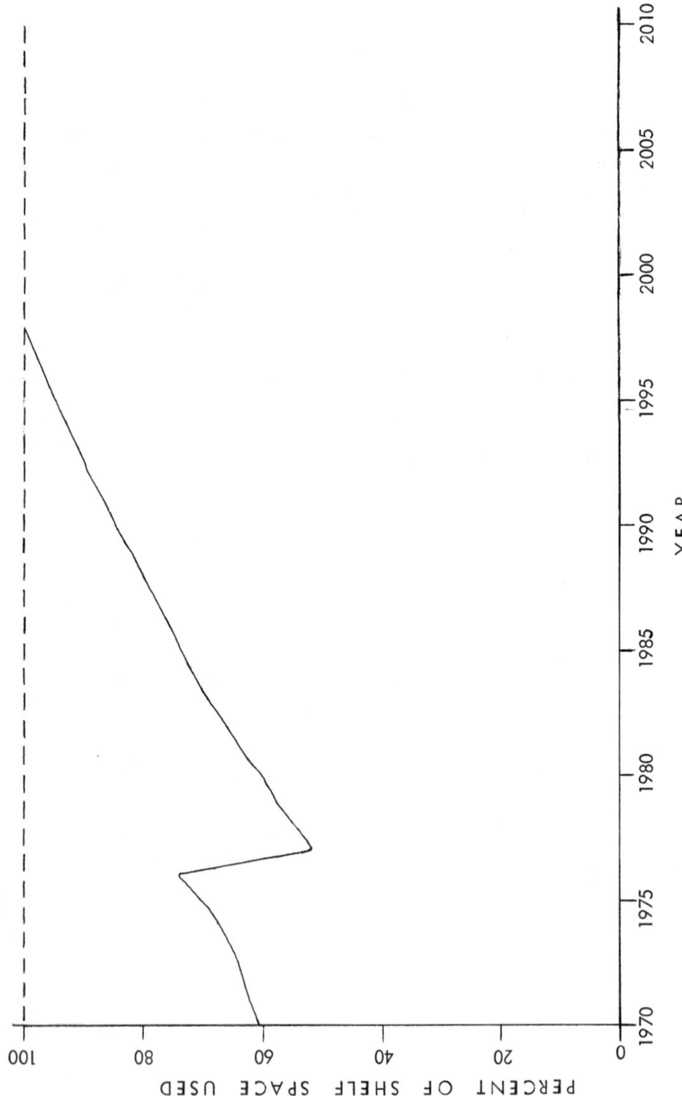

Figure 11. Future shelf space availability with pruning.

This is not the ultimate solution, as the library will still reach its limit because it is acquiring books more than twice as fast as it is retiring them. In order to reach a steady-state, some additional trade-offs must be made.

It should be noted that by decreasing the user satisfaction from the 99.5% level to the 95% level, one is not buying much time. For a high increase in projected user dissatisfaction (4.5%—a decrease in user satisfaction by a factor of 9), the increase in spaces vacated annually will be from 18,000 to 20,000, for an additional yearly saving of 2,000 spaces, assuming 40,000 acquisitions per year. This buys one-twentieth of a year's acquisition time. But on the other hand, using absolute figures, recalled books from secondary storage will increase from 200 to 2,000 per year, which is the same as recalling an average of 5.5 items per day. This may well be an acceptable volume to recall if the occasional inconvenience for the patron is deemed acceptable. This should be kept in the perspective that 40%-50% of the items the patron desires to borrow that the library owns are unavailable[36] for other reasons, such as being lost, stolen, misshelved, or checked out.

---

[36] Daniel Gore, "Zero Growth for the College Library," College Management, August-September 1974, p. 13; and Richard Trueswell, "A Quantitative...," American Documentation, January 1965, p. 24.

Chapter III

USE OF JOURNALS

Roger Flynn

A. Summary of Findings

In studying the six science and engineering libraries involved in this project to determine the use of journals, certain conclusions were seen to be generally true of all the libraries, others were unique to individual libraries.

Some of the general conclusions common to all libraries were:

Usage in General

- Usage in general is low.
- Larger collections tend to have a greater percentage of low-use journals. (However, size of the collection is not the only factor influencing the percent of usage.)
- Usage is primarily of current journals.
- Browsing is primarily of current journals, while older issues are accessed through some type of reference.
- Over 75% of the articles perused do not result in photocopying.
- In general, the amount of photocopying done increases with the age of the issue.
- Well over 90% of the photocopying of older issues is initiated by a reference, not by browsing. This indicates that these uses could have been satisfied with a copy of the article rather than access to the original journal.

Patron Characteristics

- The principal users of journals are students; and, among students, graduate students are the principal users.

- Usage among students is mainly by previous reference. Faculty do more browsing.
- Usage of the special libraries is primarily on a departmental basis, with the Physics department using the Physics Library, the Chemistry department using the Chemistry Library, and so on. While this may seem a trivial point, the fact of very little crossover among clients of the libraries suggests that resource-sharing centers designed along disciplinary lines (distributed network) are worth considering.

Some of the conclusions unique to individual libraries were:

- The Physics Library could be called "journal-intensive."
- Langley Library (Life Sciences, including Psychology) showed more browsing of older issues of journals than the other libraries.
- The Physics Library showed more usage of browsing than all other libraries. This was due in part to the librarian's marketing procedures.
- The secondary users (graduate students being the primary users in terms of number of uses) varied from library to library. For example, the Physics Library and the Mathematics Library showed very little undergraduate usage, while the Engineering Library and the Computer Science Library did show undergraduate use. The Physics and Mathematics Libraries also showed a higher rate of use by faculty, while the Computer Science Library showed very little use by faculty.
- The Computer Science Library was the only library which was used more often by members of other departments than by its own Computer Science department members.
- Also interesting along these interdisciplinary lines was the fact that the Chemistry department members used the Physics Library, but the Physics department members did not use the Chemistry Library.

B. Purpose of and Approach to Journals Study[1]

1. The Purpose of the Study

The purpose of the journals study was twofold:

a. to develop a methodology that would provide librarians with a relatively simple mechanism for discerning patterns of usage; and

b. to test this methodology by studying the patterns of usage in the Science and Engineering Libraries on the University of Pittsburgh campus.

Some of the questions we wanted to answer in defining "patterns of use" were:

Who uses the library? This question was broken down into two parts:

- What is the academic status of the user?
- What is the academic department of the user?

"Status" was broken down into undergraduate students, graduate students, faculty, post-doctoral students, visitors, and staff. Anyone not fitting into these categories was considered to be "other." The department of the user was taken from the standard list of departments at the University: for example, Physics, Chemistry, Metallurgical & Materials Engineering (abbreviated Metallurgy), Psychology, Biology.

Which journals are used? This question was concerned with four points:

- What are the titles of the most used journals?
- Which journals are not used?
- What proportion of the collection is used?

---

[1] It should be kept in mind by the reader that this study considers only journal usage in the library, since only the decision processes impacting the library budget are of interest here. Overall patterns of use for given journal titles could well be influenced by the extent of personal subscriptions. It may be that some extremely important journals exhibit low use in the library because many, or most, in a given discipline will want to have their personal copy. Some insight on the issue may be obtained from the study by Alexander Strasser ("Acquisition of Scientific Information: A Study of the Physics Department of the University of Pittsburgh," Ph.D. Dissertation, University of Pittsburgh, 1978).

- What proportion of the collection seems to be little used or not used at all?

What is the age of the journals that are used? That is, usage primarily of current journals, or of journals published years ago, or both? We refined this question in terms of: Do different users (for example, by department) use the journals differently (for example, one department using current journals, but another department using older journals)?

How do people find out about the journal articles they read? That is, are they directed to them by class assignments, browsing, references from indexes and/or abstracts, etc.?

This category was called the "Alert Method" and consisted of such methods as browsing, personal communication, class assignment, index/abstract, previous reference (e.g., journal reference or bibliography), and "other."

2. The Approach to the Study

a. The Libraries Studied: The libraries chosen for the study were the Physics Library, the Langley Library (Life Sciences, including Psychology), the Bevier Engineering Library, the Chemistry Library, the Computer Science Library, and the Mathematics Library. The study spread over three calendar years, with each library being sampled during the following trimesters of the school year:

Library	Sampling Period
Physics	Fall 1975; Winter 1976
Life Sciences	Fall 1976
Engineering	Fall 1976; Winter 1977
Chemistry	Winter 1977
Computer Science	Winter 1977
Mathematics	Winter 1977

The two-trimester samples (Fall, Winter) involved more sampling hours than the single-trimester samples.

b. Methodology: The methodology finally developed was a combination of observation, questionnaire and interview techniques. An observation form was designed, with space for recording such data as: the title of the journal; status of user; department of user; alert method; whether the user intended to photocopy the article(s) being accessed, etc. A preliminary form was developed, tested and revised, and then used in a two-trimester study of the Physics Library. Based on experience in the Physics Library, the form was again revised and the new version was used in studying all other libraries. (See sample of form in the Appendix, Figures 18 and 19.)

The form was administered by data collectors who would go to a designated library at prearranged times and watch for people who used the journal collection. In line with our definition of benefit in terms of "use," the observer was to enter the library and see if anyone was currently using the journal collection, by circulating through the library on the lookout for people reading journals. If a journal reader was observed, the observer would then either ask the person the questions from the observation sheet or have the person fill in the sheet, aided by comments from the observer. The observer would then watch for people entering the journal area and if someone did enter and take a journal off the stacks, the observer would administer the questionnaire. "Use" was defined as physical selection and the act of leafing through pages.

The data recorded on the completed forms were then keypunched onto hollerith cards, verified, and then collected in a file to be processed by a standard statistical package (in this case, SPSS).

c. Sampling: Two separate methods were used in order to select the hours in which to sample the libraries. In the case of the Physics Library, the librarian was consulted as to "heavier hours of usage." A stratified sample was used which emphasized these periods. In the case of all other libraries, the libraries were "pre-sampled" for one week, at one hour intervals, in order to determine the distribution of usage. The assignment of "observation periods" was then made in accordance with this distribution.

Once a schedule of one-hour or one-and-one-half hour observation periods had been made for an entire trimester (two trimesters for Physics and Engineering), data collectors were sent to collect the data during these hours. One observer was assigned to a library in any one observation period. There were two to four observation periods a week, depending on the library in question. Thus, the samples included only a certain percentage of the actual operating hours of the library. The approximate percentage of sampling hours per open library hour for each library was:

Physics	1/15th of the total weekly hours
Life Sciences	1/30th " " " "
Engineering	1/25th " " " "
Chemistry	1/25th " " " "
Computer Science	1/25th " " " "
Mathematics	1/20th " " " "

More exact percentages are given in the Appendix. These figures were used to arrive at both a projected trimester usage and a projected yearly usage, based on the observed sample usage.

While the number of hours of observation was set, the number of uses recorded in each hour was unlimited. If usage was light, as few as 2-5 uses might be recorded; if usage had been heavy, conceivably any number of uses could have been recorded. (We say "conceivably" because the actual usage was never so heavy as to cause us to consider putting on a second observer in order to handle the overflow of interviews, although we kept a cadre of trained data collectors available for this purpose.)

d. Differences in the Sampling Methods and Libraries Sampled: The first round of sampling was carried out in the Physics Library only. The second round was carried out in the other five libraries. The personnel and methods used to sample the Physics Library were different in some respects from those used to sample the other libraries. The principal methodological differences were:

- The basis for collecting an observation in the Physics Library was whether or not the material was in the "journal area." Both bound volumes and unbound volumes were observed, and serials were included.

  In all other libraries the observers looked either for unbound journals or for a bound volume that had volume numbers indicating that it was a serial or periodical. Again, serials were included.

- In the Physics Library, statistics were collected in one-hour periods, distributed according to the recommendation of the librarian and favoring heavier use periods. The hours were distributed over morning, afternoon, evening, all days of the week. The distribution in all other libraries was derived after a week spent sampling numbers of uses, so that the distribution of sampling hours followed the actual pattern of usage—more sampling hours in heavier used times, less hours in little used times. In either case, the sampling biases toward heavier usage statistics.

- The method of recognizing a "use" also differed: in the Physics Library, if a journal was picked up, a "use" was recorded. In the other libraries, some scanning was required before it was considered a "use"; so that there might be some bias toward higher usage in the Physics Library.

- Browsing opportunities also differed between libraries: Physics has a policy of displaying new incoming journals at 11 a.m. each day. Faculty come in and browse these new journals, thus biasing usage toward more faculty usage and more browsing than in the other libraries.

e. Computing the Statistics: In collecting the observations, some items were occasionally missed. For example, the observer might obtain the title of the journal, but not the status or department of the user. These missed observations occurred for two reasons:

(1) the user finished the journal article and left the library before the observer could reach the user, although the title of the journal was still available from the copy left behind. This occurred relatively infrequently.

(2) the user refused to divulge certain information.

These missed observations would fall into the category of "unknown." In computing many of the statistics contained in this report, the "unknown" category was removed before performing the computations.

The category of "other" also presented difficulties at times. It signified that the response given by a user to a particular question did not fit into our pre-defined categories of response. Where this category seemed to offer little information, the category of "other" was also eliminated before the statistics were computed.

Because of these deletions of certain data, the actual number of uses that the statistics were based on has been noted in our discussion of the findings. Thus, in computing usage by age, the Physics Library is listed as having only 419 uses, instead of the actual 439. This is because the category of "age unknown" was dropped before the computation. In this particular case, we have no reason to believe that the "unknown" journals were any "older" or "younger" than the rest of the journal population.

f. Definitions: Several terms which are used throughout this portion of the study are defined as follows:

Use — the use of a journal was considered to be the physical apprehension and perusal of the volume in question by the user, whether from the stacks, from the reading tables or from elsewhere. Journals checked out on loan would be included in the use statistics if the checkout took place during an observation period. Otherwise they would not be observed nor included in the results. The same applies to items removed from the shelf for photocopying. If an item was checked out to be distributed to others, only the one actually observed would be included in the sample. This biases the use data toward lower use. However, the method of observation was used in order to have an operational method which could be replicated in other studies. Reliance was not placed on impressions of use but on direct observation of the use of the journal collection.

Sample Uses — uses actually observed during the sampling period.

Projected Uses (per term or per year) — extrapolation of uses from the sample period to a larger period of time.

User — the person who accessed the journal.

Status of User — the user's position in the University, e.g., faculty, graduate student, undergraduate, staff, visitor.

Department of User — the school department with which a faculty member, student or staff member was associated.

Transaction — any use is a transaction.

Title — represents a "run of journals"; does not distinguish between different volumes of the title being used.

Titles in the Collection — represents the total number of journals in the collection, regardless of whether the library still subscribes to these journals. Thus ceased publications are involved, if these titles are still available in the collection.

Current Collection — includes only titles currently subscribed to by the library in question.

Official List of Titles in the Collection — the listing of all titles in the collection, both current and ceased, as provided by the central library administration.

Age of Journals — concerns individual volumes of a particular title. The current year is age zero, the previous year is age one, and so on.

Alert Method — the motivating factor behind the use of a particular journal at a particular time, e.g., browsing, class assignment, a reference from another book or journal, etc.

Previous Reference — a concatenation of alert methods, all of which are "non-browsing," e.g., personal communication, class assignment, bibliographic reference, etc.

Use of Photocopying — refers only to the photocopying of the particular journal being used, by the person using that journal. Does not include photocopying that might be ordered by faculty or students outside the sample observation periods.

Observation Period — periods of one or one-and-one-half hours in which a person physically observed the usage in the journal areas of the various libraries.

Sample Period — the total number of observation periods for a particular library.

Journal — probably the most difficult term to define. The method by which the observer tried to ascertain whether a library user was accessing a "journal" was a combination of the physical area of the library being used and the physical characteristics of the material being apprehended or read. The various libraries have certain areas that are primarily for the access of journals. Furthermore, in the case of unbound journals, the materials "look like a magazine." In the case of bound journals, the observer was instructed to look for volume numbers on the binding. Serials were included in the sample uses, as well as more frequently published materials. In the report, the use of the term "journal" is often as a synonym for "title." In other instances, the use is in its more generic sense. It is hoped that the context will serve to distinguish the two uses.

C. Discussion of Findings

Usage of the Journal Collection

1. Number of Uses

a. Sample Uses: The usage of the journals in the libraries studied was generally very low. The actual number of sample usages in each library was:

Library	Number of Sample Usages
Physics	439
Life Sciences	211
Engineering	172
Chemistry	160
Computer Science	24
Mathematics	30

b. Uses per Hour: By dividing the number of uses by the number of hours sampled, we can derive the average number of uses per sampling hour for each library:

Library	Sample Uses	Hours Sampled	Uses per Hour
Physics	439	120	3.7
Life Sciences	211	39	5.4
Engineering	172	81	2.1
Chemistry	160	39	4.1
Computer Science	24	39	0.6
Mathematics	30	39	0.8

Thus, in terms of raw usage, Langley Library (Life Sciences, including Psychology) is the most heavily used, followed by the Chemistry Library and then the Physics Library. The Engineering Library exhibited low usage, and the Mathematics and Computer Science Libraries were utilized less times per hour than they were sampled.

c. Projected Yearly Usage: Using the multiplying factor mentioned above (Chapter III, section B. 2. c.), we can project a yearly usage for each library as follows:

Library	Sample Uses	Projected Yearly Usage	Rounded
Physics	439	9,879	9,900
Life Sciences	211	19,413	19,400
Engineering	172	6,579	6,600
Chemistry	160	12,288	12,300
Computer Science	24	1,842	1,850
Mathematics	30	1,890	1,900
	3,683	51,891	51,950

d. Uses per Person: The amount of raw usage exhibited by each library is affected by the number of users in the departments that each library serves. In order to account for this, we have computed a use per person. The population of the library served consists of undergraduate students, graduate students, and faculty. The results are:

Library	Use per Person
Physics	16.6
Life Sciences	3.0
Engineering	0.67
Chemistry	6.4
Computer Science	2.5
Mathematics	1.7

Thus, in terms of use per person affected, the Physics Library is by far the strongest user of journals. However, as we shall see, there are some mitigating factors accounting for this. For instance, users from the Chemistry department are considered by the Physics Library to be part of their clientele; however, we have computed this table with the Chemistry department users listed separately, since they have their own library. If we restrict the sample only to Physics users, the average number of uses per person would be about 13.6 uses per person per trimester. Despite having their own library, users from the Chemistry department do account for 13% of the journal usage in the Physics Library. (However, users from the Physics department do not account for any of the Chemistry Library usage in our study; thus, the "borrowing" is not reciprocal.) Another factor to consider is that the Physics librarian has a policy of putting the new journals on display at 11 a.m. each day. Many faculty members come in to browse the index of these journals at this time and this biases the statistics in favor of greater usage, greater faculty usage, more browsing, and more usage of current journals. However, even with these reservations, Physics does seem to be a field that is "journal-intensive."

2. Usage by Title

In all six libraries studied, a high percent of usage was provided by a small percent of the collection. The number of titles in the entire collection was:

Library	Official Figures	Librarian's Figures
Physics	298	298 [2]
Life Sciences	914	835
Engineering	1,643	829
Chemistry	433	402
Computer Science	198	148
Mathematics	265	181

There was considerable discussion of the precise number of titles in the journal collections for the science and engineering libraries. The figures from the offical serials record are listed under "Official Figures" above. The departmental librarians said that there were fewer titles actually in the collections, and their figures are listed under "Librarian's Figures." In some cases, the discrepancy is not insignificant, as in the Engineering Library, where the official list has 1,643 titles while the Engineering librarian reports about half this amount (829). The librarian cites duplications in the official lists, e.g., one listing for the title in print, another for microfiche of the same title, as part of the reason for the discrepancy. Since the use of microfiche is not covered in this study, it is the opinion of this author that the estimate of the librarian is more accurate. However, in the interests of consistency, the decision was made to use the official list wherever possible. This was not possible in the Physics Library because the collection had changed considerably since the study of that library; however, the official list was used for all other libraries. We have not recalculated our figures, which are based on the "official" count. We have included the librarians' figures so that the interested reader may be in a position to recalculate the percent of usage if he wishes to do so. These discrepancies

---

[2] The estimates in Physics were originally made from a list provided by the Physics librarian and the data collectors, not from the official list.

affect the percent of collection used, both in the sample and in the estimates of yearly usage. They do not affect totals based on number of uses alone, e.g., uses per person, projected yearly number of uses, cost per use, and so on.

a. Percent of Collection Used During the Sampling Period: The percent of the titles in the collection used during the sampling period varies from under 10% to a high of 37%, depending on the library sampled. In general, a very small percentage of the collection accounted for the entire journal usage in the sampling period. Listing the libraries by the percent of the entire collection accounting for all usage in the sampling period, we have:

Library	Percent of Collection
Physics	36.9%
Life Sciences	11.9%
Engineering	6.8%
Chemistry	14.5%
Computer Science	8.6%
Mathematics	8.3%

A more detailed breakdown (Table 32) shows the percent of the collection supplying a given percent of the sample usage.

From the point of view of acquisitions decisions, a more interesting statistic is the amount of usage lost by elimination of a given percentage of the collection. In the light of the below table, an elimination of 85-90% of the collection would result in a loss of only 30% of usage (subtracting figures in line 3 from 100%).

The problem of projecting the sample percentages into yearly percentages is dealt with in subsection III. C. 2. f. below.

Table 32
Concentration of Journal Usage in Six Libraries

% of sample usage	Percent of Collection Supplying that Percentage of the Usage					
	Physics	Life Sci.	Engineering	Chemistry	Comp.Sci.	Math.
20	1.0	1.3	0.7	0.4	0.5	0.8
40	3.7	2.4	2.3	1.3	1.5	1.9
70	15.8	5.6	6.8	6.2	8.6	8.3
100	36.9	11.9	6.8	14.5	8.6	8.3

b. Usage versus Collection Size: With the exception of the Engineering Library, the raw usage parallels the collection size. That is, the larger collections do support larger usage:

Rank: Collection Size		Rank: Raw Usage	
Engineering	1,643	Life Sciences	19,400
Life Sciences	914	Chemistry	12,300
Chemistry	433	Physics	9,900
Physics	298	Engineering	6,600
Mathematics	265	Mathematics	1,900
Computer Science	198	Computer Science	1,850

The Engineering Library faces problems of a larger magnitude than those faced by other libraries. It services an entire school—The School of Engineering—while the other libraries service only certain departments within the School of Arts and Sciences. Thus, its clientele is almost equal in numbers to the combined clientele of the other five libraries. Furthermore, the funds available for support have a wider base than in the other libraries. Thus, there is some justification for maintaining such a large collection. However, the extremely low usage indicates that a smaller collection might not lead to user dissatisfaction.

c. Usage per Title: A better indication of the efficiency in acquisition policy for each library can be gleaned from consideration of the average number of uses per title in the collection. Dividing the projected yearly usage by the number of titles in the collection gives us:

Library	Uses per Title
Physics	33.2
Chemistry	28.4
Life Sciences	21.2
Computer Science	9.3
Mathematics	7.2
Engineering	4.0

d. Usage Categories: Certain titles were used repeatedly during the sample study period. However, the great majority of titles appeared only one time or not at all during the sampling period. Because the Physics and Engineering Libraries were two-trimester samples, while the other four libraries involved only one trimester, the results are listed in two different tables: for the Physics and Engineering Libraries (Table 33); for the libraries with only one trimester of sampling (Table 34).

Table 33
Uses per Title—Physics, Engineering

Number of Sample Uses	Percent of Collection supplying that Usage	
	Physics	Engineering
10 or more	3.7	0.2
5 to 9	5.0	0.0
2 to 4	13.1	2.1
1	15.1	4.5
0	63.1	93.2
	100.0	100.0

Table 34
Uses per Title—Remaining Libraries

Number of Sample Uses	Percent of Collection supplying that Usage			
	Life Sci.	Chemistry	Computer Sci.	Math.
10 or more	0.0	0.6	0.0	0.0
5 to 9	0.5	0.9	0.5	0.0
2 to 4	5.1	4.7	1.0	1.9
1	6.3	8.3	7.1	6.4
0	88.1	85.5	91.4	91.7
	100.0	100.0	100.0	100.0

e. More Economical Journals: That certain journals provide a greater return than others can be seen by constructing a table of uses per title for the various categories of usage. Again, the Physics Library is listed separately (Table 35). However, because of the low usage in the Engineering Library, we include those statistics with the libraries having only one trimester of sampling.

We have computed two averages: one counting zero-use titles (called "average, 0 or more" in Table 35); and the other not including the zero-use titles (called "average, 1 or more" in the same table). The average of interest is the one not including the zero-use titles. The rationale for this is that ideally only the used journals should remain in the collection. (The second average is included for the purpose of harmonizing this table with the first table listed in this section.) The number of uses per title has been rounded to the nearest whole number.

Table 35
Uses in Relation to Average Title Use—Physics Library

Category of Usage	Projected Uses per Title for that Category
	Physics Library
10 or more	413
4 to 9	115
1 to 3	36 *
average, 1 or more	90
average, 0 or more	33

* The asterisk indicates where the number of uses per title in a given category falls below the average for all titles used. In making decisions about whether or not to continue subscribing to a given journal, the titles giving above average service should be "safe." Titles that are not found in the sample would be the first candidates for "de-acquisition." Titles that are below average in performance would be the next likely candidates.

The decision rule for continuing or stopping subscriptions will include factors besides the number of uses. For example, cost per use should be considered. However, the uses per title offers a "first cut" at separating the "productive" from the "non-productive" journals.

The data for the other five libraries are given in Table 36. It was not possible to track the source for acquisition of each title in the collection. However, a tracking of these decisions to acquire, with the status of the person recommending acquisition indicated (e.g., faculty member, librarian, student, administrator, salesperson) would help to evaluate the various sources of recommendations.

Table 36
Uses in Relation to Average Title Use—Other Libraries

Category of Usage	Projected Uses per Title for that Category				
	Life Sci.	Engineering	Chemistry	Comp.Sci.	Math.
4 or more	498	239	653	383	251
3 uses	276	115	231	230	189
2 uses	184	77	154	153	129
1 use	92*	38*	77 *	77 *	63*
average, 1 or more	178	59	195	108	86
average, 0 or more	22	4	31	9	8

* See note bottom of Table 35.

f. Projecting Yearly Percentages of Usage: By graphing the data (method described in the Appendix), we can project the sample usage into yearly usage. The results show that most of the titles in a collection will eventually be used, but only very few titles will be used a great number of times.

The fact that nearly all titles eventually get used can be seen by considering the percent of the collection having at least two uses of a given title:

Library	% of Collection Used Two or More Times per Year
Physics	95.5
Life Sciences	97.3
Engineering	84.0
Chemistry	97.0
Computer Science	>98.0
Mathematics	>98.0

Note, however, that this is based on "titles used," not on volumes. A given title will have anywhere from a few to several hundred individual volumes, depending on frequency of publication and the number of years the library has subscribed to it. Seen in this light, a usage of "at least two times" per title is small usage indeed.

The predominantly low usage of most titles in the collection can be seen by considering the percentage of titles expected to fall below certain usage thresholds. For example, in the Physics collection, 90% of the titles will be used 100 or fewer times during the course of the year. In fact, 90% of all the library collections studied can be expected to be used 100 or fewer times. And 60% or more of the titles in the collections will be used 25 or fewer times. The expected yearly usage is given in Table 37.

Table 37
Projected Yearly Usage: 100 or Fewer Uses

Total Uses of Title during Year	Percent of Collection Providing that Usage					
	Physics	Life Sci.	Engineering	Chemistry	Comp.Sci.	Math
100 or less	90.0	90.0	98+	89.5	95.5	97.0
50 or less	80.0	79.0	95.8	78.0	82.5	88.0
25 or less	65.0	62.0	89.0	62.0	59.0	68.5
10 or less	42.0	37.0	73.0	37.0	23.0	32.5
5 or less	25.0	21.0	55.0	21.0	6.8	22.5

The Engineering Library has the lowest usage performance. This is partially a problem of size: the Engineering Library has more titles and services more users than any other library studied.

The difficulties in journal acquisition policy seem to multiply as the library grows in size. The four largest libraries (Engineering, Life Sciences, Chemistry and Physics) have the largest proportions of titles in the "low usage" categories. Furthermore, the smaller libraries (the Mathematics and Computer Science Libraries) show a greater tendency for every title in the collection to eventually be consulted.

However, every library experiences some low usage. Most of the libraries show that 30-40% of the titles in the collection will be used less than 11 times a year. For some titles, this will be less than one use per volume published during that year.

The table for "10 or fewer" uses is:

Library	Percent of Collection with 10 or Fewer Uses per Year
Engineering	73
Physics	42
Life Sciences	37
Chemistry	37
Mathematics	33
Computer Science	23

Very few journals show high usage, with 10% or less of the titles being consulted more than 100 times (Table 38).

Table 38
Projected Yearly Usage: High Usage Titles

Total Uses of Title during year	Percent of Collection supplying that Usage					
	Physics	Life Sci.	Engineering	Chemistry	Comp.Sci.	Math.
>100	10.0	10.0	<2.0	10.5	4.5	3.0
>200	4.2	4.0	<2.0	4.1	<2.0	<2.0
>300	2.5	2.1	<2.0	2.2	<2.0	<2.0

g. Identifying Individual Titles: Probably the most difficult problem in studying the journal usage is identifying the actual titles of the journals used. The extremely popular journals present no problem, nor do those that are never used. But the journals in the less used classes are a difficulty. Shaw[3] has suggested a method by which a sticker is attached to the bound volumes when they are reshelved (students using bound journals are requested not to reshelve journals). This does identify the journals that are never used (no sticker) but does not distinguish between journals that are used one time versus those used more than one time. Furthermore, Shaw has confined his method to bound journals, although this is not necessary. The findings of our study show that the predominance of usage is of current journals, so that these must also be monitored.

King and Roderer[4] have indicated that a "cut-off" point between the journals that are economical for local holdings and those more economically obtained through resource-sharing can be identified. They identified the cut-off point as six or fewer uses per year in the Physics field. Similar methods could be used to identify cut-off points in the other disciplines. Another extensive study of the cut-off point between owning and borrowing has been done by Palmour, Bellassai and Wiederkehr.[5] However, in order to make use of a cut-off threshold, we must be able to identify which journals fall above that point, and which fall below. This requires knowing the number of times a title was consulted, not just whether or not a particular title was or was not consulted "at least once."

In view of this, it would seem that a more labor-intensive, but also more fruitful method of tracking usage must be found. If it is requested that no journals be reshelved, the person who does the reshelving can carry a list of the journal titles and make a check next to the title for each volume reshelved. For most low-use libraries, this should not be a difficult task, involving under 100 volumes a day. The method would apply to bound as well as unbound journals. If a daily running total is kept, the library should have a

---

3 W. M. Shaw, Jr., "A Practical Journal Usage Technique," paper delivered to the American Library Association Research Roundtable, Detroit, June 1977.

4 Donald W. King and Nancy K. Roderer, "Economic Considerations for Interlibrary Loan Networks," paper delivered at the American Library Association meeting, June 1977.

5 Vernon E. Palmour, Marcia C. Bellassai and Robert R. V. Wiederkehr, "Costs of Owning, Borrowing and Disposing of Periodical Publications," Public Research Institute, prepared for the National Commission on New Technological Uses of Copyrighted Works, October 1977.

good picture of the actual usage of each title on an ongoing basis. This would certainly be the basis for a more reasoned decision in continuing or stopping subscriptions to the various journals. However, continuous monitoring is not a necessity. Periodic sampling, as described in the section entitled "Applying the Methodology to Journal Use Studies Elsewhere" in the Appendix, should suffice.

If the age of the journal was also a desirable item of information, a matrix (title by age group) could be included; or, more simply, a dichotomy between unbound (current) and bound (older) journals could be noted. This would necessitate merely drawing a line through the middle of the page on which journal uses were noted.

This method would not yield information on the type of user, e.g., status, department, or method by which the user was alerted to the collection. However, these items could be sampled by a method similar to our observation form (sample given in the Appendix). The patterns of usage in these categories are much easier to identify than the exact usage of given journal titles, so that a smaller sample is sufficient. This smaller sample will obviate the difficulty of the periodic monitoring inherent in identifying the high-use and low-use titles in the collection.

h. Current Subscription Titles: The number of titles in the collection is larger than the number of titles currently subscribed to. In order to see the relationship, we have computed the "percent of collection currently subscribed to" for the six libraries. The figures for all but the Physics Library are exact. The data for the Physics Library were estimated from data given by the librarian and the central administration (Table 39).

Table 39
Number of Titles in Collection

Library	Titles in the total collection	Titles : current subscriptions	% of current subscriptions to total collection
Physics	298	157	52.7
Life Sciences	914	494	54.0
Engineering	1643	737	44.9
Chemistry	433	177	40.9
Computer Science	198	126	63.6
Mathematics	265	195	73.6

If the reader wishes to adjust any of the usage percentages by percent of "current subscriptions" rather than basing the figures on the total collection, simply multiply by the following numbers:

Library	Adjustment
Physics	1.9
Life Sciences	1.9
Engineering	2.2
Chemistry	2.4
Computer Science	1.6
Mathematics	1.4

i. The Cost of Usage: While this topic is covered fully in Chapter IV, section C. ("Measuring the Cost of Journal Use"), it is appropriate to point out the strong cost differential between the journals that are used and the collection as a whole. Based on subscription costs alone, we have the following average costs:

	Average Cost per Use	
Library	Journals Used During Sample Period	Entire Collection
Physics	$ 1.83	$ 3.50
Life Sciences	$ 0.66	$ 2.52
Engineering	$ 1.25	$ 6.81
Chemistry	$ 0.95	$ 2.69
Computer Science	$ 0.36	$ 2.68
Mathematics	$ 1.32	$ 7.54

The consistently lower figures for the journals that were accessed during the sample period offers support for the weeding of little-used or no-use journals.

The above figures, based on subscription costs alone, underestimate the true cost per use. The total cost per use, including such factors as storage space, processing, administrative salaries, etc. (see Chapter IV, section C. for complete breakdown) is:

Library	Average Cost per Use Based on All Costs (Entire Collection)
Physics	$ 4.12
Life Sciences	$ 3.30
Engineering	$ 9.04
Chemistry	$ 3.33
Computer Science	$ 3.55
Mathematics	$ 10.07

3. Usage by Age

a. The primary usage is of journals published within the current year and the previous five years. With the exception of the Mathematics department, 90% of all usage is supplied by journals published within the last 15 years. The breakdown for each library is given in Table 40.

b. Use of journals older than 25 years is 5% or less, depending on the library in question (Table 41).

We have included only the aggregate statistics, to indicate the general pattern of usage. It is possible that the more highly used journals would have a longer "age-span." However, this identification is better studied by each individual library. The methodology described in the section entitled "Applying the Methodology to Journal Use Studies Elsewhere" in the Appendix is adequate for such a study.

c. Bias in the Statistics: Two types of bias enter into the statistics:

(1) journals only recently subscribed to will have only relatively recent issues available, thus biasing the statistics on age toward the current journals;

Table 40
Age of Journals Used

Age	Physics	Life Sci.	Engineering	Chemistry	Comp.Sci.	Math.
Uses	419	211	172	160	24	30
0 - 5	82.1%	66.3%	73.9%	65.7%	83.3 %	56.6 %
0 - 15	94.2%	91.4%	93.7%	93.3 %	95.8 %	80.0 %

Table 41
Use of Older Journals

	Physics	Life Sci.	Engineering	Chemistry	Comp.Sci.	Math.
Age 26+	1.7%	2.4%	1.7%	5.0%	0.0%	3.3 %
oldest use	1920	1940	1942	1935	1958	1951
age, yrs*	56	36	35	42	19	26

* The age of the oldest use is subtracted from the final year of the study in each library: 1976 (Physics and Life Sciences); 1977 (remaining four libraries).

(2) journals that have been discontinued do not have current issues available, thus biasing the statistics toward older copies.

Thus, the two biases tend to work against each other. The bias toward older usage has little effect, since there is very little older usage. However, the bias toward current usage should be accounted for. A study of the beginning year of the journals available in each of the libraries yielded the percentages given in Table 42.

By comparing the percentage of titles available with the percent actually used, we can see that the preponderence of current usage is not due to these being the only journals available (Table 43).

4. Usage by Alert Method

The means by which a user was directed to a particular journal were categorized as: browsing, personal communication, indexes/abstracts, journal reference, class assignment, bibliography, other, and unknown. By "other" we refer to a category not listed. By "unknown" we mean that the alert method was not ascertained from the user. The conclusions regarding alert method follow. In compiling these statistics, we have eliminated the categories of "other" and "unknown" before performing the calculations.

a. The relative use of browsing versus all other forms of previous reference (index/abstract, journal reference, bibliography, personal communication, and class assignment) differs among the libraries. For example, Physics is highly browsing-oriented, while Life Sciences, Chemistry, and Mathematics are greatly dependent on previous reference (over 70% of usage due to previous reference). In fact, Physics is unique in that it was the only library with less than 50% of the sample usage due to previous reference. The exact statistics are given in Table 44. The implication of the differential usage is that each library must be individually studied to ascertain its pattern of usage in regard to the alert method.

Table 42
Duration of Journal Subscription

Age of Subscription (in years)	Percent of Collection					
	Physics	Life Sci.	Engineering	Chemistry	Comp.Sci.	Math.
0 - 5	9.0	18.7	14.2	8.5	19.0	4.7
6 - 15	36.4	34.7	42.2	39.9	57.0	31.8
16 - 25	25.8	17.2	24.8	20.9	19.0	22.0
26 +	28.8	29.4	18.8	30.7	5.0	41.5
	100.0	100.0	100.0	100.0	100.0	100.0

Table 43
Comparison of Subscription Age with Actual Use

Age of Subscription (in years)	Percentage of Journals in Age Category					
	Physics	Life Sci.	Engineering	Chemistry	Comp.Sci.	Math.
0-5, available	9.0	18.7	14.2	8.5	19.0	4.7
0-5, used	82.1	66.3	73.9	65.7	83.3	56.6
16+, available	54.6	46.6	43.6	51.6	24.0	63.5
16+, used	5.8	8.6	6.3	6.7	4.2	20.0

Table 44
Alert Method Used

	Physics	Life Sci.	Engineering	Chemistry	Comp.Sci.	Math.	Total
Uses	420	201	160	153	24	30	988
%Browse	68.6	21.9	41.2	28.8	41.7	26.7	460
% Previous Reference	31.4	78.1	58.8	71.2	58.3	73.3	528

Average: Browse - 46.6%; Previous Ref. - 53.4%

The presence of the Physics data, weighted in the opposite direction to the other libraries, somewhat distorts the total average usage. While the total average is split 47-53, or almost equally, when the Physics data are included, the averages with the Physics data excluded are:

	Uses	% Usage
Browsing	172	30.3%
Previous Reference	396	69.7%
	568	100.0%

This 70% usage of previous reference in the sample portends well for alternative means of supply, such as resource sharing, which normally require a reference for efficient retrieval.

It is also interesting to note that Physics and Chemistry users were almost diametrically opposed in regard to their relative usage of browsing versus previous reference:

Alert Method	Physics	Chemistry
Browsing	68.6%	28.8%
Previous Reference	31.4%	71.2%
	100.0%	100.0%

b. In all libraries, the alert methods of personal communication and class assignment are among the lowest categories. However, the exact percentage of usage due to these categories varies widely among the libraries (Table 45).

c. Alert Method as a Function of Age: The most interesting statistics in regard to alert method are those relating to the age of the journal (volume) accessed. In this section we examine how the alert method used varies with the age of the journal accessed.

Over 60% of the browsing that occurs is with journal volumes less than two years old; and if we exclude Langley Library (Life Sciences, including Psychology), which is far below the norm in this respect, over 90% of the browsing that occurs is with journals five years old or less.

This is in contrast to the use of previous reference, where no library showed a usage as high as 30% in the first two years (year of acquisition and following year). Langley Library (Life Sciences, including Psychology) was significantly different in this respect, having more browsing of the older journals. Again, we caution that the disciplinary libraries show differing patterns of usage, and should be studied individually.

The breakdown of age of journal as a function of alert method is given in Table 46.

Table 45
Percentage of Personal Communication and Class Assignment

Library:	Physics	Life Sci.	Engineering	Chemistry	Comp.Sci.	Math.	Total
% Personal Comm.	6.4	3.5	6.3	10.5	8.3	3.3	6.4
% Class Assign.	2.1	5.5	11.3	7.2	12.5	0.0	5.3
	8.5	9.0	17.6	17.7	20.8	3.3	11.7

Table 46
Alert Method as a Function of Age

Library:	Physics	Life Sci.	Engineering	Chemistry	Comp.Sci.	Math.	Total
Uses:	401	201	160	153	24	30	969
Browsing Uses:	272	44	66	44	10	8	444
Journal Age							
0-1 yrs	93.4	65.9	68.2	95.4	90.0	62.5	86.5
2-5 yrs	6.2	2.3	25.8	2.3	10.0	37.5	9.0
6-15yrs	0.0	22.7	6.0	2.3	0.0	0.0	3.4
16+ yrs	0.4	9.1	0.0	0.0	0.0	0.0	1.1
	100.0	100.0	100.0	100.0	100.0	100.0	100.0
Previous Ref. uses:	129	157	94	109	14	22	525
Journal Age							
0-1 yrs	17.8	26.1	21.3	12.8	28.6	9.1	19.8
2-5 yrs	29.5	42.1	40.4	38.5	42.9	31.8	37.5
6-15yrs	36.4	24.8	27.7	38.5	21.4	31.8	31.2
16+ yrs	16.3	7.0	10.6	10.1	7.1	27.3	11.4
	100.0	100.0	100.0	100.0	100.0	100.0	100.0

d. Relative Use of Alert Method as a Function of Age: If we vary the age of the journal, then examine the alert method used, contrasting browsing with previous reference, we see the declining use of browsing and the increasing use of previous reference as the journals grow older. The averages for all libraries together are given in Table 47. Thus, we may conclude that about 80% of the journals two years old and more will be accessed through some type of previous reference. In regard to the implications for resource-sharing, this previous reference could just as readily be submitted to a resource-sharing partner as to the local collection. Furthermore, even 20% of the current journals (0 - 1 year old) are accessed through previous reference. These items, if they proved to be low-use journals, might also be held in an alternate collection.

The impact on permanent storage is staggering. If all items were stored after two years, we would lose 17% of the browers in the period 2 - 5 years old, 8 1/2% in the age bracket 6 - 15 years old, and about 8% for all journals over 15 years old. In absolute percentages, this represented 60 uses of the 969 uses in the sample, or an absolute loss of 6.2% of the uses. Thus, if we had an alternate means of supply for all journals older than one year, we could still supply 94% of the requests, with a tremendous reduction in storage and maintenance. The concept of a "temporary" collection for local storage could be considered.

Table 47
Relative Use of Alert Method as a Function of Age

Age	% Browsing	% Previous Reference	Total Uses
0-1 yrs	78.7	21.3	488
2-5 yrs	16.9	83.1	237
6-15yrs	8.4	91.6	179
16 + yrs	7.7	92.3	65
			969

Even the Langley Library (Life Sciences, including Psychology), which does more browsing of older journals in relative terms, would not be greatly affected by a decision rule to relegate journals two years old or older to a secondary source. The absolute amount of browsing lost at Langley Library would be about 7 1/2% (15 uses out of 201). This smaller absolute loss is due to the fact that Life Sciences/Psychology patrons do not do a heavy amount of browsing. The Engineering Library would be the hardest hit by such a rule, with a loss of 13.1% (21 uses out of 160 in absolute terms). Again, we point out the desirability of having decision rules tailored to individual libraries.

5. Photocopying of Journals

a. The majority of the users do not photocopy the articles they access. The statistics for each library, including the category of "unknown" are given in Table 48. The category of "unknown" consists primarily of two situations:

(1) the respondent did not yet know whether or not (s)he would photocopy the article;

(2) the observer was unable to obtain the information.

If we eliminate the "unknown" category, we see that in over 75% of the cases, the individual does not plan to photocopy the article (Table 49).

It is clear from interdepartmental charges that some photocopying takes place over and above that shown by our sample. These would be copies supplied by the librarian. However, the sample usage does indicate that the majority of uses do not result in photocopying of the article in question.

Table 48
Journal Photocopying

Library:	Physics	Life Sci.	Engineering	Chemistry	Comp.Sci.	Math.
Uses:	439	211	172	160	24	30
% No	73.6	59.2	66.9	58.8	83.3	70.0
% Yes	15.0	27.0	20.9	30.6	12.5	26.7
% Unknown	11.4	13.7	12.2	10.6	4.2	3.3

Table 49
Journal Photocopying (Excluding "Unknown")

Library:	Physics	Life Sci.	Engineering	Chemistry	Comp.Sci.	Math.	Total
Uses:	389	182	151	143	23	29	917
% No	83.0	68.7	76.2	65.7	87.0	72.4	76.1
% Yes	17.0	31.3	23.8	34.3	13.0	27.6	23.9

b. Photocopying in Relation to Age of Article: There is an aging factor in the use of photocopying, though the increase in the amount of photocopying that occurs is not as dramatic as the drop-off that occurs in the use of browsing versus previous reference. There is an increase of about 13% in the percentage of photocopying done after the two initial years (acquisition and one year old), then another increase of about 11% for journals over 15 years old (Table 50).

Table 50
Photocopying Relative to Age
of Article: All Libraries

Age	Total Uses	% No	% Yes
0 - 1	453	83.2	16.8
2 - 15	384	70.1	29.9
16 +	65	60.0	40.0

With some fluctuations (e.g., Physics has more "No's" in the "16+" category than in the "2 - 15 years" category), the individual libraries follow a similar pattern (Table 51).

Table 51
Photocopying Relative to Age
of Article: Individual Libraries

Library	Age	Uses	% No	% Yes
Physics	0 - 1	254	87.4	12.6
	2 -15	97	71.1	28.9
	16 +	23	82.6	17.4
		374		
Life Sci.	0 - 1	66	71.2	28.8
	2 -15	101	67.3	32.7
	16 +	15	66.7	33.3
		182		
Engineering	0 - 1	62	82.3	17.8
	2 - 15	80	73.8	26.3
	16 +	9	55.6	44.4
		151		
Chemistry	0 - 1	51	74.5	25.5
	2 -15	81	66.7	33.3
	16 +	11	18.2	81.8
		143		
CompSci.	0 - 1	13	92.3	7.7
	2 -15	9	77.8	22.2
	16 +	1	100.0	0.0
		23		
Math.	0 - 1	7	100.0	0.0
	2 -15	16	75.0	25.0
	16 +	6	33.3	66.7
		29		

One implication is that the 30% of users who would have photocopied the older articles (anything older than two years) would be willing to invest this sum in a photocopy obtained through a resource-sharing mechanism if the time for delivery was not excessive. However, the 70% who would not wish to photocopy would not be as willing to incur the cost of copying in a resource-sharing scheme utilizing duplication for dissemination.

c. Relationship of Alert Method and Photocopying: Photocopying is much less used among journals that are browsed than among journals accessed through previous reference. Of all journals that were photocopied, over 75% were accessed through previous reference (Table 52).

Furthermore, within the category of "Previous Reference," almost 35% of the journals were photocopied, while only slightly over 11% of the browsed materials were copied (Table 53).

Table 52
Alert Method in Relation to Photocopying

Photocopied?	Alert Method		Total Uses
	Browsing %	Previous Ref. %	
Yes	22.4	77.6	210
No	54.1	45.9	676
			886

Table 53
Photocopying in Relation to Alert Method

Alert Method	Photocopy?		Total Uses
	Yes %	No %	
Browsing	11.4	88.6	413
Previous Ref.	34.5	65.5	473
			886

d. Photocopying by Year Published by Alert Method: The results are even more dramatic when we consider the use of photocopying in conjunction with both age and alert method. In fact, we can almost categorically say that items photocopied that are "old" were accessed by previous reference (Table 54, for all libraries). Thus, while 40% of the photocopying of relatively new journals is initiated by browsing, over 90% of all photocopying of journals more than two years old is initiated by a previous reference. Presumably, in these cases, a photocopy of the original article could have substituted for the actual journal.

The totals given in the right-hand column indicate the relative proportions of photocopying between new and old journals. This is close to an even split in photocopying between the new journals (46%) and the older journals (53%). However, the alert method is predominantly "previous reference" for the older journals.

The totals in the bottom row give the relative proportion of photocopying initiated by the two methods of alert in the total sample. Thus, about 4 of every 5 articles photocopied (77.4%) were articles accessed through previous reference; 1 out of 5 (22.6%) being due to browsing.

Patron Characteristics

6. Usage by Academic Status

Usage by academic status breaks down as given in Table 55. The following statements highlight the conclusions drawn about status:

- Students are the heaviest users of the journals.
- Among students, graduate students are the heaviest users.

Table 54
Photocopying in Relation to Age and Alert Method

Yes, photocopy			
Age (yrs.)	Alert Method		Total
	Browse	Previous Ref.	
0 - 2	39.6%	60.4%	46.2%
3 +	8.0%	92.0%	53.8%
Total:	22.6%	77.4%	

- Usage by both faculty and undergraduate students varies among libraries.
- Usage by visitors and staff is relatively small.

a. Usage by Students: Students account for the majority of usage. Creating a single category from the three groups, graduate, undergraduate and post-doctoral, we have the data given in Table 56.

b. Usage by Graduate Students: Among students, graduate students are the heaviest users. As is evident from the main table on status, graduate usage ranges between 40% and 65% of all usage, depending on the library studied. Furthermore, if we combine the graduate students with the post-doctoral students, we obtain the totals for "advanced" students as given in Table 57. The relatively low usage among advanced students in Engineering is not due to the size of the graduate population alone. Engineering ranks third in percentage of graduate students (23.8%) but last in graduate student usage. On the other hand, Life Sciences ranks last in percentage of graduate students (11.5%) but second in percent of usage due to advanced students (69.2%).

Table 55
Use by Academic Status

Library:	Physics	Life Sci.	Engineering	Chemistry	Comp.Sci.	Math.
Uses:	384	211	172	160	24	30
Status%:						
Graduate	62.8	57.8	45.9	41.3	50.0	63.3
Undergrad	1.8	19.9	40.7	11.9	33.3	0.0
Post-Doc	7.0	11.4	1.7	23.1	8.3	0.0
Faculty	26.3	4.7	8.7	16.9	0.0	36.7
Visitor	1.0	4.7	2.9	1.9	8.3	0.0
Staff	1.0	1.4	0.0	5.0	0.0	0.0

Table 56
Student Usage

Library:	Physics	Life Sci.	Engineering	Chemistry	Comp.Sci.	Math.
Status%: all students	71.6	89.1	88.3	76.3	91.6	63.3

Table 57
Graduate Student Usage

Library:	Physics	Life Sci.	Engineering	Chemistry	Comp.Sci.	Math.
Status%: advanced students	69.8	69.2	47.6	64.4	58.3	63.3

c. Usage by Undergraduate Students: Usage by the undergraduate students was heaviest in Engineering (40%), with substantial usage in Computer Science (33.3%) and Life Sciences (20%). Chemistry had about 12% usage, but both Physics and Mathematics were extremely low in undergraduate usage, Mathematics having none at all during the sample period.

The extremely high usage among undergraduates in Engineering (40.7%) cannot be explained by numbers alone. Both Life Sciences and Computer Science have proportionately more undergraduates, yet have a lower usage by these undergraduates than has Engineering. However, size does play a part. Life Sciences, Computer Science and Engineering have the largest proportion of undergraduates; they also show the largest undergraduate usage.

The author is indebted to Miriam A. Drake for pointing out that many of the titles used in the Engineering Library sample were popular titles, such as Aviation Week and Engineering News Record. Furthermore, the percentage of class assignment is higher in Engineering than in any other library except Computer Science. Engineering and Computer Science ranked one and two in percent of undergraduate usage, respectively, and ranked two and one in percent of class assignment. Thus, this explanation that the undergraduate usage is affected by class assignment is particularly plausible.

In fact, both leads proved fruitful. In examining undergraduate usage in the Engineering and Computer Science Libraries, the percent of undergraduate usage due to class assignment was 18% in Engineering and 15% in Computer Science. This pattern was followed in Chemistry (16%) and Life Sciences/Psychology (10%). The two libraries that had no class assignment of undergraduate usage were Physics and Mathematics, which showed only 1.8% and 0.0% undergraduate usage, respectively, during the sample period.

In the general population of all six libraries, 15% of the undergraduate usage (21 of 144 uses) was due to class assignment. The average of all uses due to class assignment was about 5% in the general population, so that class assignment does play a greater role in undergraduate usage. Among graduate students, the class assignment resulted in a little over 8% of the usage in Engineering and Computer Science, and about 5% in the general population.

In checking the popular titles, both Aviation Week and Engineering News Record were among the most popular journals in the undergraduate usage at the Engineering Library. The most popular titles among undergraduates were:

Civil Engineering — 9 uses in sample
Aviation Week — 5 uses in sample
Engineering News Record — 3 uses in sample
Datamation — 3 uses in sample
Electronics — 3 uses in sample

The two most popular titles in the sample for graduate students were:

Photochemistry and Photobiology — 4 uses in sample
Fluid Mechanics — 3 uses in sample

There was very little overlap between the items read by either group (undergraduate or graduate students) and the remainder of the population. The six most popular titles among Engineering undergraduates accounted for 27 undergraduate uses in Engineering, and 30 uses in the entire population, so that 90% of the usage was due to the undergraduate students.

The undergraduates in Engineering showed a usage pattern more similar to that of the Physics Library users: 6 titles accounted for 39% of the sample usage, 11 titles accounted for 53% of sample usage, and 33 titles accounted for the entire sample usage.

The graduate Engineering students had 65 titles accounting for 79 uses, an average of 1.2 uses per title. Only the two titles already mentioned had more than two uses. Thus, the graduate usage seems scattered while the undergraduate usage seems more concentrated.

A study concentrating on the user patterns of individual groups on such matters as methods of alert, overlap of titles, etc., in more depth than the current study was able to provide, is indicated.

Another factor is the nature of the courses. For example, the undergraduate courses in Mathematics are usually textbook centered. As a result, the Mathematics department, which has an undergraduate population of over 70% of the department, shows no undergraduate usage of the journals during our sampling period.

d. Usage by Faculty: Usage by the faculty was substantial in Mathematics, Physics and Chemistry. It was less than 10% in the other libraries, with Computer Science showing no faculty uses in the sample.

Again, the relative size of the population is a factor in usage, but not the only factor. Physics, Chemistry and Mathematics have the largest proportion of faculty; they also have the highest faculty usage. However, Physics has proportionately twice as many faculty as Mathematics, yet Mathematics had a higher proportion of faculty usage.

A second factor in the higher usage by Physics faculty was the practice of displaying new journals at 11 a.m. each day. Many faculty would come in at this time, browse the index, and leave. Whether these "uses" should be considered in the same class as a use involving the reading of an entire article is a moot question. However, we operationalized the term "use" as "any use," because of the difficulties in rating the quality of usage. This practice of browsing the index of new journals also contributed to a higher percentage of both "browsing" and usage of "current journals" in the Physics Library.

The extent to which personal subscriptions, by faculty, graduate students, or other users, affects the usage of the collection was not investigated. However, the number of titles owned personally and the amount of overlap in this personal collection with the libraries' collection, can be useful knowledge in helping the library eliminate duplication, where the duplication seems unwarranted.[6]

e. Normalizing the Usage: In order to take the size of the population into consideration, we have computed a use per person per trimester for the three groups: graduate, faculty and undergraduate users (Table 58). From this table, it is evident that Physics is "journal intensive" in its graduate program (almost 25 uses per student), while Engineering seems to rely very little on the journals even for graduate studies. Undergraduate usage is generally low, with one or fewer uses per student for all libraries. Faculty usage is high in both Physics and Chemistry, but relatively low in the other libraries.

In terms of percent of usage versus percent of population, the faculty accounts for more usage than its population in every library except Computer Science (Table 59).

---

[6] Robert W. Frase, personal communication in review of this report.

Table 58
Uses per Person

Status	Uses per Person pertrimester for that particular Status Group					
	Physics	Life Sci.	Engineering	Chemistry	Comp.Sci.	Math.
Graduate	24.8	19.1	1.37	17.3	9.0	6.0
Faculty	18.5	3.6	1.7	19.7	0.0	5.6
Undergrad	1.1	0.75	0.38	1.2	1.2	0.0

Table 59
Faculty Usage

	Physics	Life Sci.	Engineering	Chemistry	Comp.Sci.	Math.
Pop.* %	24.1	4.2	3.5	5.8	5.4	11.2
Usage %	26.9	5.1	9.0	18.1	0.0	36.7

* The population consisted of faculty, graduate students, and undergraduates, as found in the statistics of the University.

In all the libraries studied, the graduate student usage was well above their percentage in the population. Life Sciences was the most notable, with the graduate students comprising 11.5% of the population, but 73.7% of the sample usage. Physics and Engineering were the least impressive in this respect. The graduate students in Physics accounted for over 70% of the usage, but they comprise almost 50% of the population. Engineering was the only library in which the graduate students supplied less than 60% of the usage. In fact, they accounted for less than half the usage, 49.1%, while comprising over 20% of the population (23.8%), Table 60.

Table 60
Graduate Student Usage

	Physics	Life Sci.	Engineering	Chemistry	Comp.Sci.	Math.
Pop. %	47.7	11.5	23.8	25.4	17.9	18.0
Usage %	71.2	73.7	49.1	69.2	63.6	63.3

The undergraduate students consistently supply less than their proportion in the population. In fact, only three libraries—Engineering, Computer Science, Life Sciences—showed an undergraduate usage above 20%, while in five of the libraries, the undergraduates make up over 65% of the population (Table 61).

f. Usage by Staff:[7] Usage by staff and visitors was low. The combined usage of both groups was under 10% in all libraries (Table 62).

The Mathematics Library was the most "self-enclosed," with all usage being due either to the Mathematics graduate students or the Mathematics faculty. Computer Science was the most "open" to visitors (over 8%), as well as the most open to other departmental users, as will be made evident in the section on departmental usage.

Table 61
Undergraduate Student Usage

	Physics	Life Sci	Engineering	Chemistry	Comp.Sci.	Math.
Pop. %	28.2	84.3	72.7	68.8	76.7	70.8
Usage %	1.9	21.2	41.9	12.7	36.4	0.0

Table 62
Staff Usage

	Physics	Life Sci.	Engineering	Chemistry	Comp.Sci.	Math.
Status: % visitors & staff	2.0	6.1	2.9	6.9	8.3	0.0

[7] Staff—Anyone working for the University who was not faculty or student, e.g., secretaries.

The usage by staff raises some obvious questions. While a percentage of staff usage may be for the staff member's own interests, very often the staff member is retrieving on behalf of the faculty member. The type of usage most commonly occurring when the staff member acts in this role of "agent" falls into two categories:

(1) The faculty member wishes to read the journal personally, in which case staff usage would simply add into the faculty usage on a one-for-one basis.

(2) The faculty member has directed the staff member to photocopy the journal for either distribution to the class, or for placement on a reserve file. In this case, the staff usage would increment the student usage on a many-to-one basis.

While our study did not address this investigation of staff usage, it remains a useful question for libraries attempting to track their usage patterns.

g. Variation in Usage Patterns: The category of status seems to illustrate the variability in usage patterns more than any other category. For example, Physics is high in faculty usage, low in undergraduate usage; while Life Sciences is low in faculty usage, medium in undergraduate usage; and Engineering is high in undergraduate usage. The Mathematics Library catered to only graduates and faculty during the sampling period.

These differences are due to a variety of factors: the demographics of the student population; the physical placement of the library; the nature of the disciplines involved; individual marketing strategies of the various libraries; and so on. It is these differences in the characteristics of both the population served and the library servicing that require an individual study of each library.

h. Predicting Usage (Physics Library): In the Physics Library the single best predictor of usage was the graduate student population. The distribution of graduate usage was essentially the same as the distribution of usage in the total population in regard to most used journals, usage by age, and alert method. The significance of this fact is that the Physics Library could simplify their task of monitoring journal usage by considering a somewhat restricted population, the 80-90 graduate students who use the library.

7. Alert Method as a Function of Status

With the exception of the Physics department, the graduate students use previous reference more than browsing as an alert mechanism (Table 63).

Table 63
Alert Method for Graduate Students

	Graduate Students and Postdoctoral					
Library:	Physics	Life Sci.	Engineering	Chemistry	Comp.Sci.	Math.
Uses:	262	142	74	66	14	19
%Browse	64.9	18.3	29.7	45.5	28.6	5.3
%Reference	35.1	81.7	70.3	54.5	71.4	94.7

Table 64
Alert Method for Undergraduates

	Undergraduate Students					
Library:	Physics	Life Sci.	Engineering	Chemistry	Comp.Sci.	Math.
Uses:	7	42	67	19	8	0
%Browse	42.9	40.5	47.8	15.8	50.0	0.0
%Reference	57.1	59.5	52.2	84.2	50.0	0.0

The undergraduate students are closer to a 50-50 split between browsing and references as the access mechanism, except in Chemistry, where over 80% of the undergraduate uses were through previous reference (Table 64).

It is worth noting that, with the exception of the Physics graduate students , students in general show much more use of previous reference than of browsing. This is not true of the faculty. In Physics, Engineering and Mathematics the primary use of the journal collection by faculty was through browsing. Only Life Sciences and Chemistry showed a high reference usage among faculty; and, in Life Sciences, although the percentage of previous reference was high (90%) among faculty, the absolute usage is low (9 or 10 total uses by faculty—less than 5% of the total usage of this collection), Table 65.

The obvious significance of the fact that faculty browse while students are directed to the collection by reference, is that any use of alternate mechanisms that impinge on browsing will affect the faculty more than the students. The references submitted by the students could as easily be submitted to a remote storage area as to a local one. However, any curtailment of browsing in the Physics Library would decrease usage dramatically.

Table 65
Alert Method for Faculty

	Faculty					
Library:	Physics	Life Sci.	Engineering	Chemistry	Comp.Sci.	Math.
Uses:	95	10	14	23	0	11
%Browse	70.5	10.0	71.4	43.5	0.0	63.6
%Reference	29.5	90.0	28.6	56.5	0.0	36.4

The preference of students for reference and faculty for browsing is made more salient when the statistics from all six libraries are aggregated:

	Alert Method	
	Browse	Reference
Undergraduate	41.3%	58.7%
Graduate	43.8%	56.2%
Faculty	62.1%	37.9%

As we have said, the Physics graduate students act in a significantly different manner from the other graduate students. If we eliminate the Physics graduate students, the proportion of browsing done by graduate stu- ents falls to 26.3%, with the use of reference rising to 73.7%. Thus, the behavior of the Physics graduate students was almost diametrically opposed to that of the general graduate student population.

8. Usage by Department

a. Nucleus of Users: The greatest percentage of use in each of the six libraries is by a small nucleus of departments. In fact, with the exception of the Computer Science and Life Sciences Libraries, over 75% of the usage is by the departments designated as the "primary users." These primary users were designated as follows:

Library	Primary Users
Physics[8]	Physics; Chemistry
Langley	Psychology; Life Sciences

[8] The Physics Library now services Earth and Planetary Science in addition to the Physics users, but this addition was made after the study in the Physics Library was carried out.

Library (cont.)	Primary Users (cont.)
Engineering	All Types of Engineering
Chemistry	Chemistry
Computer Science	Computer Science
Mathematics	Mathematics

Table 66 shows each library, its departmental users, and the percentage of usage by each department, illustrating the heavy usage by the nucleus of users.

Restricting the table to "own users" versus "other department," we have Table 67.

Table 66
Journal Use by Department of User

LIBRARY	USAGE		
	Department	% Use	Cumulative %
Physics (395 uses)	Physics	78.0	78.0
	Chemistry	13.1	91.2
	Other	8.9	100.0
Langley (204 uses)	Life Sciences	53.9	53.9
	Psychology	20.6	74.5
	Other	25.5	100.0
Engineering (167 uses)	All types of Engineering	84.4	84.4
	Other	15.6	100.0
Chemistry (158 uses)	Chemistry	94.3	94.3
	Other	5.7	100.0
Comp.Sci. (22 uses)	Computer Science	40.9	40.9
	Other	59.1	100.0
Mathematics (30 uses)	Mathematics	100.0	100.0
	Other	0.0	100.0

Table 67
Percent of "Own" versus "Other" Users

Library:	Physics	Life Sci.	Engineering	Chemistry	Comp.Sci.	Math.	Total
Uses:	395	204	167	158	22	30	976
%own users	91.1	74.5	84.4	94.3	40.9	100.0	86.2%
%other users	8.9	25.5	15.6	5.7	59.1	0.0	13.8%

The Computer Science Library is the only library serving more outside users than its own departmental users (60 - 40). This is probably an indication of the wide use of the computer as a tool in other disciplines. However, the absolute usage (24 sample uses, less than two-thirds use per sampling hour) somewhat lessens the impact of this statistic. This outside usage of journals might be an indication that the library also services a number of outside users in book usage (this has been confirmed in informal observation) and could lead to a costing scheme amortized over a wider population than that of Computer Science alone.

The Life Sciences Library also services a good number of outside users (almost 25%), while the Mathematics Library serviced nobody outside the Mathematics department during our 39 hours of sampling in that library.

According to the librarian, the overlap in journal titles between the Mathematics and Engineering Libraries is not large.

It was not possible, during the course of this study, to relate the usage of the journal collection in each library to the amount of research done by the departments using those libraries.

b. Crossover Among the Libraries: We can examine the crossover among the clientele of the various libraries by constructing a matrix of "library versus patrons of that library" (Table 68).

Table 68
Crossover Matrix

Library	Patrons of that Library							
	Physics	Life Sci.	Engineering	Chemistry	Comp.Sci.	Math.	Other	Total
Physics	-	0.3	1.0	13.1	0.0	0.8	6.8	22.0
Life Sci.	0.0	-	1.0	0.0	0.0	0.0	24.5	25.5
Engineering	0.0	1.8	-	1.8	0.6	2.4	9.0	15.6
Chemistry	0.0	1.3	0.6	-	0.0	0.0	3.8	5.7
CompSci.	0.0	0.0	22.7	13.6	-	4.5	18.2	59.0
Math.	0.0	0.0	0.0	0.0	0.0	-	0.0	0.0

As we have already indicated, the Computer Science Library is taxed more by people outside the department than within. Among the libraries studied, the clientele of Engineering, Chemistry, and Mathematics all place demands on the Computer Science collection.

However, in terms of absolute usage the demands are not great, since the Computer Science Library is expected to have only 1,800 - 1,900 uses in a year's time. Yet, it is interesting to note that the engineers, with a library of 1,643 titles, account for over 20% of the usage in the Computer Science Library. While the engineers are expected to account for only 6,600 journal uses in their own library, they will also have about 420 uses in the Computer Science Library, or 6% of the combined engineering usage in both libraries.

In constructing this crossover matrix, we have treated Chemistry as an "outside" user in the Physics Library. The reason for this is that while chemistry people use the Physics Library (13.1%), the Physics people do not utilize the Chemistry Library (0.0%). Thus, crossover is not a reciprocal affair. This lack of reciprocality can be further illustrated by noting that the Computer Science people make almost no use of the other libraries in the sample (with one use in the Engineering Library being the only incidence of a Computer Science person found outside the Computer Science Library).

The relative lack of crossover among the clientele of the various libraries suggests that specialized centers, designed along disciplinary lines, are feasible in considering alternative methods of providing journals, e.g., through resource-sharing centers.

Even the strong use of the Computer Science Library indicates that a disciplinary scheme will not hinder outside usage to the extent that it would be impossible. The Computer Science Library is located in a remote part of the campus, up a steep hill, thus making access both time-consuming and physically exertive. However, people who need the resources do seek them out. Yet, the remote physical location may be a contributing factor to the low absolute usage. The moral seems to be that the people with a strong need will seek, but attrition will occur as the difficulty of access imposes a cost equivalent to the benefit of access. A resource-sharing system with convenient local access and delivery of document (or copy) in a reasonable length of time might easily lead to greater and more widespread usage of a field with multi-disciplinary interest, such as Computer Science.

Missing Observations

9. Observations Missed When Recording Data on Forms (For sample forms, see Appendix)

It may be of interest to note how many observations were missed on any particular form. The forms used in the Physics Library provided space for 25 items to be recorded; the forms used in all other libraries provided space for 20 pieces of data. Some of the data had to be obtained from the user, e.g., "status," "department," "name," "alert method," etc. Other data could be obtained from the journal itself, e.g., "title," "ISSN," "volume number," etc.

The entire interaction with a user took one to two minutes. Any data items that could not be obtained were listed as "missing observations." In the Physics Library, the question of missed observations was not addressed. However, in the other five libraries, a record of the number of missing observations was kept. The cumulative percentage of missed observations shows that in 90% of the cases, there were three or fewer missed items (Table 69). The items accounting for the majority of the missed observations were the name and phone number of the individual user. Thus, the return on non-identifying information approached 90%.

This high return of "full" or "nearly full" forms indicates that the methodology of observation and interview is a viable technique for studying library activity. However, it does have the drawback of requiring the time and effort of a human observer.

Table 69
Missing Data Items

Missed Observations	Life Sci.	Engineering	Chemistry	Comp.Sci.	Math.
None	67.8	47.1	66.9	37.5	53.3
One	92.4	67.4	90.7	62.5	90.0
Two	98.1	94.7	99.5	83.3	90.0
Three	98.1	98.8	100.0	91.6	100.0
Four	98.1	99.4	100.0	91.6	100.0
Five	100.0	100.0	100.0	100.0	100.0

An unattended form would remove the imposition on the observer's time. Furthermore, it would have the added advantage of being available during all hours that the library was open. However, it would probably yield a lower percentage return. This lower percentage might be offset by the increase in hours observed. The unattended form might also raise questions about the truthfulness of the usage reported. However, this could be monitored periodically by the librarian. In any case, experimentation with an unattended form might prove useful for an individual library.

Confirmation of Results

10. Sampling of Engineering Library During Summer Months

Some objections were raised that we did not include the summer months in our sample. It was decided, therefore, that we should sample the Engineering Library during the summer months in order to ascertain any unique patterns of usage.

While some interesting differences in the Summer usage did appear, the general form of the results was similar. For example, in terms of usage in general, the Summer study would project a yearly usage of 5,730 uses; the projection from our two-trimester study during the regular school year was 6,600 uses.

The actual number of uses was 172 in the regular-year sample, 50 in the Summer. The multiplying factor for the regular year was 38.25; for the Summer it was 114.6. The Engineering Library has the same hours of opening in the Summer as during the regular year; this was not true of the other libraries in the study, which all have shorter hours in the Summer.

The percent of the collection used was again low, only 2.9% of the titles in the collection being touched during our 27 hours of sampling. During the regular year, 6.8% of the collection was used. The lower percentage during the Summer sample is due to the smaller sample size. The number of titles sampled in a collection grows as the sample size increases. The sample during the Fall and Winter (regular) trimesters consisted of 81 hours over a two-trimester period. The Summer sample consisted of 27 hours over a two-week period.

The smaller sample also affects our method of graphing in order to project yearly usage. However, the effect is in the opposite direction. The line from a smaller sample tends to predict more of the collection achieving a greater number of uses than the larger sample (Table 70). Thus, the regular year figures predict that 73% of the collection will have 10 or fewer uses, while the Summer sample says that only 40% of the collection will have such low usage.

Table 70
Projected Yearly Usage:
Fall/Winter versus Summer Sample

No. of Uses	% of collection having that no. of uses	
	Fall/Winter	Summer
100 or less	> 98.0	95.0
50 or less	95.8	85.0
25 or less	89.0	69.5
10 or less	73.0	40.0
5 or less	55.0	20.0
1 or zero	4.5	< 2.0

Table 71
Projected Usage by Age of Journal:
Fall/Winter versus Summer Sample

Age	Cumulative % of usage by that age grouping	
	Fall/Winter	Summer
0 - 1	41.3	42.0
2 - 5	73.9	74.0
6 - 10	87.3	88.0
11 - 15	93.7	98.0
16 - 20	96.0	100.0
21 - 25	98.3	100.0
26 +	100.0	100.0

This tendency of a smaller sample to over-estimate the usage percentages should be kept in mind when studying the usage of the Mathematics and Computer Science Libraries. Because of the extremely small number of journal uses in these libraries, the projected figures are somewhat less reliable than the figures obtained in the libraries with a greater number of sample uses.

The smaller sample does predict the age distribution of the journals used fairly well (Table 71). The major difference lies in the fact that more of the older uses turn up in the larger sample. These are the more rarely occurring uses and are less likely to show up in a small sample. However, the general usage patterns of the more heavily used age-groups are already apparent in the small sample.

In regard to the alert method, there is more use of previous reference in the Summer sample, less browsing:

Alert Method	Fall/Winter	Summer
Browse	41.2%	23.4%
Reference	58.8%	76.6%

There seem to be at least two reasons for this. The first reason is that there are fewer undergraduate students and faculty using the library during the Summer. Both of these categories use a greater proportion of browsing than the graduate students. Thus, when they go, the browsing declines. Furthermore, all undergraduate students using the journal collection during the Summer did so as a result of a reference; none browsed. This would indicate that "leisure reading" might be somewhat replaced by outside activities during the nicer weather months.

The comparison of alert method versus status indicates the greater proportion of previous reference during the Summer (Table 72). The faculty usage was only one use. Undergraduates had 11 uses, visitors 10, and graduate students 22 uses in this table.

One interesting factor is that browsing went up among graduate students during the Summer. It has not been ascertained whether this was due to sampling error or to some deviation in behavior patterns, e.g., graduate students having more free time to pursue their own interests in the Summer. However, it is more likely that the difference is attributable to the small sample size.

In regard to status, the graduate students remained the primary user population. Undergraduate and faculty usage went down, and visitor usage increased (Table 73).

Table 72
Alert Method by Academic Status:
Fall/Winter versus Summer Sample

Status	Alert Method			
	Fall/Winter		Summer	
	Browse	Reference	Browse	Reference
Undergrad	47.8%	52.2%	0.0%	100.0%
Graduate	29.7%	70.3%	40.9%	59.1%
Faculty	71.4%	28.6%	0.0%	100.0%
Visitor	40.0%	60.0%	20.0%	80.0%

Table 73
Academic Status of Users:
Fall/Winter versus Summer Sample

Status	Fall/Winter	Summer
Undergrad	40.7%	22.0%
Graduate	47.6%	50.0%
Faculty	8.7%	2.0%
Visitor	2.9%	20.0%
Staff	0.0%	6.0%

The decrease in faculty and undergraduate usage can be attributed to a population that declines in the Summer. The faculty is decreased to one-third of its normal size, the undergraduate population to half its normal size; while the graduate student population declines only slightly in numbers during the Summer. Why there is such an increase in usage by visitors can only be surmised. Perhaps students and faculty, as well as out of town visitors, have more time to visit the libraries of schools other than their own during the Summer. The increase does seem to be due to exceptional circumstances, since only 5 visitors were observed in 172 uses during the 81-hour sampling period of the regular school year. Yet, 10 out of 50 uses were due to visitors during the 27-hour sampling period of the Summer.

Usage by department was still primarily due to the users designated as the primary users (Table 74). The amount of photocopying done (or not done) was also similar (Table 75).

Table 74
Departmental Uses: Fall/Winter versus Summer Sample

User Department	Fall/Winter	Summer
Engineering (all types)	84.4%	73.3%
Other	15.6%	26.7%

Table 75
Photocopying: Fall/Winter versus Summer Sample

Photocopying?	Fall/Winter	Summer
No	76.2%	64.9%
Yes	23.8%	35.1%

At least two studies have been initiated by the librarians at the University of Pittsburgh since the appearance of the first Progress Report on this study. One is taking place in the Engineering Library.[9] The intent is to collect a year's data on collection usage, utilizing all hours the library is open. Thus, the usage will not be based on sampling, but on full usage, and the results will be compared with the results of this study. Preliminary results indicate that the projected number of yearly uses given here might be slightly high, but are reasonable. The projections on percent of collection used have not yet been compared with the data listed here.

---

[9] Homer Bernhardt, Engineering Librarian, personal conversation.

Chapter IV

THE ECONOMICS OF MATERIALS' USE

Jacob Cohen

A. On Measuring Costs

Overall Costs

The data on uses discussed in previous sections become most meaningful when combined with the cost data. This involves analyzing and augmenting library budgetary data to produce consistent cost figures.[1]

The underlying budgetary data are given in Tables A1, A2 and A3 in the Data Appendix to this chapter, for the three fiscal years 1973-74, 1974-75, and 1975-76.

Library expenditures were divided into variable and fixed costs and "excluded" costs. The latter represent costs unrelated to Hillman Library book use. Fixed costs are those independent of use. Variable costs on the other hand depend on use.

From the tables it is seen that variable cost has two main elements: acquisitions and circulation. The former in turn include book purchase and processing costs. Under fixed costs are administration, maintenance and imputed cost.

An economic accounting for fixed costs goes beyond the costs found in a university's financial records. The latter provide data on such operating costs as administration and maintenance but omit imputed costs—the "opportunity costs" of the fixed investment in the library, for example. Such costs measure what the university could have earned had the funds been

---

[1] Special acknowledgment must be made of the contribution of Robert Neumann, Assistant to the Director of Libraries at the University of Pittsburgh, in furnishing the basic library data.

lent out rather than being invested in the library. Depreciation (which appears in private accounting statements but not in university accounts) is another imputed cost that has to be estimated. Imputed costs have been incorporated in the tables on library expenditures.

The question whether acquisition costs should be treated as a fixed rather than a variable cost will have a substantial effect on the measurement of the cost of book use. If treated as a variable cost, such costs will only be germane to new book use. On the other hand, if treated as a fixed cost, the average cost per new and old book use will be uniform. (In this chapter, section B., book use costs measured by these alternative methods are compared.) When acquisitions are treated as a fixed cost, an opportunity interest rate is applied to the total library investment in books to give an estimate of imputed interest (as shown in Tables 76 and 77 below). Each year's acquisitions are cumulated with previous year's acquisitions to secure total book investment and thus such fixed costs will accelerate with time. Moreover, compound interest—i.e., interest being earned on interest—will cause such costs to rise exponentially.

Either approach has its rationale. If the acquisition of books depends directly on use, one can argue that such costs are variable costs. On the other hand, as is more likely, if acquisitions are not directly related to use, then acquisition costs should be treated as an investment with the potential interest return being considered a fixed cost.

When books are treated as an investment, various "price-level" accounting questions arise. Should books be valued at original cost or at their current market value, the latter also measuring replacement value? Replacement cost can be expected to be above original cost because of books going out of print and because of the effects of inflation on "old" book prices. The effect of using market value in measuring the cost of book use would be to increase this cost since the imputed interest cost would be figured on the higher replacement cost basis. (The interest rate used in calculating implicit interest cost is the AAA corporate bond rate.) On the other hand, the library makes a "paper profit" from appreciation of its book investment. Conceivably, the annual imputed profit could be offset against book use cost. A less confusing treatment, however, would be to show such profits in the library's balance sheet under its "net worth." The estimates in this report are based on original cost, thus avoiding these questions.

B. Measuring the Cost of Book Use

1. Combining Cost and Book Use Data

The tables below combine cost data with book use data. Table 76 treats acquisitions as part of fixed costs, while Table 77 treats them as part of variable costs. Costs for book use are analyzed in detail by each method for three years, with two years' data also being deflated by salary increases and by increases in book costs so that comparisons can be made in "real" terms, that is, in terms of real resources utilized.

The total number of new book transactions in 1974-75 (the year on which the statistical analysis has generally focussed) is seen to have been 13,769 (Table 76, line 1), as compared with 197,577 old book transactions (line 2). "Items circulated" refers to the number of books circulated. Thus, dividing transactions by books circulated yields the "average times circulated" for new and old items (lines 5 and 7).

The importance of acquisition costs is reflected in the vast reduction in variable costs when acquisitions are treated as a fixed cost (Table 76). This can be seen by comparison of the amounts of variable costs shown in line 15 of Table 76 and line 13 of Table 77 respectively, and the amounts of fixed costs shown on line 21 of Table 76 and line 19 of Table 77 respectively.

The "bottom line" in these calculations is the total cost per item circulated ("average item cost"), or the cost per transaction ("average transaction cost"). In the case of Method 1 (acquisitions treated as part of fixed cost), the total cost per transaction or per item will be uniform for new and old items. In the case of Method 2 (acquisitions treated as a variable cost), the cost estimates will obviously be higher for new items.

If we examine lines 25 and 26 of Table 76, average transaction cost is $16.02 in 1974-75 and average item cost is $28.56. On the other hand, line 26 in Table 77 shows the new item total cost when acquisitions are a variable cost to be $128.20. The average transaction cost is $71.48 (line 28, Table 77).

Table 76
Book Cost and Book Use for the Hillman Library, Three Fiscal Years, Acquisitions Treated as Part of Imputed Fixed Cost (Method 1)(A)

Line		Footnote*	(1) 1973---1974	(2) 1974---1975 (Nominal)	(3) 1974---1975 (Deflated)	(4) 1975---1976 (Nominal)	(5) 1975---1976 (Deflated)
1	Total New Item Transactions		15218	13769	13769	11072	11072
2	Total Old Item Transactions		206249	197577	197577	197276	197276
3	Total Transactions		221467	211346	211346	208348	208348
4	Total New Items Circulated		7762	7666	7666	6112	6112
5	Average Times New Items circulated	1	1.96	1.80		1.81	
6	Total Old Items Circulated		114498	110868	110868	110589	110589
7	Average Times Old Items circulated	2	1.80	1.78		1.78	
8	Total Items Circulated		122260	118534	118534	116701	
8a	Average Items circulated, All Items	3	1.81	1.78		1.79	
9	Total Circulation Cost (TCC)		359336	410914	373219	429050	365553
10	TCC per All Transactions	4	1.62	1.94	1.77	2.05	1.75
11	TCC per Item Circulated	5	2.93	3.46	3.15	3.67	3.13
12	Total Variable Cost (TVC)	6	359336	410914	373219	429050	365553
13	TVC Attributable to New Items	7	22782	26545	24137	22439	19145
14	TVC per New Item Circulated	8	2.93	3.46	3.15	3.67	3.13
15	TVC Attributable to New Item Trans.	9	24686	26751	24315	22783	19426
16	TVC per New Item Transaction	10	1.62	1.94	1.77	2.05	1.75
17	TVC Attributable to Old Items	11	336554	384369	349082	406611	346408
18	TVC per Old Item Circulated	12	2.93	3.46	3.15	3.67	3.13
19	TVC Attributable to Old Item Trans.	13	334650	384163	348904	406267	346127
20	TVC per Old Item Transaction	14	1.62	1.94	1.77	2.05	1.75
21	Total Fixed Cost Adjusted (TFC)	15	2615315	2974361	2927207	3109937.08	3024018
22	TFC Adjusted per All Transactions	16	11.81	14.07	13.85	14.93	14.51
23	TFC Adjusted per All Items circulated	17	21.39	25.09	24.69	26.64	25.91
24	Total Cost (TC)		2974651	3385274	3300426	3538987.08	3389572

Line		Footnote*	(1) 1973---1974	(2) 1974---1975 (Nominal)	(3) 1974---1975 (Deflated)	(4) 1975---1976 (Nominal)	(5) 1975---1976 (Deflated)
25	TC per All Transactions	18	13.43	16.02	15.62	16.99	16.27
26	TC per All Items Circulated	19	24.33	28.56	27.84	30.33	29.04
27	TC Attributable to New Items	20	188593	218689	213450	185347	177522
28	TC per New Item Circulated	21	24.33	28.56	27.84	30.32	29.04
29	TC Attributable to New Item Trans.	22	204358	220381	215019	188068	180128
30	TC per New Item Transaction	23	13.43	16.01	15.62	16.99	16.27
31	TC Attributable to Old Items	24	2786058	3166585	3086976	3353638	3212049
32	TC per Old Item Circulated	25	24.33	28.56	27.84	30.33	29.04
33	TC Attributable to Old Item Trans.	26	2770293	3164893	3085406	3350918	3209443
34	TC per Old Item Transaction	27	13.43	16.02	15.62	16.99	16.27
35	Reported New Book Use		15218	13769	13769	11072	11072
36	Adjusted New Book Use	28	30436	27538	27538	22144	22144
37	Adjusted Total Book Use	28	236685	225115	225115	219420	219420
38	Total Circulation Cost (TCC)		359336	410914	373219	429050	365553
39	TCC per Adjusted Total Transactions	29	1.52	1.83	1.66	1.96	1.67
40	Total Variable Cost (TVC)		359336	410914	373219	429050	365553
41	TVC Attributable to New Items Trans.	30	46175	50255	45655	43291	36892
42	TVC per New Item	31	1.52	1.83	1.66	1.96	1.67
43	Total Fixed Cost Adjusted (TFC)		2615315	2974362	2927207	3109937.08	3024018
44	TFC per All Transactions	32	11.05	13.21	13.00	14.17	13.78
45	Total Cost (TC)		2974651	3385274		3538987.08	3389572
46	TC per All Transactions	33	12.56	15.04	14.66	16.13	15.45
47	TC Attributable to New Item Trans.	34	382243	414019	403736	357757	342078
48	TC per New Item Transaction	35	12.56	15.03	13.55	16.16	16.51

* Footnotes explaining the calculations in Table 76 are given in the Data Appendix.

Footnotes to Table 76

A1 Calculation of Imputed Interest:

In Method 1, acquisitions were treated as part of imputed fixed costs. Imputed interest for the three years was estimated as follows:

1.	Number of volumes, July 1, 1973	621,704
2.	Average value of a volume, July 1, 1973	$ 12.20
3.	Total value of books	$ 7,584,788.80
4.	Ratio of processing costs to book cost, 1973-74 fiscal year data	2.43
5.	Total investment in books, including processing (line 3 x line 4)	$18,431,036.78
6.	Imputed interest (total investment times 7.9%, based on Moody's Seasoned AAA Corporate Bond rate)	$ 1,456,051.91
7.	Acquisition cost for 1973-74	$ 917,939.27
8.	Imputed interest on 1973-74 acquisitions[2]	$ 36,258.60
9.	Total imputed interest, fiscal year 1973-74	$ 1,492,310.51
10.	Total investment in books, including processing, as of July 1, 1974 ($18,431,036.78 + $917,939.27)	$19,348,976.05
11.	Imputed interest cost (total investment times 8.9%)	$ 1,722,058.87
12.	Acquisition cost for 1974-75	$ 878,563.58
13.	Imputed interest on 1974-75 acquisitions[2]	$ 39,096.08
14.	Total imputed interest, fiscal year 1974-75	$ 1,761,154.95
15.	Total investment in books, including processing, as of July 1, 1975 ($19,348,976.05 + $878,563.58)	$20,227,539.63
16.	Imputed interest cost (total investment times 8.7%)	$ 1,759,795.95
17.	Acquisition cost for 1975-76	$ 1,083,232.75
18.	Imputed interest on 1975-76 acquisitions[2]	$ 47,120.12
19.	Total imputed interest, fiscal year 1975-76	$ 1,806,916.57

[2] Imputed interest on fiscal acquisitions was calculated by taking half of yearly acquisitions costs, lines 7, 12 and 17 above, and multiplying the result by 7.9%, 8.9% and 8.7% respectively. The acquisition costs were halved since it was assumed that outlays were made continuously over the fiscal year.

Footnotes to Table 76 (continued)

A2 Deflation Procedure:

In columns 3 and 5, figures for 1974-75 and 1975-76 were deflated in order to eliminate the effect of inflation on cost comparisons with 1973-74. The deflation method was as follows:

Method 1: (Acquisitions Treated as Part of Fixed Cost)

1. Imputed fixed costs (imputed interest on buildings and book acquisitions) were not deflated since it was assumed that they did not increase on account of inflation, thus not requiring any correction for given increases.

2. Variable costs and other fixed costs were deflated by 10.1% and 6.6% in 1974-75 and 1975-76 respectively, the estimated percentage increase in salaries for the Hillman Library. The deflation procedure was to divide the 1974-75 figures by 1.101 where appropriate and the 1975-76 figures by 1.1737 so that all deflated figures are expressed uniformly in 1973-74 dollars.

The figures are as follows:

	1974-75	Adjusted for Omitted items (36%)	Adjusted for Inflation (10.1%)	1975-76	Adjusted for omitted items (32%)	Adjusted for Inflation (6.6%)
	$	$	$	$	$	$
(1) Imputed Fixed Costs						
A. Library	1,092,480.00	699,187.20		1,062,445.00	722,462.60	
B. Books	1,761,154.95	1,761,154.95		1,806,916.57	1,806,916.57	
Total:	2,853,634.95	2,460,342.15	2,460,342.15	2,869,361.57	2,529,379.17	2,529,379.17
(2) Other Fixed Costs						
A. Administration	305,366.10	195,434.30		291,427.73	198,170.86	
B. Maintenance	497,787.75	318,584.16		562,333.90	382,387.05	
Total Other:	803,153.85	514,018.46	466,865.09	853,761.63	580,557.91	494,639.10
Total Fixed:	3,656,788.80	2,974,360.61	2,927,207.24	3,723,123.20	3,109,937.08	3,024,018.27
(3) Variable Cost (circulation)	410,913.63	410,913.63	373,218.56	429,049.97	429,049.97	365,553.35
TOTAL:	4,067,702.43	3,385,274.24	3,300,425.80	4,152,173.17	3,538,987.05	3,389,571.62

Table 77

Book Cost and Book Use for the Hillman Library, Three Fiscal Years

Acquisitions Treated as Part of Variable Cost

(Method 2)(B)

Line		Footnotes *	(1) 1973 --- 1974	(2) 1974 - - - 1975 (Nominal)	(3) 1974---1975 (Deflated)	(4) 1975---1976 (Nominal	(5) 1975---1976 (Deflated)
1	Total New Item Transactions		15218	13769	13769	11072	11072
2	Total Old Item Transactions		206249	197577	197577	197276	197276
3	Total Transactions		221467	211346	211346	208348	
4	Total New Items Circulated		7762	7666	7666	6112	6112
	Average Times New Items Circulated	1	1.96	1.80		1.81	
5	Total Old Items Circulated		114498	110868	110868	110589	110589
	Average Times Old Items Circulated	2	1.80	1.78		1.78	
6	Total Items Circulated		122260	118534	118534	116701	116701
	Average Times Circulated, all items	3	1.81	1.78		1.79	
7	Total Circulation Cost (TCC)		359336	410914	373209	429050	365553
8	TCC per All Transactions	4	1.62	1.94	1.76	2.05	1.75
9	TCC per Item Circulated	5	2.93	3.46	3.15	3.67	3.13
9a	Acquisition Cost	5a	917939.27	878563.58	782957 59	1083232.75	879294.25
10	Total Variable Cost (TVC)	6	1277276	1289477	1156167	1512282	1244848
11	TVC Attributable to New Items	7	940753	905139	807094	1105703	898439
12	TVC per New Item Circulated	8	121.20	118.07	105.28	180.91	147.00
13	TVC Attributable to New Item Trans.	9	942631	905334	807271	1106033	898720
14	TVC per New Item Transaction	10	61.94	65.75	58.63	99.89	81.17
15	TVC Attributable to Old Items	11	336523	384138	349072	406579	
16	TVC per Old Item Circulated	12	2.94	3.47	3.15	3.68	3.13
17	TVC Attributable to Old Item Trans.	13	334645	384143	348895	406249	346127
18	TVC per Old Item Transaction	14	1.62	1.94	1.77	2.06	1.75
19	Total Fixed Cost	15	1123004	1213206	1166052	1303021	1217102
20	TFC per All Transactions	16	5.07	5.74	5.52	6.25	5.84
21	TFC per All Items Circulated	17	9.18	10.24	9.84	11.17	10.43
22	Total Cost (TC)		2400280	2502683	2322219	2815303	2461949
23	TC per All Transactions	18	10.84	11.84	10.99	13.51	11.82

Line		Footnotes *	(1) 1973 -- 1974	(2) 1974 --- 1975 (Nominal)	(3) 1974---1975 (Deflated)	(4) 1975---1976 (Nominal	(5) 1975---1976 (Deflated)
24	TC per All Items Circulated	19	19.63	21.11	19.59	24.12	21.10
25	TC Attributable to New Items	20	1011502	982784	882507	1173460	962182
26	TC per New Item Circulated	21	130.31	128.20	115.12	191.99	157.43
27	TC Attributable to New Item Trans.	22	1068995	984192	883238	1175093	963399
28	TC per New Item Transaction	23	66.96	71.48	64.15	106.13	87.01
29	TC Attributable to Old Items	24	1388778	1519899	1439712	1641843	1499766
30	TC per Old Item Circulated	25	12.13	13.71	12.99	14.85	13.56
31	TC Attributable to Old Item Trans.	26	1381285	1518491	1439157	1640151	1498831
32	TC per Old Item Transaction	27	6.70	7.69	7.28	8.31	7.60
33	Reported New Book Use		15218	13769	13769	11072	11072
34	Adjusted New Book Use	28	30436	27538	27538	22144	22144
35	Adjusted Total Book Use	28	236685	225115	225115	219420	219420
36	Total Circulation Cost (TCC)		359336	410914	373209	429050	365553
37	TCC per Adjusted Total Trans.	29	1.52	1.83	1.68	1.96	1.67
38	Total Variable Cost (TVC)		1277276	1289477	1156167	1512282	1244848
39	TVC Attributable to New Item Trans.	30	963934	928695	828612	1126138	916186
40	TVC per New Item	31	31.67	33.72	30.09	50.86	41.37
41	Total Fixed Cost Adjusted		1123004	1213206	1166052	1303021	1217102
42	TFC per All Transactions	32	4.74	5.38	5.18	5.93	5.55
43	Total Cost (TC)		2400280	2502683	2322219	2415303	2461949
44	TC per All Transactions	33	10.14	11.18	10.32	12.83	11.22
45	TC Attributable to New Item Trans.	34	1107679	1076706	971253	1256440	1039019
46	TC per New Item Transaction	35	36.39	39.10	35.27	56.74	46.92

* Footnotes explaining the calculations in Table 77 are given in the Data Appendix.

Footnotes to Table 77

B. Deflation Procedure:

1. Book purchases were deflated by 15.5% and 14.9% in 1974-75 and 1975-76 respectively, representing average increases in book prices during those years, based on the Bowker annual index.

2. All other variable costs were deflated by 10.1% and 6.6% in 1974-75 and 1975-76 respectively, the estimated value of the wage increase for the Hillman Library.

3. Fixed costs except imputed costs were also deflated by 10.1% in 1974-75 and by 6.6% in 1975-76.

4. Imputed cost (depreciation and interest) were left unchanged since they were assumed to be unaffected by inflation.

Later year figures were adjusted in the same way as was described in footnote A2 above.

The underlying figures are as follows:

	1974-75	Adjusted for omitted items (36%)	Adjusted for Inflation (10.1%) except for books (15.5%)	1975-76	Adjusted for omitted items (32%)	Adjusted for Inflation (6.6%) except for books (14.9%)
(1) Imputed Fixed Costs						
A. Library	1,092,480.00	699,187.20	699,187.20	1,062,445.00	722,462.60	722,462.60
(2) Other Fixed Costs						
A. Administration	305,366.10	195,434.30		291,427.73	198,170.86	
B. Maintenance	497,787.75	318,584.16		562,333.90	382,387.05	
Total Other:	803,153.85	514,018.46	466.865.09	853,761.63	580,557.91	494,639.10
Total Fixed:	1,895,633.85	1.213.205.66	1,166,052.29	1,916,206.63	1,303,020.51	1,217,101.70
(3) Book Purchases	353,500.07	353,500.07	306,060.67	442,987.44	442,987.44	333,801.10
(4) Circulation Cost	410,913.63	410,913.63	373,209.47	429,049.97	429,049.97	365,553.35
(5) Processing Cost	525,063.51	525,063.51	476,896.92	640,245.31	640,245.31	545,493.15
TOTAL VARIABLE COSTS (3)+(4)+(5)	1,289,477.21	1,289,477.21	1,156,167.06	1,512,282.72	1,512,282.72	1,244,847.60
TOTAL COSTS:	3,185,111.06	2,502,682.87	2,322,219.35	3,428,489.35	2,815,303.23	2,461,949.30

The cost of new items and transactions will be overstated (apart from assigning acquisition costs exclusively to one year's use as is done in Method 2) because books will have been available for only part of the year, assuming that book purchases are made evenly throughout the year. To compensate for this overstatement, the figures for annual new book use have been doubled.[3] The adjusted figures are shown beginning in line 36 in Table 76 and line 34 in Table 77. The downward effect is most substantial under Method 2, as seen by comparing the difference between lines 28 and 46 in Table 77 with the difference between lines 30 and 48 in Table 76. These figures are still an overestimate, since they do not allow for unrecorded transactions via in-house browsing.[4]

2. Inter-Year Comparisons

The tables reveal a decline in new book transactions (Table 77, line 1) in 1975-76 which, coupled with the increase in total variable costs associated with new book transactions (Table 77, line 10), results in a sharp increase in average variable costs for new transactions (Table 77, line 14) and new items circulated (Table 77, line 12). The total cost per new item circulated (Table 77, line 26) is now \$191.99 as compared with \$128.20 in 1974-75 and per transaction (Table 77, line 28) the comparison is \$106.13 versus \$71.48. On the most liberal accounting basis, after adjusting new transactions upwards (Table 77, line 46), the average new transaction cost is \$56.74, as compared with \$39.10 in the earlier year.

The increases in the latter year are not as great when acquisitions are treated as a fixed cost (Table 76). The increase in average total cost per new item transaction is only \$1.13 beyond the \$15.03 level of 1974-75.

3. Allowing for Inflation

The effects of inflation have been allowed for in the estimates by correcting the latter two years for the effects of salary increases and increases in book

---

[3] The author is indebted to H. A. Olsen, San Jose State Library, for this suggestion.

[4] See Chapter II above for a discussion of in-house browsing.

Nor do the figures reflect manual checkouts in the Reserve Book Room or special libraries, such as the East Asian Library. On the other hand, the costs of operating these libraries have been excluded from the estimates of cost. (See Tables A1, A2 and A3, and note 15 to Table 76.)

costs. The deflated figures[5] measure costs in real terms—e.g., amount of labor input, per each unit of book use. The conclusions drawn when costs were measured in nominal (current) dollars are not affected by measurement in deflated dollars. That is, the increases in book-use cost over time are "real"—implying more physical resources per item circulated or per book use.

Of course, the effects of inflation can be stated in an obverse and more familiar way. In order to buy the same number of books and hire the same personnel, money outlays have to increase. Inflation exacerbates the library's budgetary problem!

C. Measuring the Cost of Journal Use

1. Subscription Costs

The study of journal usage in six branch libraries—Langley (Life Sciences), Physics, Engineering, Computer Science, Chemistry and Mathematics—discussed in earlier sections classified journals according to frequency of use. Once the cost of journal subscriptions is estimated for these different use categories, the subscription cost per use is secured by dividing costs by total uses in each frequency category.[6]

Tables 78 - 83 summarize subscription costs and journal use for each of the six libraries. The (a) section of each table details uses and costs in terms of frequency categories. The (b) section of the tables cumulates these data for each library.

The frequency of use sections of the tables do not demonstrate what one might have expected—that journal costs per use vary inversely with the number of times that a given journal is used—the more journal use, the less will be the average cost. The reason for the irregular cost behavior going down column (8) is the sharp variation in journal costs for different frequency of use categories. When the figures are cumulated in the second section of the tables, however, with a few exceptions the rise in the average cost of journal use as journals become less frequently used is evident.

If we concentrate on the ultimate figures of average subscription costs, it is seen that the ranking going from highest cost per use to lowest is: Mathematics, Engineering, Physics, Chemistry, Computer Science, and Life Sciences. For Mathematics the cost is $7.54 in contrast to $2.52 for Life Sciences. These "finite" costs prevail despite the "infinite" cost of the zero-use categories since only totals are involved.

---

[5] The methods for deflation are explained in the notes A, B to the tables.

[6] Subscription costs are for the fiscal year 1976-77. See Table A4 and A5.

Table 78
Journal Subscription Costs and Journal Use—Physics Library

(a) By Frequency of Use Categories

(1) No. of times journal used in sample	(2) No. of titles	(3) % of collection	(4) No. of sample uses	(5) Projected no. of total uses [8]	(6) % of usage	(7) Subscription cost [7]	(8) Subscription cost per use [9]
						$	$
40	1	0.33	40	900.0	9.1	90.00	0.10
29	1	0.33	29	652.5	6.6	85.00	0.13
25	1	0.33	25	562.5	5.7	98.00	0.17
20	1	0.33	20	450.0	4.6	195.00	0.43
17	1	0.33	17	382.5	3.9	41.31	0.11
15	1	0.33	15	337.5	3.4	646.65	1.90
13	1	0.33	13	292.5	3.0	(no cost - gift)	
12	1	0.33	12	270.0	2.7	859.32	3.18
11	1	0.33	11	247.5	2.5	201.28	0.81
10	2	0.7	20	450.0	4.6	59.00	.13
8	1	0.33	8	180.0	1.8	195.00	1.08
7	2	0.7	14	315.0	3.2	50.00	0.16
6	3	1.0	18	405.0	4.1	453.00	1.12
5	9	3.0	45	1012.5	10.25	2290.18	2.26
4	8	2.7	32	720.0	7.3	1598.61	2.22
3	13	4.4	39	877.5	8.9	2371.61	2.70
2	18	6.0	36	810.0	8.2	1737.00	2.14
1	45	15.1	45	1012.5	10.25	7066.84	6.98
0	188	63.1	0	0	0	16565.78	∞
228	298	100.0	439	9877.5	100.00	$ 34603.58	$ 3.50

(b) Cumulative Percentages

(1) Frequency Category	(2) No. of Titles	(3) % of collection	(4) Projected No. of uses	(5) Cumulative % Usage	(6) Subscription Cost	(7) Subscription Cost/Use (6) ÷ (4)
10 +	11	3.7	4545	46.0	$ 2275.56	$0.50
8 +	12	4.0	4725	47.8	2470.56	0.52
7 +	14	4.7	5040	51.0	2520.56	0.50
6 +	17	5.7	5445	55.1	2973.56	0.55
5 +	26	8.7	6457.5	65.4	5263.74	0.82
4 +	34	11.4	7177.5	72.7	6862.35	0.96
3 +	47	15.8	8055	81.5	9233.96	1.15
2 +	65	21.8	8865	89.7	10970.96	1.24
1 +	110	36.9	9877.5	100.0	18037.80	1.83
0 +	298	100.0	9877.5		34603.58	3.50

---

[7] The figures in column (7) are aggregate subscription costs per annum for the number of titles in col. (2), excluding costs for 105 of 298 titles in the Journal Use Study. Most of the uncosted journals were cancelled. Others were "classed," i.e., they are no longer treated as journals. Some ceased publication, while a few others were gifts to the library.

[8] Column (5) = col. (4) x 22.5, the "blow-up factor." The latter was obtained by first dividing the number of hours the library was open in a week, times 15 weeks, by the number of hours sampled. The dividend is then multiplied by the number of trimesters per year, divided by the number of trimesters sampled. For the Physics Library, these figures were 15 x 1.5 = 22.5.

[9] Column (8) = col. (7) ÷ col. (5).

Table 79
Journal Subscription Costs and Journal Use
Langley (Life Sciences) Library

(a) By Frequency of Use Categories

(1) No. times journal used in sample	(2) No. Titles	(3) % of collection	(4) No. of sample uses	(5) Projected no. of total uses [11]	(6) % of Usage	(7) Subscription Cost [10]	(8) Subscription Cost per use [12]
						$	$
13	1	0.1	13	1196.13	6.2	(no cost listed)	
8	1	0.1	8	736.08	3.8	200.00	0.27
6	1	0.1	6	552.06	2.8	1907.50	3.46
5	2	0.2	10	920.1	4.7	310.50	0.3
4	7	0.8	28	2576.28	13.3	760.93	0.30
3	10	1.1	30	2760.3	14.2	1293.04	0.47
2	29	3.2	58	5336.58	27.5	3762.69	0.71
1	58	6.3	58	5336.58	27.5	4597.13	0.86
0	859	88.1	0	0	0	36190.78	∞
Total	914	100.0	211	19414.11	100.0	$49022.59	$2.52

(b) Cumulative Percentages

(1) Frequency Category	(2) No. of Titles	(3) % of Collection	(4) Projected no. of uses	(5) Cumulative % Usage	(6) Subscription Costs	(7) Subscription Cost/Use (6) ÷ (4)
5 +	5	0.5	3404.37	17.5	$2418.00	$0.71
4 +	12	1.3	5980.65	30.8	3178.93	0.53
3 +	22	2.4	8740.95	45.0	4471.97	0.51
2 +	51	5.6	14077.53	72.5	8234.66	0.58
1 +	109	11.9	19414.11	100.0	$12831.79	0.66
0 +	914	100.0	19414.11	100.0	$49022.59	$2.42

[10] Total subscription costs do not include costs for 14 journals, subscriptions for which were either cancelled or "classed."

[11] Column (5) = col. (4) x 92.01, the "blow-up factor": 30.67 x 3 = 92.01.

[12] Column (8) = col. (7) ÷ col. (5).

Table 80
Journal Subscription Costs and Journal Use—Engineering Library[13]

(a) By Frequency of Use Categories

(1) No. times journal used in sample	(2) No. of titles	(3) % of Collection	(4) No. of sample uses	(5) Projected no. of total uses[15]	(6) % of usage	(7) Subscription Cost [14] $	(8) Subscription Cost/Use [16] $
10	1	0.06	10	382.5	5.8	5.60	0.01
7	1	0.06	7	267.75	4.1	40.00	0.15
4	2	0.1	8	306.0	4.7	142.50	0.47
3	7	0.4	21	803.25	12.2	689.55	0.86
2	26	1.6	52	1989.0	30.2	2616.20	1.32
1	74	4.5	74	2830.5	43.0	4716.63	1.67
0	1532	93.2	0	0	0	36576.15	∞
Total:	1643	100.0	172	6579.0	100.0	44786.63	6.81

(b) Cumulative Percentages

(1) Frequency Category	(2) No. of Titles	(3) % of Collection	(4) Projected no. of uses	(5) Cumulative % Usage	(6) Subscription Cost $	(7) Subscription Cost/Use (6) ÷ (4)
10 +	1	0.1	382.50	5.8	5.60	$0.01
7 +	2	0.1	650.25	9.9	45.60	0.07
4 +	4	0.3	956.25	14.5	188.10	0.20
3 +	11	0.7	1759.50	26.7	877.65	0.50
2 +	37	2.3	3748.50	57.0	3493.85	0.93
1 +	111	6.8	6579.00	100.0	8210.48	1.25
0 +	1643	100.0	6579.00		44786.63	6.81

---

13 On the basis of new information supplied as this report was being completed (December 7, 1977) by the Head of the Engineering and Mathematics Libraries, Engineering journal costs are overstated by the inclusion of the cost of indexing and abstracting services which were not covered in the use survey. The cost of such services was $9,072 in 1976/77.

14 Total subscription costs shown here do not include costs for 15 journals which were probably gifts. Figures in column (7) are aggregate subscription costs for the number of titles in col. (2).

15 Column (5) = col. (4) x 38.25, the "blow-up factor": 25.5 x 1.5 = 38.25.

16 Column (8) = col. (7) ÷ col. (5).

Table 81
Journal Subscription Costs and Journal Use—Chemistry Library

(a) By Frequency of Use Categories

(1) No. times journal used in sample	(2) No. of titles	(3) % of Collection	(4) No. of sample uses	(5) Projected No. of Total Uses[18]	(6) % of Usage	(7) Subscription Cost[17] $	(8) Subscription Cost/Use $[19]
27	1	0.2	27	2073.6	16.9	112.00	0.05
13	1	0.2	13	998.4	8.1	475.00	0.48
10	1	0.2	10	768.0	6.3	12.00	0.02
6	3	0.7	18	1382.4	11.3	292.74	0.21
5	1	0.2	5	384.0	3.1	96.00	0.25
4	3	0.7	12	921.6	7.5	716.55	0.78
3	5	1.2	15	1152.0	9.4	615.6	0.53
2	12	2.8	24	1843.2	15.0	2776.79	1.51
1	36	8.3	36	2764.8	22.5	6538.98	2.37
0	370	85.5	0	0	0	21410.74	∞
Total:	433	100.0	160	12288.0	100.0	33046.40	2.69

(b) Cumulative Percentages

(1) Frequency Category	(2) No. of Titles	(3) % of Collection	(4) Projected no. of uses	(5) Cumulative % Usage	(6) Subscription Cost $	(7) Subscription Cost/Use (6) ÷ (4)
27 +	1	0.2	2073.6	16.9	112.00	$ 0.05
13 +	2	0.4	3072.0	25.0	587.00	0.19
10 +	3	0.6	3840.0	31.3	599.00	0.16
6 +	6	1.3	5222.4	42.5	891.74	0.17
5 +	7	1.5	5606.4	45.6	987.74	0.18
4 +	10	2.2	6528.0	53.1	1704.29	0.26
3 +	15	3.4	7680.0	62.5	2319.89	0.30
2 +	27	6.2	9523.2	77.5	5096.68	0.54
1 +	63	14.5	12288.0	100.0	11635.66	0.95
0 +	433	100.0	12288.0		33046.40	2.69

[17] Total subscription costs do not include costs for seven journals which were either gifts, cancelled or "classed." Figures in column (7) are aggregate subscription costs per annum for the number of titles in col. (2).

[18] Column (5) = col. (4) x 76.8, the "blow-up factor": 25.6 x 3 = 76.8.

[19] Column (8) = col. (7) ÷ col. (5).

Table 82
Journal Subscription Costs and Journal Use
Computer Science Library

(a) By Frequency of Use Categories

(1) No. times journal used in sample	(2) No. of titles	(3) % of Collection	(4) No. of sample uses	(5) Projected No. of Total Uses[21]	(6) % of usage	(7) Subscription Cost[20] $	(8) Subscription Cost/Use[22] $
5	1	0.5	5	384.0	20.8	13.14	0.04
3	1	0.5	3	230.4	12.5	12.00	0.05
2	1	0.5	2	153.6	8.3	15.00	0.10
1	14	7.1	14	1075.2	58.3	628.13	0.58
0	181	91.4	0	0	0	4277.05	∞
Total:	198	100.0	24	1843.2	100.0	$4945.32	$2.68

(b) Cumulative Percentages

(1) Frequency Category	(2) No. of Titles	(3) % of Collection	(4) Projected no. of uses	(5) Cumulative % Usage	(6) Subscription Cost	(7) Subscription Cost/Use (6) ÷ (4)
					$	$
5 +	1	0.5	384.0	20.8	13.14	0.03
3 +	2	1.0	614.4	33.3	25.14	0.04
2 +	3	1.5	768.0	41.7	40.14	0.05
1 +	17	8.6	1843.2	100.0	668.27	0.36
0 +	198	100.0	1843.2		4945.32	2.68

[20] Total subscription costs do not include costs for journals which appeared to be gifts. Figures in column (7) are aggregate subscription costs per annum for the number of titles in col. (2).

[21] Column (5) = col. (4) x 76.8, the "blow-up factor": 25.6 x 3 = 76.8.

[22] Column (8) = col. (7) ÷ col. (5).

Table 83
Journal Subscription Costs and Journal Use
Mathematics Library

(a) By Frequency of Use Categories

(1) No. times journal used in sample	(2) No. of titles	(3) % of Collection	(4) No. of sample uses	(5) Projected No. of Total Uses[24]	(6) % of Usage	(7) Subscription Cost[23] $	(8) Subscription Cost/Use[25] $
4	1	0.4	4	252.0	13.3	67.50	0.27
3	1	0.4	3	189.0	10.3	395.00	2.10
2	3	1.1	6	378.0	20.0	394.65	1.04
1	17	6.4	17	1071.0	56.7	1635.99	1.53
0	243	91.7	0	0	0	11766.40	∞
Total:	265	100.0	30	1890.0	100.0	14259.54	7.54

(b) Cumulative Percentages

(1) Frequency Category	(2) No. of Titles	(3) % of Collection	(4) Projected no. of uses	(5) Cumulative % Usage	(6) Subscription Cost $	(7) Subscription Cost/Use (6) ÷ (4)
4 +	1	0.4	252.0	13.3	67.50	$ 0.27
3 +	2	0.8	441.0	23.3	462.50	1.05
2 +	5	1.9	819.0	43.3	857.15	1.05
1 +	22	8.3	1890.0	100.0	2493.14	1.32
0 +	265	100.0	1890.0		14259.54	7.54

---

23 Figures in column (7) are aggregate subscription costs per annum for the number of titles in column (2). Total subscription costs do not include cost of 3 journals which are being paid by the department.

24 Column (5) = col. (4) x 63, the "blow-up factor": 21 x 3 = 63.

25 Column (8) = col. (7) ÷ col. (5).

2. Other Costs

We have also obtained other variable and fixed costs for the six branch libraries. These are shown in Table 84. Omitted are the fixed costs associated with the imputed return on the investment in building space and depreciation costs. Nonetheless, per-use costs are substantially increased when "other" costs are considered. The cost-ranking of the six libraries is not substantially altered. Mathematics and Engineering are at the high end of the range ($10.07 and $9.04 respectively) and Life Sciences and Chemistry are at the low end ($3.33 and $3.30 respectively).

Table 84
Total Costs per Journal Use: Six Branch Libraries[32]

LIBRARY	(1) Subsc Costs[26] $	(2) Fixed Costs[27] $	(3) Costs[28] $	(4) Total Costs[29] $	(5) Total Uses[30]	(6) Cost per use[31] $
Computer Science	4945.32	409.28	1188.16	6542.76	1843.2	3.55
Chemistry	33046.40	2734.97	5110.47	40891.84	12288.0	3.33
Mathematics	14259.54	1180.13	3593.07	19032.74	1890.0	10.07
Langley (Life Scs)	49022.57	4057.19	10992.90	64072.66	19414.11	3.30
Engineering	44786.63	3706.61	10975.55	59468.79	6579.0	9.04
Physics	31522.18	2608.83	6529.77	40660.78	9877.5	4.12
TOTAL:	177582.64	14697.01	38389.92	230669.57	51891.81	4.45

26 Data for this column were taken from the "1976-1977 Analysis of Acquisitions for Six Libraries" provided by Hillman Library (see Table A5, Data Appendix to this section).

27 Fixed costs were derived by a two-step computation: Step 1: Take the ratio of each library's budget to the total University library budget. The former was computed by adding together variable expenditures for each library as provided in Table A4 "1976-77 Serial Costs—Science Libraries" to expenditures for books, subscriptions, standing orders for each library, plus excluded costs for each; the ratio was multiplied by the total administration costs (fixed costs) of $293,494.00. Step 2: Multiply the product of Step 1 by the percentage importance of

subscriptions in each library's budget to obtain the fixed costs attributable to each library. (For subscription costs, see Table A5 "Analysis of Acquisitions for Six Science Libraries 1976-77".)

28 Variable costs for each library were derived by multiplying variable expenditures for each (source: Table A4 "Serial Costs—Science Libraries") by the percentage importance of subscriptions in each library's budget.

29 Total costs = (1) + (2) + (3).

30 Data for this column were taken from the cumulative number of uses shown in previous tables.

31 Cost per use = (4) ÷ (5).

32 Costs for subscriptions include the costs of indexes and abstracts in all libraries, whereas the sample survey did not cover indexes and abstracts. If this cost were removed, the cost per use would be lower. The figures for the Engineering Library (the only figures available) are suggestive of the effects of making such an adjustment.

The cost of subscriptions in the Engineering Library was listed as $44,786.63. Deducting the $9,072 cost for indexing and abstracting services reduces the cost of subscriptions to $35,714.63. The cost per use, based on subscriptions alone, would be $5.43 instead of $6.81 (Table 80).

The total costs would be similarly affected. For example, the Engineering costs in Table 84 (above) would be:

(1) Subscriptions	(2) Fixed	(3) Variable	(4) Total	(5) Uses	(6) Cost per Use
$35,714.63	$2,954.27	$8,747.80	$47,416.70	$6,579.00	$7.21

D. Towards a Library Decision Model for Book Purchase *

1. Introduction

When cost and circulation data are disaggregated by LC Class and Cost Center, the analysis becomes specific enough to offer some guidance for book ordering. The Cost Center is the basic administrative unit in the ordering of books for the Hillman Library. Such centers have a rough correspondence to university departments (except for those cost centers which play purely a bookkeeping role).[33] In the order process, the final say in purchases is exercised by the bibliographers administering the cost centers.

2. The Underlying Data

An extensive data matrix was constructed having LC Classes (26 in number) along its rows and Cost Centers (55) across the columns. By merging three data files—one for book orders by Cost Center, one for their subsequent LC classification, and one on circulation by LC Class—13 bits of information were produced for each cell of the matrix. Seven bits of information refer to a particular LC Class and a particular Cost Center: total amount spent (per LC Class per Cost Center), number of items purchased, mean cost per item, standard deviation of mean cost per item, number of transactions, mean cost per transaction, and standard deviation of mean cost per transaction. The remaining six pieces of information are percentages: amount spent (for an LC Class within a given Cost Center) ÷ total amount spent on a given Cost Center; amount spent (on a Cost Center within an LC Class) ÷ total amount spent on a given LC Class; number of items purchased ÷ total number of items purchased for a given LC Class; number of items purchased ÷ total number of items purchased for a given Cost Center; number of

---

* James R. Kern co-authored this section.

[33] While not included in this report, detailed analysis was done of the interconvertibility of LC Classes and Hillman Library Cost Centers in terms of acquisitions. As might be expected, the convertibility is highly imperfect with limited "two-directional" correspondence between these categories. That is, rarely does one find that a single LC category corresponds to a single Cost Center's orders or that the latter's orders are confined to a single LC category. For example, Cost Center 44 which is identified with Political Science orders only 35% of books in the LC category J which covers Political Science, and 65% of books from other LC categories. Conversely, 61% of LC category J was ordered by Cost Center 44.

transactions ÷ total number of transactions within a given LC Class; number of transactions ÷ total number of transactions within a given Cost Center.[34]

Tables 85 and 86 summarize this information. Table 85 summarizes the mean acquisition costs and standard deviations across the LC rows of the large-scale matrix; Table 86 does the same down the Cost Center columns. The first half of each table is on an item basis, the second half is on a transaction basis. Circulation costs and fixed costs (in Table 85) are those estimated in subsection C. above. They are assumed to be the same for all LC Classes. Total cost per item (col. 4, Table 85) is the sum of mean acquisition cost per item (col. 1) plus circulation cost per item (col. 2) plus fixed cost per item (col. 3). Total cost per transaction (col. 10) is the sum of columns 7, 8 and 9.

3. Decision Variables

The decision variables chosen for this study are:

a. Mean Acquisition Cost/Transaction: Since all LC rows and Cost Centers are assumed to have equivalent circulation costs and fixed costs on a per-item basis, the only variable is acquisition cost. The mean acquisition cost refers to the mean of a particular LC or Cost Center row in Tables 85 and 86. Mean acquisition cost/transaction can be lowered either by decreasing the numerator (mean acquisition cost) or increasing the denominator (mean number of transactions). As is shown in the analysis, differences in the number of transactions across the LC and Cost Center rows of Tables 85 and 86 are more important than differences in book purchase price in determining the ratio.

---

[34] The computer program which "matched" and "merged" intersecting files covered acquisitions for a 21-month period—July 1, 1974 to March 31, 1976. Initially the matrix covered 14,610 volumes and was limited to cost data and LC classifications. Subsequently, circulation data by LC Class was added. Now the overlapping data files covered 6,369 volumes. It is this more limited matrix which underlies the present discussion.

From time to time, specific items are reclassified. Reclassification does not affect transaction or item counts but could affect distribution of items or transactions by LC Class over time. However, since such a small number of items are reclassified (approximately 9,000 or about 1.5% of the circulating collection in 1976), and an even smaller amount are reclassified so drastically as to change their class, it is our belief that reclassification will not significantly alter the findings of this study.

Table 85
Cost Analysis of Book Use
by LC Category

LC Class	SUBJECT MATTER	Rank	Cost per Item (1) Mean Acquisition Cost	(2) Circulation Cost	(3) Fixed Cost
			$	$	$
A	General Works	9	10.01	3.67	11.17
B	Philosophy	7	9.82	3.67	11.17
C	Auxiliary Sciences of History	3	8.64	3.67	11.17
D	History	16	11.35	3.67	11.17
E	History: America (general)	6	9.19	3.67	11.17
F	History: America (by country)	5	8.99	3.67	11.17
G	Geography/Anthropology/Recreation	4	8.86	3.67	11.17
H	Social Sciences	8	9.98	3.67	11.17
J	Political Science	17	11.50	3.67	11.17
K	Law	13	10.42	3.67	11.17
L	Education	2	7.98	3.67	11.17
M	Music	1	7.05	3.67	11.17
N	Fine Arts	15	11.18	3.67	11.17
P	Language & Literature	11	10.38	3.67	11.17
Q	Science	18	11.74	3.67	11.17
R	Medicine	12	10.40	3.67	11.17
S	Agriculture	20	12.88	3.67	11.17
T	Technology	14	10.45	3.67	11.17
U	Military Science	19	12.54	3.67	11.17
V	Naval Science	10	10.12	3.67	11.17
Z	Bibliography & Library Science		00.0		

Source of Data: Columns (1), (5), (7) and (11) are derived from the matrix prepared by Stephen Bulick and W. N. Sabor based on their April 1975—July 1976 sampling data.

Table 85 (continued)

LC Class	SUBJECT MATTER	Cost per Item (4) Total Cost = (1) + (2) + (3)	Rank	(5) Standard Deviation of Cost	Rank	(6) Number of Items Acquired
		$		$		
A	General Works	24.85	18	8.55	2	15
B	Philosophy	24.66	15	7.62	18	759
C	Auxiliary Sciences of History	23.48	3	5.43	6	36
D	History	26.19	17	8.26	16	467
E	History: America (general)	24.03	6	5.60	14	300
F	History: America (by country)	23.83	5	5.56	12	193
G	Geography/Anthropology/Recreation	23.70	7	5.69	15	364
H	Social Sciences	24.82	9	5.90	19	1300
J	Political Science	26.34	19	15.82	13	266
K	Law	25.26	10	5.94	7	69
L	Education	22.82	2	4.44	17	674
M	Music	21.89	1	4.24	5	32
N	Fine Arts	26.02	14	7.32	9	83
P	Language & Literature	25.22	20	50.71	20	1468
Q	Science	26.58	16	7.78	11	167
R	Medicine	25.24	8	5.81	10	169
S	Agriculture	27.72	13	7.21	3	22
T	Technology	25.29	4	5.48	8	72
U	Military Science	27.38	12	6.48	4	27
V	Naval Science	24.96	11	6.08	1	4
Z	Bibliography & Library Science			0.00		0

Columns (2), (3), (8) and (9) are based on FY 1975-1976 data furnished by Hillman Library (see Table 77, col. 4).

Table 85 (continued)

LC Class	SUBJECT MATTER	*Rank*	(7) Mean Acquisition Cost	(8) Circulation Cost	(9) Fixed Cost	(10) Total Cost = (7)+(8)+(9)
			$	$	$	$
A	General Works	19	7.15	2.05	6.25	15.45
B	Philosophy	8	4.46	2.05	6.25	12.76
C	Auxiliary Sciences of History	11	4.93	2.05	6.25	13.23
D	History	18	6.89	2.05	6.25	15.19
E	History: America (general)	7	4.40	2.05	6.25	12.70
F	History: America (by country)	14	5.45	2.05	6.25	13.75
G	Geography/Anthropology/Recreation	3	3.38	2.05	6.25	11.68
H	Social Sciences	6	4.06	2.05	6.25	12.36
J	Political Science	16	6.29	2.05	6.25	14.59
K	Law	9	4.79	2.05	6.25	13.09
L	Education	2	3.08	2.05	6.25	11.38
M	Music	1	2.25	2.05	6.25	10.55
N	Fine Arts	13	5.33	2.05	6.25	13.63
P	Language & Literature	10	4.87	2.05	6.25	13.17
Q	Science	12	5.45	2.05	6.25	13.75
R	Medicine	5	3.95	2.05	6.25	12.25
S	Agriculture	20	7.45	2.05	6.25	15.75
T	Technology	4	3.87	2.05	6.25	12.17
U	Military Science	15	6.04	2.05	6.25	14.34
V	Naval Science	11	6.75	2.05	6.25	15.05
Z	Bibliography & Library Science		0.00			

Table 85 (continued)

LC Class	SUBJECT MATTER	Rank	Cost per Transaction (11) Standard Deviation of Mean Acquisition Cost/Trans.	Rank	(12) Coefficient of Variation (11) ÷ (7)	(13) Number of Transactions	Rank	(14) Average No. Transactions per Item = (13)÷(6)
			$		$			
A	General Works	18	8.53	5	1.19	21	1	1.4
B	Philosophy	12	7.09	16	1.58	1669	13	2.2
C	Auxiliary Sciences of History	4	5.93	6	1.20	63	6	1.75
D	History	17	8.49	7	1.23	769	3	1.646
E	History: America (general)	5	6.01	8	1.366	626	9	2.09
F	History: America (by country)	8	6.17	3	1.132	318	4	1.647
G	Geography/Anthropology/Recreation	3	5.56	17	1.64	953	17	2.62
H	Social Sciences	9	6.18	12	1.52	3194	15	2.46
J	Political Science	19	13.02	19	2.07	486	7	1.82
K	Law	10	6.58	9	1.374	150	12	2.17
L	Education	2	4.76	13	1.55	1744	16	2.59
M	Music	1	4.07	18	1.81	100	20	3.13
N	Fine Arts	13	7.53	10	1.41	174	10	2.10
P	Language & Literature	20	35.12	20	7.21	3128	11	2.13
Q	Science	15	7.82	11	1.43	374	14	2.23
R	Medicine	7	6.19	15	1.57	445	18	2.63
S	Agriculture	16	8.42	2	1.13	38	5	1.73
T	Technology	6	6.05	14	1.56	194	19	2.69
U	Military Science	14	7.13	4	1.18	56	8	2.07
V	Naval Science	11	7.03	1	1.04	6	2	1.5
Z	Bibliography & Library Science		0.00			0		0

Table 86

Cost Analysis of Book Use by Cost Center

	COST CENTER	Rank	COST PER ITEM (1) Mean Cost	Rank	(2) Standard Deviation of Mean Cost	Rank	(3) Items Purchased
			$		$		
99	Adjustment *		6.84		2.47		5
87	Administration of Justice	18	10.62	9	6.13	3	25
01	Alldred		0		0		0
02	Anthropology	17	10.58	18	7.52	22	189
03	Astronomy		0		0		0
83	Biochemistry		0		0		0
36	Life Sciences		4.60		0		1
81	Biophysics		14.50		0		1
04	Black Studies	11	9.51	2	4.43	14	84
05	Business		0		0		0
06	Computing & Data Processing		0		0		0
07	Chemistry		0		0		0
09	Classics	29	13.53	28	10.21	9	51
82	Comparative Literature	2	6.94	1	4.35	1	16
11	Center for Regional Economic Studies		0		0		0
84	Dance		8.84		4.90		11
14	East Asian	20	11.18	15	6.80	12	58
15	Economics	25	12.84	12	6.35	15	86
16	Education	3	8.02	3	4.53	30	982
17	Engineering		9.05		0		1
18	English	9	9.25	20	7.70	28	400
19	Earth & Planetary Sciences		0		0		0
90	Film		0		0		0
20	Fine Arts		0		0		0
22	French	30	37.10	30	197.81	16	94
23	Geography	21	11.35	13	6.46	19	29
24	German	26	12.85	23	8.17	11	57
25	Gift & Exchange		0		0		0
26	Government Documents		0		0		0
27	Hillman (General)	15	10.06	15	6.80	26	350
28	Hillman (Reference)		11.56		5.80		3
29	Hillman (Reserve)	4	8.09	29	12.73	23	281
30	Hispanic	7	8.64	17	6.82	7	47
31	History	23	12.11	19	7.57	24	297
32	History of Science	27	13.28	24	8.64	4	28
21	Italian	16	10.36	21	7.80	10	56
88	Judaica		11.40		9.44		5
89	Langley replacement/periodicals		0		0		0
35	Latin America	1	6.64	14	6.66	21	181
37	Linguistics	24	12.66	25	8.93	5	30
39	Mathematics		9.05		0		1
40	Music		6.86		0		1
41	Philosophy	28	13.48	26	8.99	17	110
42	Physics		0		0		0
44	Political Science	19	10.69	22	8.12	29	516
45	Psychology		11.86		6.96		3
46	Religious Studies	8	8.70	5	4.91	8	48
66	Replacement /Lost Books	5	8.10	11	6.30	18	114
47	Russian and East European	12	9.53	7	5.18	6	32
49	Slavic	10	9.33	10	6.19	2	23
50	Special Collections		4.72		3.14		2
51	Sociology	14	9.95	6	5.17	27	379
52	Speech	6	8.48	4	4.74	20	163
53	Social Work	13	9.87	8	5.47	25	338
55	Technical Services		0		0		0
86	Women's Studies	22	11.63	27	9.16	13	67

* "Adjustment" is an account for bookkeeping purposes only.

Source of Data: Computer program prepared by W. Sabor and S. Bulick.

Table 86 (continued)

Cost per Transaction

Rank	(4) Coefficient of Variation, Mean Cost	*Rank*	(5) Mean Cost	*Rank*	(6) Standard Deviation of Mean Cost	*Rank*	(7) Number of Transactions	*Rank*	(8) Transactions per Item
	$		$		$				
	1.34		2.85		3.82		12		2.40
24	1.59	7	4.02	11	6.39	6	66	27	2.64
			0		0		0		0
22	1.51	13	4.87	17	7.34	23	410	21	2.17
			0		0		0		0
			0		0		0		0
	1.41		2.30		3.25		2		0
	1.73		4.83		8.37		3		0
14	1.33	9	4.20	5	5.57	15	190	22	2.26
			0		0		0		0
			0		0		0		0
			0		0		0		0
12	1.30	27	7.93	27	10.27	11	87	11	1.71
8	12.73	5	3.70	1	4.71	1	30	13	1.88
			0		0		0		0
	1.64		3.14		5.15		31		0
10	12.77	19	5.89	18	7.46	12	110	14	1.90
11	1.28	20	6.06	20	7.76	14	182	19	2.12
28	1.60	1	2.96	2	4.75	30	2658	29	2.71
			9.05		0		1		0
13	1.54	12	4.65	15	7.16	26	795	15	1.99
			0		0		0		0
			0		0		0		0
			0		0		0		0
30	6.96	30	24.22	30	168.58	13	144	5	1.53
13	1.31	17	5.54	16	7.25	18	264	17	2.05
1	0.82	29	10.77	24	8.86	7	68	2	1.19
			0		0		0		0
			0		0		0		0
27	1.78	4	3.65	12	6.50	27	890	26	2.54
	0.86		8.67		7.47		4		0
26	1.73	25	7.04	30	12.18	21	323	1	1.15
9	12.75	16	5.34	14	6.81	9	76	8	1.62
7	1.20	24	6.90	23	8.28	24	521	12	1.75
4	1.07	28	8.85	27	9.45	3	42	4	1.50
3	1.04	26	7.84	23	8.12	8	74	3	1.32
	1.42		6.33		8.98		9		0
			0		0		0		0
16	14.45	11	4.31	10	6.23	19	279	6	1.54
17	14.47	22	6.12	24	8.86	5	62	18	2.07
			9.05		0		1		0
	1.74		2.28		3.96		3		0
19	1.45	23	6.28	26	9.10	17	236	20	2.15
			0		0		0		0
21	1.48	15	5.30	22	7.82	28	1041	16	2.02
	1.74		3.95		6.87		9		0
5	1.11	14	5.15	6	5.71	10	81	10	1.69
28	1.80	2	3.07	4	5.52	20	301	28	2.64
2	1.01	21	6.10	9	6.19	4	50	7	1.56
6	1.18	18	5.64	13	6.64	2	38	9	1.65
	0.67		4.72		3.14		2		0
18	14.49	8	4.08	7	5.91	28	923	25	2.44
20	1.47	3	3.51	3	5.17	22	393	24	2.41
15	1.41	10	4.30	8	6.08	23	775	23	2.29
			0		0		0		0
29	1.94	6	3.95	19	7.66	16	197	30	2.94

NOTE: Only those cost centers purchasing 15 or more items are included in the rankings.

b. The Standard Deviation and the Coefficient of Variation: In the case of the analysis of items in Tables 85 and 86, the standard deviation measures the extent to which individual item cost deviates from average item cost for a given LC or Cost Center category. In the case of transactions, again the items are involved, but now departures of item transaction costs from mean transaction costs (for all items) are being analyzed.

The standard deviation is thus important as a measure of costs around the mean. Better than the standard deviation, for purposes of comparing LC categories or Cost Centers, is the coefficient of variation. By dividing the standard deviation by mean cost, this concept adjusts for differences in standard deviations due to simply the average book being more expensive in one category than another. The coefficient of variation is a standardized measure of dispersion and thus of risk in ordering from one LC category or Cost Center rather than another. Thus, if Class A had a coefficient of variation higher than Class B, other things being equal, it involves more of a risk to order a book from Class A.

4. Risk in Ordering Books on the Basis of Their LC Classification

Mean transaction costs and their coefficients of variation provide a possible guide to future "average" transaction costs and the range of possible variation in such costs.[35] The lower the mean transaction cost and its coefficient of variation, the greater can be the librarian's confidence in a decision to order a book in a given LC or Cost Center category.

As shown by the stub of Table 87, LC Classes are divided into 9 "risk in ordering" categories. The 20 LC Classes were ranked and divided into "low" (meaning low relative mean costs per transaction or low coefficients of variation)—ranks 1-7; "medium"—ranks 8-14; and "high"—ranks 15-20. Since each of the two criteria variables is divided into 3 subclasses, combining them results in 9 possible orderings.

---

[35] Mean transaction costs may be a biased guide to book ordering if transactions are supply—rather than demand—determined. The availability of books in various LC categories may determine use, in which case certain LC categories would perpetually be favored in the acquisition process. (See Thomas J. Pierce, The Economics of Library Acquisitions: A Book Budget Allocation Model for University Libraries, University of Notre Dame, Ph.D. Thesis, 1976, p. 77; William E. McGrath, "A Pragmatic Book Allocation Formula for Academic and Public Libraries with a Test for Its Effectiveness," Library Resources and Technical Services, 19, 356-690, 1975.) Since the number of books was not available by LC Classes, no attempt is made in the present study to correct for this bias.

Table 87
Analysis of Mean Cost per Transaction
and Risk by LC Class

Category	Mean Cost per Transaction *	Coefficient of Variation	LC Categories
Case 1	Low (ranks 1-7)	Low (ranks 1-7)	
Case 2	Low (ranks 1-7)	Medium (ranks 8-14)	E, H, L, T
Case 3	Low (ranks 1-7)	High (ranks 15-20)	G, M, R
Case 4	Medium (ranks 8-14)	Low (ranks 1-7)	C, F, V
Case 5	Medium (ranks 8-14)	Medium (ranks 8-14)	K, N, Q
Case 6	Medium (ranks 8-14)	High (ranks 15-20)	B, P
Case 7	High (ranks 15-20)	Low (ranks 1-7)	A, D, S, U
Case 8	High (ranks 15-20)	Medium (ranks 8-14)	
Case 9	High (ranks 15-20)	High (ranks 15-20)	J

*NOTE: For all subsequent tables, ranks entered under mean cost per transaction apply also to coefficient of variation ranks for "low," "medium" and "high."

The easiest decisions would involve case 1, characterized by low mean cost per transaction and low coefficient of variation. No LC Class fits this case; however, LC Classes E (History, Amer.), H (Social Sciences), L (Education) and T (Technology) fit case 2, low mean cost and medium coefficient of variation.

The other extreme is demonstrated by case 9 with high mean acquisition cost per transaction and high coefficient of variation. LC Class J (Political Science) fits this case. Here not only is mean cost per transaction higher but there is a high risk in ordering a given title.

Some of the intermediate cases represent trade-off situations, as in case 3 (Class G: Geography, Anthropology, Recreation; Class M: Music and Books on Music; and Class R: Medicine) and case 4 (Class C: Auxiliary Sciences of History; Class F: History; and Class V: Naval Science). In the first case, one has low mean costs but a high coefficient of variation with the reverse being true for case 4.

Whether mean costs per transaction are more strongly influenced by transactions in a given item than by book prices can be tested by calculating the appropriate Spearman rank correlation coefficients. The correlations of mean transaction costs with transactions per item and mean costs per item (a measure of book prices) were -.905 and .566 respectively. The influence of item circulations on mean cost is thus seen to outweigh that of book prices.

5. Risk in Ordering Books on a Cost Center Basis

Using the same procedure as outlined above, a similar analysis was made of Cost Centers. In this table, Cost Center ranks 1-11 = "low"; 12-21 = "medium"; and 22-31 = "high." The results are shown in Table 88.

The results are widely dispersed. Cost Center 82 (Comparative Literature) is clearly the easiest decision, with low mean cost and low coefficient of variation. At the other extreme, Cost Centers 22 (French) and 29 (Hillman Reserve) are the most difficult decisions. Between these two extremes are a wide variety of possible decisions and trade-offs between relative degrees of cost and risk. Of course, in both the LC and Cost Center analysis we could assert that mean cost per transaction is more significant a variable than the coefficient of variation. In such a case, decision making would follow the 1 - 9 order of the categories.

Table 88
Analysis by Cost Centers

Category	Mean Cost per Transaction	Coefficient of Variation	Cost Centers
Case 1	Low (ranks 1-11)	Low	82
Case 2	Low (ranks 1-11)	Medium	04, 51, 52, 53
Case 3	Low (ranks 1-11)	High	87, 16, 27, 00, 66, 86
Case 4	Medium (ranks 12-21)	Low	14, 15, 30, 46, 47, 49
Case 5	Medium (ranks 12-21)	Medium	23, 35
Case 6	Medium (ranks 12-21)	High	02, 18, 44
Case 7	High (ranks 22-31)	Low	24, 31, 32, 21
Case 8	High (ranks 22-31)	Medium	09, 37, 41
Case 9	High (ranks 22-31)	High	22, 29

The risk-ordering by Cost Centers has little relationship to the similar ordering by LC Class. What relationship one finds reflects a two-directional relationship between LC Classes and Cost Centers. Thus, Cost Center 16 (Education) has an association with LC Class L (Education). This shows up in the former's third position in the categories, and the latter's second position. A relationship also exists between Cost Center 18 (English) and LC Class P (Language and Literature) and this may explain their respective sixth place category positions.

Similar correlations for Cost Centers to determine the primary influence on mean transaction costs (transactions versus book costs) shows a smaller margin in favor of transactions per item as compared with book prices. The correlations are, respectively, -.778 and .642.

6. Analysis by LC Subclasses

Results from studies of usage patterns by LC Class indicate that LC Classes P (Language and Literature) and H (Social Sciences) accounted for respectively 27.1% and 18.7% of total usage in 1974. The next most important classes were: Class B (Philosophy, Psychology, Religion) - (10.6%); Class D (History: General and Old World) - (8.5%); and Class L (Education) - (8.10%). Remaining classes accounted individually for only 3.4% or less of total usage.

Because of the importance of Classes P and H, it was decided to study these two classes in more depth. A matrix similar to the original matrix was prepared, with the same 13 pieces of information—only this time two-letter subclasses were analyzed (PA, PB, etc. and HA, HB, etc.)

The new decision models are shown in Tables 89 to 92. Again, mean costs per transaction and coefficients of variation were used as the decision variables. And each of these variables was again divided into three categories of low, medium and high. Although this division of the ranks is only a rough categorization of relative groups of ranks, it does allow one to make some simple rankings of different LC subclasses and Cost Centers.

The interpretation of these tables can proceed in the same manner as the interpretations made on earlier tables (87 - 88). Looking first at Table 89, one can see that LC subclass HM (Sociology: Theoretical and General) falls into case 2—low mean cost per transaction and medium coefficient of variation. Subclass HF (Commerce), HQ (The Family, Marriage, Women), and HV (Social Pathology, Social and Public Welfare, Criminology), all case 3, represent a trade-off situation with low mean cost but a high probability that any given transaction cost could be higher than the mean. Into case 4—medium mean cost per transaction, low coefficient of variation—falls HM

(Social History, Social Problems, Social Reform). Subclasses HC (Economic History and Conditions, National Production) and HD (Land, Agriculture, Industry)—case 5—represent the intermediate cases of medium mean cost per transaction and mean coefficients of variation. Case 6 includes subclass HE (Transportation and Communication). Subclasses HG (Finance), HJ (Public Finance) and HX (Socialism, Communism, Anarchism) and case 7—are again trade-off situations where one has high mean transaction costs but such costs do not vary much from the mean. Subclass HB (Economic Theory)—case 9—represents the most unfavorable of cases where one has both high mean transaction costs and a high deviation from the mean.

Turning to Table 90 (analysis of the H rows down the Cost Center columns of the underlying matrix) one finds that three cases predominate. Case 3, a trade-off situation of low mean transaction cost but high coefficient of variation, is typified by Cost Centers 16 (Education), 18 (English), 27 (Hillman General) and 86 (Women's Studies). Case 5 is the intermediate case of medium mean transaction cost and medium coefficient of variation and is exemplified by Cost Centers 87 (Administration of Justice), 44 (Political Science), 51 (Sociology) and 53 (Social Work). Case 7 is a trade-off situation of high mean transactions costs but low coefficient of variation and is represented by Cost Centers 02 (Anthropology), 15 (Economics), 29 (Hillman Reserve) and 66 (Replacement Periodicals).

Table 89
Analysis by LC Subclasses HA, HB,......HZ

Category	Mean Cost per Transaction	Coefficient of Variation	LC Sub-Categories
Case 1	Low (ranks 1-4)	Low	
Case 2	Low (ranks 1-4)	Medium	HM (Sociology, General and Theoretical)
Case 3	Low (ranks 1-4)	High	HF (Commerce) HQ (The Family, Marriage, Women) HV (Social Pathology, Social and Public Welfare, Criminology)
Case 4	Medium (ranks 5-8)	Low	HN (Social History, Social Problems, Social Reform)
Case 5	Medium (ranks 5-8)	Medium	HC (Economic History & Conditions, National Production) HD (Land, Agriculture, Industry)
Case 6	Medium (ranks 5-8)	High	HE (Transportation & Communication)
Case 7	High (ranks 9-13)	Low	HG (Finance) HJ (Public Finance) HX (Socialism, Communism, Anarchism)
Case 8	High (ranks 9-13)	Medium	HT (Communities, Classes, Races)
Case 9	High (ranks 9-13)	High	HB (Economic Theory)

Table 90
Analysis of H Subclasses by Cost Center

Category	Mean Cost per Transaction	Coefficient of Variation Costs per Transaction	Cost Centers
Case 1	Low (ranks 1-5)	Low	
Case 2	Low (ranks 1-5)	Medium	
Case 3	Low (ranks 1-5)	High	16 (Education) 18 (English) 27 (Hillman General) 26 (Government Documents)
Case 4	Medium (ranks 6-10)	Low	35 (Latin America)
Case 5	Medium (ranks 6-10)	Medium	87 (Administration of Justice) 44 (Political Science) 51 (Sociology) 53 (Social Work)
Case 6	Medium (ranks 6-10)	High	
Case 7	High (ranks 11-15)	Low	02 (Anthropology) 15 (Economics) 29 (Hillman Reserve) 66 (Replacement Periodicals)
Case 8	High (ranks (11-15)	Medium	23 (Geography)
Case 9	High (ranks 11-15)	High	31 (History)

Table 91 is an analysis of the P subclasses (PA, PB,.... PZ). One finds that the ten subclasses analyzed are widely dispersed among all cases, with the exception of case 9 (high mean transaction cost and high coefficient of variation) which contains two LC subclasses: PA (Classical Language and Literature) and PL (Language and Literature of East Asia, Africa, Oceania). The easiest decision in Table 91 is that of case 1, represented by subclass PE (English) where one has low mean transaction cost and low coefficient of variation. PS (American Literature) in case 3 is a clear trade-off situation where one has a low mean cost but a high probability that a given transaction will have a cost substantially higher than the mean. PT (Germanic Literature) in case 7 is also a clear trade-off situation where one has high mean transaction cost but low coefficient of variation.

Table 92 is an analysis of the P subclasses by Cost Center. The majority of the entries fall into cases 2, 6 and 7. Case 2 (low mean transaction cost and medium coefficient of variation) is typified by Cost Centers 82 (Comparative Literature), 16 (Education) and 30 (Hispanic). Case 6 (medium mean transaction cost and high coefficient of variation) is represented by Cost Centers 18 (English), 66 (Replacement Periodicals) and 52 (Speech). Case 7 has the highest mean transaction cost but at the same time the lowest coefficient

Table 91
Analysis of LC Subclasses PA, PB,......PZ

Category	Mean Cost per Transaction	Coefficient of Variation	LC Sub-Categories
Case 1	Low (ranks 1-3)	Low	PE (English)
Case 2	Low (ranks 1-3)	Medium	PN (Literary History & Collections)
Case 3	Low (ranks 1-3)	High	PS (American Literature)
Case 4	Medium (ranks 4-6)	Low	PG (Slavic. Baltic & Albanian)
Case 5	Medium (ranks 4-6)	Medium	PJ (Oriental Languages & Literature, General Works)
Case 6	Medium (ranks 4-6)	High	PR (English Literature)
Case 7	High (ranks 7-10)	Low	PT (Germanic Literature)
Case 8	High (ranks 7-10)	Medium	PC (Romance Languages)
Case 9	High (ranks 7-10)	High	PA (Classical Language & Literature) PL (Languages & Literature of East Asia, Africa, Oceana)

Table 92
Analysis of P Subclasses by Cost Center

Category	Mean Cost per Transaction	Coefficients of Variation Costs per Transaction	Cost Centers
Case 1	Low (ranks 1-5)	Low	
Case 2	Low (ranks 1-5)	Medium	82 (Comparative Literature) 16 (Education) 30 (Hispanic)
Case 3	Low (ranks 1-5)	High	27 (Hillman General) 35 (Latin America)
Case 4	Medium (ranks 6-10)	Low	49 (Slavic)
Case 5	Medium (ranks 6-10)	Medium	31 (History)
Case 6	Medium (ranks 6-10)	High	18 (English) 66 (Replacement Periodicals) 52 (Speech)
Case 7	High (ranks 11-15)	Low	24 (German) 29 (Hillman Reserve) 21 (Italian) 27 (Hillman General)
Case 8	High (ranks 11-15)	Medium	09 (Classics)
Case 9	High (ranks 11-15)	High	

of variation, indicating that there is less risk that the cost of a given transaction will deviate substantially from the mean. This case is represented by Cost Centers 24 (German), 29 (Hillman Reserve), 21 (Italian) and 47 (Russian and East European).

As in the case of the collection as a whole, mean costs per transaction for the H and P subclasses are in most instances more strongly correlated with transactions per item than with book purchase prices. For H subclasses, the comparative coefficients are -.802 vs. .632 (LC classification) and -.814 vs. .20 (Cost Center classification). For the P subclasses the comparative coefficients are -.575 vs. .89 (LC classification) and -.800 vs. .768 (Cost Center classification). It is noted that for the P subclasses (LC basis) book prices have the stronger influence (.89 vs. .575).

DATA APPENDIX FOR CHAPTER IV

Table A1
Budgetary Data—Hillman Library
1973-1974

Variable Costs

		Footnotes	Amount
	I. ACQUISITIONS (Lib.Mtls.)		$
	Hard Money, Books		205963.55
	Hard Money, Standing Ord.		108390.58
	Soft Money		64143.48
	Total Acquisition Costs		378497.61
	II. PROCESSING		
60020	Technical Services	(3)	56076.38
60021	Library Resources	(3)	97871.50
60022	Gift & Exchange	(3)	26182.47
60023	Order Services	(3)	39456.75
60026	Bibliographic Control	(3)	94979.56
60027	Card & Book Prep.	(4)	41258.78
60028	OCLC	(3)	12271.24
60029	Original Cataloging	(3)	12209.37
60060	Lib. Systems Development	(5)	72267.83
64604	Social Work Library	(14)	1175.57
65611	Black Studies	(14)	1143.07
65601	East Asian	(14)	34549.44
	Total Processing Cost		539441.66
	Sub Total: Acquisitions & Processing:		917939.27
	III. CIRCULATION		
60024	Card Catalog Mtl.		28085.52
60027	Card & Book Prep.	(4)	10314.62
60040	Information Services	(6)	17490.44
60044	Lending		164604.34
60050	Coordinator–Undergrad. Lib.		8448.42
60052	Undergrad. Library		13325.03
60060	Library Systems Development	(5)	89431.44
64604	Social Work Library	(14)	3526.71
65601	East Asian Library	(14)	20729.67
65611	Black Studies Library	(14)	3429.19
			359336.38
	Total Variable Cost:		**1277275.65**

Fixed Costs

		Footnotes	Amount
	I. ADMINISTRATION		$
60010	Director's Office		183023.45
60080	Adm & Fiscal Control		47531.47
60081	Supply Room		17557.77
60082	Records		20874.97
60083	Photocopy		(10244.66)
60084	Staff Services		19614.84
60085	Publications		9305.68
	Total Administration Cost		287663.52
	II. MAINTENANCE COST		
	$1.50 per sq. ft.	366739.50	
	10% extra	36673.95	
	10c extra	24449.30	
	Total Maintenance	427862.75	427862.75
	III. IMPUTED COST		
	Imputed Interest on Library		900995.00
	Depreciation on Library		85000.00
	Total Imputed Cost		985995.00
	Total Fixed Cost		1701521.27
	Adjustment for Omitted Items (34%)		578517.23
	Total Adjusted Fixed Cost		1123004.04

RECAP

	$
Total Hard Money Costs	3007668.00
Total Soft Money Costs	81526.00
	3089194.00
Total Variable Costs	1277275.65
Total Fixed Costs	287663.52
Total Excluded Costs	1524254.83
	3089194.00

Table A1 (continued)

Excluded Costs

7	8	9 (Footnotes)	10 (Amount)
	I. ACQUISITIONS (Lib.Mtl)		$
	Hard Money, Books		55493.93
	Hard Money, Standing Ord.		39481.00
	Soft Money		17382.52
	Hard Money, Subscriptions		223844.74
	Hard Money, Binding		47383.21
	Total Acquisitions Excluded		383585.40
	II. PROCESSING		
60020	Technical Services	(3)	18692.13
60021	Library Resources	(3)	32623.83
60022	Gift & Exchange	(3)	8727.49
60023	Order Services	(3)	13152.25
60025	Serials		63640.88
60026	Bibliographic Cont.	(3)	31659.85
60027	Card & Book Prep.	(3), (4)	17191.04
60028	OCLC	(3)	4090.41
60029	Original Cataloging	(3)	20736.46
	Total Processing Excluded		210514.34
	III. CIRCULATION		
60040	Information Service	(6)	11660.29
60041	Reference		80405.46
60042	Inter Library Loan		6933.35
60043	Documents		44805.60
60047	Stark Listening Center		778.50
60051	ReserveBook Room		37532.43
	Total Circulation Excluded		182115.63
	IV. BRANCH LIBRARIES		
61603	Fine Arts		74454.76
61604	Music		38283.66
62602	Langley		31666.10
62604	Chemistry		21539.43
62606	Mathematics		7189.03
62607	Physics		16813.68
64603	Engineering		42235.79
64604	Social Work	(14)	7053.41

(Continued in next column)

11	12	13 (Footnotes)	14 (Amount)
	IV. BRANCH LIBS. (contd)		$
65601	East Asian	(14)	13819.78
65603	Economics	(14)	30138.23
65611	Black Studies	(14)	6858.39
66601	Darlington		19374.72
66602	Archives		331.38
66605	Special Collections		57068.11
	Total Branch Libraries		366926.47
	V. OTHER EXCLUDED COSTS		
60010	Excluded Adm. Exp.		24921.19
60060	Library Systems Dev.	(5)	18970.31
60070	Truck Delivery		3196.69
60090	Inst. & Res. Svc.		45207.28
60091	Instructional Prin. Svc.		48046.47
60092	Audiovisual Svc.		94882.08
60093	Graphics		68012.37
60094	Instructional Dev. Svc.		50359.13
60095	Engineering Svc.		27517.47
	Total Other Excluded Costs		381112.99
	Total Excluded Costs		1524254.83
	Imputed Storage		13805.00
	Total Omitted Costs		1538059.83

Table A2
Budgetary Data—Hillman Library
1974-1975 (Revised)

Variable Costs

		Footnotes	Amount ($)
	I. ACQUISITION (Lib. Mtls.)		
	Hard Money, Books	(1)	114551.93
	Hard Money, Standing Ord.	(1)	128100.69
	Soft Money	(2)	110847.45
	Total Acquisitions		353500.07
	II. PROCESSING		
60020	Technical Services	(3)	56936.81
60021	Library Resources	(3)	77546.43
60022	Gift & Exchange	(3)	27940.73
60023	Order Services	(3)	43279.69
60026	Bibliographic Control	(3)	94799.92
60027	Card & Book Prep.	(4)	41069.31
60028	OCLC	(3)	8593.89
60029	Cataloging, Original	(3)	57218.99
60060	Library Systems Dev.	(5)	76346.44
64604	Social Work Library	(14)	861.72
65611	Black Studies Library	(14)	1743.48
65601	East Asian Library	(14)	38726.10
	Total Processing Cost		525063.51
	Sub Total Acquisitions & Processing		878563.58
	III. CIRCULATION		
60024	Card Catalog Mtce.		32901.80
60027	Card & Book Preparation	(4)	13689.77
60040	Information Services	(6)	20352.01
60044	Lending		199066.58
60050	Coord. Resv. & Undergraduate		15660.52
60052	Undergraduate Library		3713.00
60060	Library Systems Development	(5)	94478.72
64604	Social Work Library	(14)	2585.14
65611	Black Studies Library	(14)	5230.43
65601	East Asian Library	(14)	28235.66
	Total Circulation Cost		1289477.21

Fixed Costs

		Footnotes	Amount ($)
	I. ADMINISTRATION		
60010	Director's Office	(7)	178064.29
60011	Other		259.31
62080	Adm. & Fiscal Cont.		52124.54
60081	Supply Room		31561.43
60082	Records		24015.06
60083	Photocopy		(4746.65)
60084	Staff Services		24088.12
	Total Administration Cost		305366.10
	II. MAINTENANCE COST		
	$1.76 per sq. ft.		430307.68
	10% extra		43030.77
	$0.10 extra		24449.30
	Total Maintenance Cost		497787.75
	III. IMPUTED COST		
	Imputed Interest on Library		1007480.00
	Depreciation on Library		85000.00
	Total Imputed Cost		1092480.00
	Total Fixed Cost		1895633.85
	Adjustment for Omitted Items (36%)		682428.19
	Total Adjusted Fixed Cost		1213205.66

RECAP

	$
Total Hard Money Costs	3187173.95
Total Soft Money Costs	217657.00
	3404830.95
Total Variable Costs	1289477.21
Total Fixed Costs	305366.10
Total Excluded Costs	1809987.64
	3404830.95

Table A2 (continued)

7	8	9	10
			Excluded Costs
		Footnotes	Amount
			$
	I. ACQUISITIONS (Lib. Mtls)		
	Hard Money, Books	(1)	65230.00
	Hard Money, Standing Ord.	(1)	42248.00
	Soft Money	(2)	60181.50
	Hard Money–Subs.	(1)	250774.62
	Hard Money–Binding	(1)	70075.62
	Hard Money–Film	(1)	2936.55
	Hard Money–Data Bases	(1)	3366.00
	Total Acquisitions Excl.		494812.38
	II. PROCESSING		
60020	Technical Services	(3)	18978.94
60021	Library Resources	(3)	52848.81
60022	Gift & Exchange	(3)	9313.58
60023	Order Services	(3)	14426.56
60025	Serials		70407.67
60026	Bibliographic Cont.	(3)	31599.98
60027	Card & Book Prep.	(3), (4)	13689.77
60028	OCLC	(3)	28646.63
60029	Cataloging, Original	(3)	19073.00
	Total Processing Costs Excl.		233202.94
	III. CIRCULATION		
60040	Information Services	(6)	13568.00
60041	Reference		89848.20
60042	Inter Library Loan		9049.12
60043	Documents		47845.60
60047	Stark Listening Center		4585.95
60051	Reserve Book Room		44996.47
	Total Circulation Costs Excl.		209893.34
	IV. BRANCH LIBRARIES		
61603	Fine Arts		77702.88
61604	Music		39928.26
62602	Langley		35877.98
62604	Chemistry		22284.04
62606	Mathematics		8782.89
62607	Physics		17779.48
64603	Engineering		57683.75
	(continued)		

11	12	13	14
		Footnotes	Amount
			$
	IV. BRANCH LIBRARIES (contd.)		
61604	Social Work	(14)	5170.30
65611	Black Studies	(14)	10460.87
65601	East Asian Library	(14)	15490.45
65603	Economics		35966.16
65604	Computer Science		2710.29
66601	Darlington		21111.12
66602	Archives		67.35
66603	Curtis Theatre Collection		17.25
66605	Special Collections		72350. 85
	Total Branch Libraries Excl.		423403.92
	V. OTHER EXCLUDED COSTS		
60010	Administration	(7)	26790.50
60060	Library Systems Dev.		20040.94
60070	Truck Rental/TWX		3653.48
60090	Instructional and Res. Svce.		54553.62
60091	Instructional Prod.		24636.95
60092	Audio Visual Svce.		101713.39
60093	Graphics		71991.70
60094	Instructional Development		66501.50
60095	I & R Engineering		32164.93
	Soft Money other than Lib.Mtls.		46628.05
	Total Other Costs Excl.		448675.06
	Total Excluded Costs		1809087.64
	Imputed Storage Cost		13805.00
	Total Omitted Costs		1823792.64

Table A3
Budgetary Data—Hillman Library
1975-1976

	Variable Costs	Footnotes	Amount
			$
	I. ACQUISITIONS (Lib. Mtls.)		
	Hard Money, Books	(1)	226712.89
	Hard Money, Standing Ord.	(1)	112560.17
	Soft Library Funds	(2)	103724.38
	Total Acquisitions Costs		442987.44
	II. PROCESSING		
60020	Processing	(3)	44419.38
60021	Coordinator's Office	(3)	18357.56
60022	OCLC	(3)	11018.14
60023	Order Service	(3)	44831.17
60026	Bibliographic Control	(3)	96911.59
60027	Card & Book Prep.	(4)	49073.60
60028	Gift & Exchange	(3)	12991.04
60030	Original Cataloging	(3)	9345.94
60031	Original Cataloging	(3)	62905.48
60060	Library Systems Development	(5)	134054.80
64604	Social Work Library	(14)	1392.83
65611	Black Studies Library	(14)	2188.52
65601	East Asian Library	(14)	40565.19
60050	Library Resources	(3)	19853.08
60051	Coordinator's Office	(3)	6698.08
60053	Bibliographers	(3)	82214.16
60054	Gift & Exchange	(3)	13424.75
	Total Processing Costs		640245.31
	Sub Total Acquisitions & Processing		1083232.75
	III. CIRCULATION		
60024	Card Catalog Mtce.		24370.86
60027	Card & Book Preparation	(4)	12268.40
60040	Information Services	(6)	31765.40
60041	Coordinator's Office	(6)	7579.18
60045	Lending		86103.05
60060	Library Systems Development	(5)	165892. 81
64604	Social Work Library	(14)	4178.51
65611	Black Studies Library	(14)	6565.56
65601	East Asian Library	(14)	24339.12
60049	Stack Operations	(6)	65987.08
	Total Circulation Costs		429049.97
	Total Variable Cost		1512282.72

	Fixed Costs		Amount
			$
	I. ADMINISTRATION		
60010	Director's Office		22978.00
60011	Dir.Office/Mgt. Staff		160766.15
60080	Adm. & Fiscal Control		13147.57
60081	Asst. to Director Office		11249.09
60082	Records		27742.49
60083	Photocopy		7648.54
60084	Staff Services		23984.44
60085	Supply Room		35902.25
60086	Coin-op Photocopy		(9488.05)
60087	Coin-op Microfilm		(2393.45)
60088	Coin-op Pen Machines		(79.30)
	Total Administration Cost		291427.73
	II. MAINTENANCE COST		
	$2 per sq. ft.	488986.00	
	10% extra	48898.60	
	10c extra	24449.30	
	Total Maintenance Cost		562333.90
	III. IMPUTED COST		
	Imputed Interest on Library		977445.00
	Depreciation on Library		85000.00
	Total Imputed Cost		1062445.00
	Total Fixed Cost		1916206.63
	Adjustment for Omitted Items (32%)		613186.12
	Total Adjusted Fixed Cost		1303020.51
	RECAP		$
	Total Hard Money Costs		3237665.47
	Total Soft Money Costs		184718.57
			3422384.04
	Total Variable Costs		1512282.72
	Total Fixed Costs		291427.73
	Total Excluded Costs		1618673.59
			3422384.04

Table A3 (continued)

Excluded Costs

7	8	9	10
		Footnotes	Amount
			$
	I. ACQUISITIONS (Lib.Mtls.)		
	Hard Money, Books	(1)	43332.80
	Hard Money, Standing Ord.	(1)	50724.14
	Soft Library Funds	(1)	39505.58
	Hard Money – Subscriptions	(1)	288064.50
	Hard Money – Binding	(1)	74986.46
	Hard Money – Film	(1)	(250.00)
	Hard Money – Data Bases	(1)	4407.00
	Total Acquisitions Excluded		500770.48
	II. PROCESSING		
60020	Processing	(3)	14806.46
60021	Coordinator's Office	(3)	2785. 85
60022	OCLC	(3)	3672.71
60023	Order Service	(3)	14943.73
60025	Serials		103423.08
60026	Bibliographic Control	(3)	32303.87
60027	Card & Book Prep.	(3), (4)	20447.33
60028	Gift & Exchange	(3)	4330.35
60030	Original Cataloging	(3)	3115.31
60031	Original Cataloging	(3)	20968.49
60050	Library Resources	(3)	6617.69
60051	Coordinator's Office	(3)	2232.70
60053	Bibliographers	(3)	27404.72
60054	Gift & Exchange	(3)	4474.92
	Total Processing Excluded		261527.21
	III CIRCULATION		
60040	Information Services	(6)	21176.94
60041	Coordinator's Office	(6)	5052.79
60042	Reference		93025.61
60043	Inter Library Loan		12886.90
60044	Documents		42207.46
60046	Microform Area		28142.83
60047	Periodicals Reading Room		98.05
60048	Stark Listening Center		22012.12
60049	Stack Operations		43991.39
60052	Reserve Book Room		44079.45
	Total Circulation Excluded		312673.54
	IV. BRANCH LIBRARIES (continued in next column)		
61603	Fine Arts		68531.15
61604	Music		45141.88
62602	Langley-Life Sciences		54001.49

11	12	13	14
		Footnotes	Amount
			$
	IV. BRANCH LIBRARIES (contd.)		
62604	Chemistry		24531.21
62606	Mathematics		9989.08
62607	Physics		19375.60
64603	Engineering		41979.03
64604	Social Work	(14)	8357.01
65601	East Asian Library	(14)	16226.08
65603	Economics		37534.45
65604	Computer Science		10600.05
65611	Black Studies	(14)	13131.13
66601	Darlington		18334.22
66602	Archives		13283.02
66603	Curtis Collection		7268.60
66605	Special Collections		49472.43
	Total Branch Libraries Excluded		437756.43
	V. OTHER EXCLUDED COSTS		
60060	Library Systems Dev.	(5)	35189.39
60071	Truck Rental		2059.25
60072	TWX/Telephone Service		25190.63
60019	Earth & Planetary Move		2008.05
	Soft Money other than Lib. Mtls.		41498.61
	Total Other Excluded Costs		105945.93
	Total Excluded Costs		1618673.59
	Imputed Storage Cost		13805.00
	Total Omitted Costs		1632478.59

Footnotes to Tables A1 - A3

(1) Items in this category record book purchases for Hillman only. The book purchases for the branch libraries are recorded in omitted costs.

(2) Soft library funds are soft money accounts under the control of the library administration. Soft non-library funds are soft money accounts not under the administration's control.

(3) Items in this category represent 75% of total expenditures for processing the estimated amount of processing expenditures associated with Hillman Library. The remaining 25% is associated with branch libraries, and placed in omitted costs.

(4) Eighty percent of "Card and Book Preparation" was considered to be processing cost and 20% circulation cost.

(5) Forty percent of employee time in Library Systems Development was estimated as being spent in processing, 49.5% in circulation, and 10.5% doing other duties. Budgetary expenditures were allocated in these proportions to processing, circulation, and "omitted" cost.

(6) This account has been allotted between circulation (60%) and omitted data (40%).

(7) Excludes administration expenses of $26,790.50 unrelated to book use cost in Hillman or branch libraries.

(8) Maintenance and operation, including utilities, are estimated to cost $1.76 per square foot for the Hillman Library building. Square footage related to library operations are estimated as 244,493 sq. ft. The 10% extra is a correction factor for additional services and the $ .10 extra per foot is for major maintenance.

(9) Imputed cost is the amount of interest that would have been earned had the dollar investment in the library and its books been made in an interest-bearing security. An interest return of 9% is assumed for fiscal year 1974-75. This 9% rate was applied to $11,320,000 (land value of $3.5 million and building value of $8.5 million, less eight years' depreciation, assuming a depreciation rate of 1% per year on the building).

(10) Considering that 36% of the total library expenditures are omitted items, total fixed costs are reduced in the same proportion to secure fixed costs related to Hillman book use.

Footnotes to Tables A1 - A3 (continued)

(11) A section of the Anthropology Building is used for storage of seldom-used books. The imputed rate per square foot was $6 on 2,301 gross square feet.

(12) By summing all the hard money accounts found on the page, one arrives at the total hard money budget.

(13) The study includes all pertinent soft money accounts used in acquisitions.

(14) The Social Work, Black Studies, and East Asian library expenditures were allocated among processing, circulation and omitted cost in the following proportions:

	Social Work	Black Studies	East Asian
Processing	10%	10%	50%
Circulation	30%	30%	30%
Omitted	60%	60%	20%

Table A4
1976-1977 Serials Costs—Science Libraries (Computer Science, Chemistry, Engineering, Mathematics, Langley Life Sciences, Physics)

Variable Costs

		Footnote	Amount
			$
	I. ACQUISITIONS (Lib.Mtls.)		
	Hard Money, Subscriptions	(1)	177582.64
	Hard Money, Binding	(1)	16222.00
	Total Acquisition Expenditures		193804.64
	II. PROCESSING		
60020	Processing (FB only)	(3)	3230.93
60021	Coordinator:s Office	(4)	1033.44
60022	OCLC	(5)	335.92
60025	Serials	(6)	19483.36
60060	Library Systems Development	(8)	7915.26
	Total Processing Expenditures		31998.91
	III. CIRCULATION		----------
	IV. BRANCH LIBRARIES		
62602	Langley Life Sciences	(9)	27046.15
62604	Chemistry	(10)	13203.54
62606	Mathematics	(11)	7814.63
62607	Physics	(12)	14263.96
64603	Engineering	(13)	31466.92
65604	Computer Science	(14)	4132.71
	Total Branch Libraries		97927.91
	Total Variable Expenditures		323731.46

Fixed Costs

		Footnote	Amount
			$
	I. ADMINISTRATION		
60010	Director's Office		29274.16
60011	Director's Office/Mgt. Staff		158288.80
60080	Adm. & Fiscal Control		14778.70
60081	Asst. to Director Office		13152.36
60082	Records		27210.60
60083	Photocopy		19819.92
60084	Staff Services		27511.07
60085	Supply Room		29043.76
60086	Coin-op Photocopy		(10811.59)
60087	Coin-op Microfilm		(3030.94)
60088	Coin-op Penn Machine		(99.40)
60089	4th Floor Photocopy		(11643.44)
	Total Administration Expenditures		293494.00

RECAP

	$
Total Hard Money Exps.	3438674.49
Total Soft Money Exps.	107576.18
	3546250.67
Total Variable Exps.	323731.46
Total Fixed Cost Exps.	293494.00
Total Excluded Exps.	2929025.21
	3546250.67

Table A4 (continued)

7	8	9	10	11	12	13	14
		Excluded Costs					
		Footnote	Amount			Footnote	Amount
			$				$
I.	ACQUISITIONS (Lib.Mtls.)				IV. BRANCH LIBRARIES		
	Hard Money, Books	(1)	346789.70	61603	Fine Arts	(7)	79665.36
	Hard Money, Subscriptions	(1)	128943.15	61604	Music	(7)	48687.25
	Hard Money, Standing Ord.	(1)	173181.19	62602	Langley Life Sciences	(9)	15816.21
	Hard Money, Binding	(1)	63261.24	62604	Chemistry	(10)	11157.23
	Hard Money, Film	(1)	15.00	62606	Mathematics	(11)	3160.97
	Hard Money, Data Bases	(1)	2860.00	62607	Physics	(12)	7185.60
	Hard Money, Documents	(1)	24044.41	64603	Engineering	(13)	21507.70
	Soft Library Funds	(2)	90511.95	64604	Social Work	(7)	17949.93
	Total Acquisitions Expensitures Excluded		829606.64	65601	East Asian	(7)	87628.43
				65603	Economics	(7)	38912.49
II.	PROCESSING			65604	Computer Science	(14)	3694.40
60020	Processing (FB only)	(3)	63729.13	65611	Black Studies	(7)	25836.94
60021	Coordinator's Office	(4)	19635.31	66601	Darlington	(7)	19994.54
60022	OCLC	(5)	16992.84	66602	Archives	(7)	22265.63
60023	Order Service	(7)	64537.05	66603	Curtis Collection	(7)	5891.20
60024	Catalog Mtce.	(7)	34268.98	66605	Special Collections	(7)	53149.01
60025	Serials	(6)	98597.58		Total Branch Libraries Excluded		462502.89
60026	Bibliographic Services	(7)	118757.99				
60027	Card & Book Prep.	(7)	57979.34		V. OTHER EXCLUDED COSTS		
60028	Gift & Exchange	(7)	36538.74	60060	Library Systems Dev.	(8)	255926.61
60030	Original Cataloging	(7)	15431.77	60071	Truck Rental		3652.00
60031	Original Cataloging	(7)	92264.76	60072	TWX/Telephone		23332.43
60050	Library Resources	(7)	28757.74	60090	Students		32.80
60051	Coordinator's Office	(7)	10849.39		Soft Money other than Library Mtls.		17064.23
60053	Bibliographers	(7)	129161.29				
	Total Processing Expenditures Excl.		787501.91		Total Other Excluded Costs		300008.07
	III. CIRCULATION – HILLMAN				Total Excluded Costs		2929025.21
60040	Information Services	(7)	48525.00				
60041	Coordinator's Office	(7)	13191.78				
60042	Reference	(7)	76704.95				
60043	Inter Library Loan	(7)	11834.36				
60044	Documents	(7)	52614.09				
60045	Lending	(7)	91355.92				
60046	Microform Area	(7)	32202.77				
60047	Information Bank	(7)	19039.49				
60048	Stark Listening Center	(7)	19776.84				
60049	Stack Operations	(7)	134391.34				
60052	Reserve Book Room	(7)	49769.16				
	Total Circulation Excluded		549405.70				

Footnotes to Table A4: 1976-77

(1) Items in this category represent actual expenditures for subscriptions and binding in the 6 departmental science libraries. The actual expenditures for the other departmental libraries and the Hillman Library are contained in the Excluded Costs.

(2) Soft Library Funds are soft money accounts under control of the Library Administration or other administrative areas which allocate specific amounts to the library to be used for acquisitions to be placed in the library's collection.

(3) Fringe Benefits for all processing departments are charged to this account. The allocation between Variable and Excluded Costs is based on actual expenditures.

(4) It is estimated that 5% of the efforts of the Coordinator of Processing are applicable to the serials function of the six science libraries.

(5) Variable Costs include 10% of 1/3 of the telecommunications and maintenance costs of the serials terminal plus 10% of the acquisition of one line printer for use with the serials terminal. Remainder of expenditures for OCLC are in Excluded Costs.

(6) Allocated on the basis that 16.5% of personnel effort is applicable to serials for the six science libraries.

(7) No expenditure applicable to serials in the six science libraries.

(8) It is estimated that 3% of the total efforts of Library Systems Development department is devoted to processing serials information for the six science libraries. All other Library Systems Development expenditures are excluded.

(9) 63.1% of the total acquisition of Library Materials purchased for the Langley Library was for subscriptions. The cost of operation of the library has been allocated accordingly.

(10) 54.2% of the total acquisition of Library Materials purchased for the Chemistry Library was for subscriptions. The cost of operation of the library has been allocated accordingly.

(11) 71.2% of the total acquisition of Library Materials purchased for the Mathematics Library was for subscriptions. The cost of operation of the library has been allocated accordingly.

Footnotes to Table A4 (continued)

(12) 66.5% of the total acquisition of Library Materials purchased for the Physics Library was for subscriptions. The cost of operation of the library has been allocated accordingly.

(13) 59.4% of the total acquisition of Library Materials purchased for the Engineering Library was for subscriptions. The cost of operation of the library has been allocated accordingly.

(14) 52.8% of the total acquisition of Library Materials purchased for the Computer Science Library was for subscriptions. The cost of operation of the library has been allocated accordingly.

Table A5
Analysis of Acquisitions for Six Science Libraries—1976-1977

	Computer Science		Chemistry		Engineering		Langley Life Scs.		Mathematics		Physics	
	Amount	%	Amount	%	Amount	%	Amount	%	Amount	%	Amount	%
BOOKS	$ 3,375.80	36.0	$ 7,762.25	12.7	$ 19,243.35	25.5	$ 20,564.78	26.4	$ 3,080.68	15.4	$ 10,415.27	22.0
SUBSCRIPTIONS	4,945.32	52.8	33,046.40	54.2	44,786.63*	59.4	49,022.57	63.1	14,259.54	71.2	31,522.18	66.5
STANDING ORDERS	1,052.84	11.2	20,210.06	33.1	11,398.75	15.1	8,161.88	10.5	2,697.46	13.4	5,472.18	11.5
TOTAL:	$ 9,373.96		$61,018.71		$ 75,428.73		$77,749.23		$ 20,037.68		$ 47,409.63	

Source: This table was supplied by Hillman Library.

* This figure includes the $9,072 for indexes and abstracts. See footnote 32, page 125.

Footnotes Explaining Calculations—Table 76

1. Line 1 divided by line 4.
2. Line 2 divided by line 6.
3. Line 3 divided by line 8.
4. Line 9 divided by line 3.
5. Line 9 divided by line 8.
6. Total variable costs in the case of Method 1 = circulation costs.
7. Line 4 divided by line 8 multiplied by line 12.
8. Line 13 divided by line 4.
9. Line 1 divided by line 3 multiplied by line 12.
10. Line 15 divided by line 1.
11. Line 6 divided by line 8 multiplied by line 12.
12. Line 17 divided by line 6.
13. Line 2 divided by line 3 multiplied by line 12.
14. Line 19 divided by line 2.
15. A portion of fixed costs were reduced by 34% in 1973-74, 36% in 1974-75 and 32% in 1975-76. These percentages are the ratio of expenditures unrelated to Hillman Library divided by the total library budget. They reflect the fact that a portion of fixed costs associated with administration and maintenance are not related to Hillman book use. The portion of fixed costs represented by the imputed interest value of books was not reduced.
16. Line 21 divided by line 3.
17. Line 21 divided by line 8.
18. Line 24 divided by line 3.
19. Line 24 divided by line 8.
20. Line 4 divided by line 8 multiplied by line 24.
21. Line 27 divided by line 4.
22. Line 1 divided by line 3 multiplied by line 24.
23. Line 29 divided by line 1.
24. Line 6 divided by line 8 multiplied by line 24.
25. Line 31 divided by line 6.

Footnotes Explaining Calculations—Table 76 (continued)

26. Line 2 divided by line 3 multiplied by line 24.

27. Line 33 divided by line 2.

28. New book transactions were doubled, on the assumption that new book purchases were available, on the average, for only half a year. Thus, recorded new book transactions would be half of what they could be expected to be, had the books been available for the full year.

29. Line 38 divided by line 37

30. Line 36 divided by line 37 multiplied by line 40.

31. Line 41 divided by line 36.

32. Line 43 divided by line 37.

33. Line 45 divided by line 37.

34. Line 36 divided by line 37 multiplied by line 45.

35. Line 38 divided by line 36.

Footnotes Explaining Calculations—Table 77

1. See Footnote 1, Table 76.

2. See Footnote 2, Table 76.

3. See Footnote 3, Table 76.

4. Line 7 divided by line 3.

5. Line 7 divided by line 6.

5a. Acquisition costs include processing costs.

6. Variable costs in Method 2 equal circulation plus acquisition costs. Acquisition costs include book purchases and book processing costs.

7. Total acquisition cost plus (line 4 divided by line 6 multiplied by line 7).

8. Line 11 divided by line 4.

9. Total acquisition cost plus (line 1 divided by line 3 multiplied by line 7).

10. Line 13 divided by line 1.

11. Line 5 divided by line 6 multiplied by line 7.

12. Line 15 divided by line 5.

Footnotes Explaining Calculations—Table 77 (continued)

13. Line 2 divided by line 3 multiplied by line 7.

14. Line 17 divided by line 2.

15. All fixed costs in Method 2 were adjusted according to the percentages mentioned in Footnote 15, Table 76.

16. Line 19 divided by line 3.

17. Line 19 divided by line 6.

18. Line 22 divided by line 3.

19. Line 22 divided by line 6.

20. Line 11 plus (line 4 divided by line 6 multiplied by line 19).

21. Line 25 divided by line 4.

22. Line 13 plus (line 1 divided by line 3 multiplied by line 19).

23. Line 27 divided by line 1.

24. (Line 5 divided by line 6 multiplied by line 19) plus (line 5 divided by line 6 multiplied by line 7).

25. Line 29 divided by line 5.

26. (Line 2 divided by line 3 multiplied by line 19) plus (line 5 divided by line 6 multiplied by line 7).

27. Line 31 divided by line 2.

28. See Footnote 28, Table 76.

29. Line 36 divided by line 35.

30. Total acquisitions cost plus (line 34 divided by line 35 multiplied by line 36).

31. Line 39 divided by line 34.

32. Line 41 divided by line 35.

33. Line 43 divided by line 35.

34. (Line 34 divided by line 35 multiplied by line 41) plus line 39.

35. Line 45 divided by line 34.

Chapter V

A COST BENEFIT MODEL OF LIBRARY OPERATIONS*

Jacob Cohen

A. The Ubiquitous Economist

The economist brings to librarians his own peculiar theology. It is not a new theology—the economist's paradigm is uniquely constant.[1] But it is a pervasive theology laying down conditions for rational human behavior. Its pervasiveness is demonstrated by recent extension to supposedly "non-economic" areas. Thus a new introductory text in economics eschews traditional topics such as inflation and unemployment and teaches economics in terms of the more titillating subjects of sex, the family, crime and dishonesty, politics, bureaucracy, committee meetings and the learning process.[2] Nothing is sacred for the economist. All (rational) human actions are motivated by a cost-benefit calculus.

One eminent librarian challenges this singlemindedness.[3] The economist goes off the track, according to Hayes, because he equates cost (price)

---

* Subsections A, B, C, D are based on the author's paper "Book Cost and Book Use: The Economics of a University Library," from A. Kent and T. Galvin, eds., Library Resource Sharing, Marcel Dekker, Inc., New York, 1977, Chapter 17.

1 Cf. Michael C. Lovell, "The Production of Economic Literature: An Interpretation," Journal of Economic Literature, 11, March 1973, p. 27, fn. 2.

2 See Lawrence H. Officer and Leanna Stiefel, "The New World of Economics: A Review Article," Journal of Economic Issues, 10, March 1976, 149ff. The book reviewed is Richard B. McKenzie and Gordon Tullock, The New World of Economics: Explorations into the Human Experience (Homewood, Ill., 1973).

3 Robert N. Hayes, The National Library Network, Its Economic Rationale and Funding, National Commission on Libraries and Information Science, National Program for Libraries and Information Services, Related Paper No. 9, Washington, D.C., 1974, esp. pp. 25ff.

with value.[4] Hayes would apply Oscar Wilde's definition of a cynic to the economist: he knows the price of everything and the value of nothing.[5] The word "value" for Hayes goes beyond the price the buyer of services or goods is willing to pay. It includes a value to society—a social benefit. Computers and cars have such a social benefit (and the motives of IBM and GM therefore are loftier than mere profit-seeking).[6] This distinction between private and social benefit was pioneered by the economist but he insists on measurement. Professor Hayes denies the possibility of measurement in library matters.[7]

One can concede the problems of measurement but the response should be similar to Maurice Chevalier's response to inquiries about the infirmities of old age—does anyone have a better alternative?[8]

B. The Economic Model

In constructing an economic model of a library's operations it makes a difference how one defines a library's output. Defining it as "books" is different from defining it as "book use."[9] In the former case, the benefit consists of the utility from using books plus the utility of having books available for use. These functions of books can be referred to as their <u>use function</u> and <u>museum function</u>, respectively.

---

[4] Ibid., p. 26.

[5] This definition is quoted by Paul A. Samuelson, Economics, 5th ed. (New York, 1961), p. 435.

[6] Hayes, op. cit., p. 26.

[7] Not all librarians spurn the idea of measurement. One author speaks of the "Zens-Kelvin" schism in library budgetary matters and is critical of the former approach. John Kountz, "Library Cost Analysis: A Recipe," Library Journal, 97, p. 463, February 1, 1972.

[8] Alan Williams, "Cost-benefit Analysis: Bastard Science? And/or Insidious Poison in the Body Politick?," Cost Benefit and Cost Effectiveness, ed. by J. N. Wolfe (London, 1973), p. 58.

[9] While the economic model is phrased in terms of books, it should apply equally to journals.

"Book use" has been chosen as the measure of output because the overall study reported here has focussed on book use (and non-use). A casualty is the museum function.[10] Figure 12 speculates on the relationships between benefits, costs (measured on the vertical axis) and amounts of book use (measured along the horizontal axis). The diagram is in two sections, one for the services of existing books and one for those of new books. The diagram measures costs and benefits (uses) per period of time, say for one month or one year.

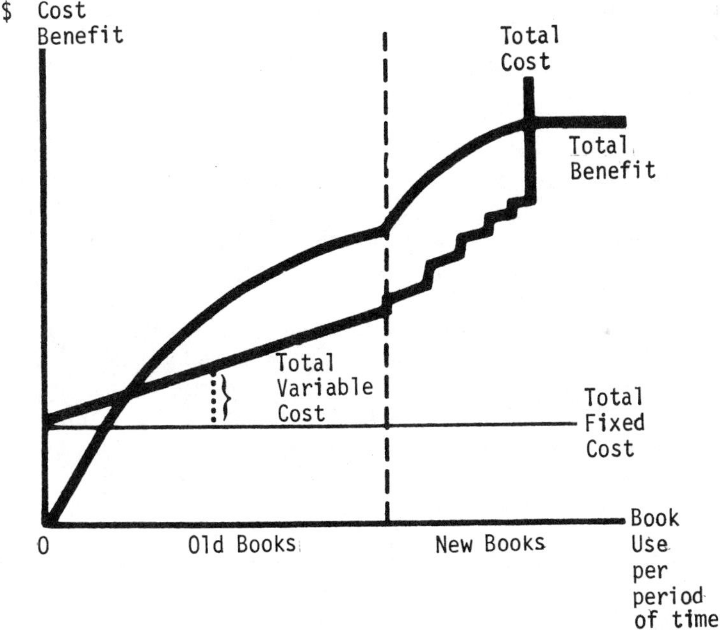

Figure 12. Cost and benefit of book use: acquisition cost included in variable cost.

---

[10] It is an interesting question, however, whether the museum value of the library is independent of book-use value. If no one ever entered a museum, what would its utility be? The analogue, in the theory of finance, is the corporation that has never paid dividends and is not expected to pay them. Apart from the psychology of other buyers—which may still make a market for the stock—would anyone buy it?

The total benefit curve cumulates the benefits from book use. Each book has multiple uses but each additional book (proceeding to the right along the book-use axis) is assumed to have less circulations ("transactions") than the preceding book. Each successive use of a given book is also assumed to confer a diminishing benefit. The overall shape of the curve for old books thus depicts total benefits increasing at a decreasing rate.[11] The curve has been smoothed out instead of being shown as a series of "bumps" with each bump representing the utility from successive uses of a single book. These bumps would get progressively flatter and shorter as one moves to the right of the curve and depict books with less total utility and fewer uses. Finally, the curve for old books comes to an abrupt end signifying no further book use. At such a point a large percentage of books may not have circulated in the current period.

The flow (new book) portion of the diagram measures benefits from current acquisitions. The shape of the total benefit curve parallels that for "old" books. Again, the curve ends when new books are no longer used. Since books get used less often as they age, the "bumps" for new books would be more substantial than for old books.

On the cost side (as previously discussed in Chapter IV), total costs consist of fixed and variable costs. Fixed costs are independent of "output" and are represented as a horizontal line on the diagram. The variable costs on the other hand depend on book use. These costs are superimposed on the fixed cost curve so that the vertical difference between the total cost curve and the fixed cost curve measures the total variable costs for any amount of book use.

The total cost curve for the "existing" library is drawn as a straight line, suggesting that the only variable costs are circulation costs and that these vary in proportion to book use.[12] In the "new" portion of the diagram we have allowed for book acquisitions. As each new book is acquired costs increase (including processing costs), as shown by the vertical segments of the curve. The sloped portions of the total cost curve indicate circulation

---

[11] On the diagram, ranking of books by their utility does not necessarily correspond to the order in which they circulate. In effect, the diagram takes all the books that have circulated in a given period of time and rearranges them, beginning with the book having the most transactions and which is assumed to have the highest total utility.

[12] More precisely, the variable cost curve would be a "staircase" function since library staff and other circulation costs would increase <u>discontinuously</u> with increases in use.

costs which are again proportional to book use. Since each successive book will have diminishing transactions (the diagram arranges books in the order of the number of their circulations, beginning with books with the highest circulations), the slopes become shorter in length as we move to the right in the diagram. Finally, when total benefits reach a maximum (no further book use), the total cost curve is vertical—the unlimited cost of unused books.

As mentioned in Chapter IV, section A. above (and measured in section B.), this independence of acquisition costs in relation to book use suggests that acquisition costs should be treated as a capital cost rather than as a current (variable) cost. Books are bought in contemplation of use but not in a fixed relation to such use. Now variable costs would be limited to circulation costs for both old and new book use as indicated by the total cost curve of Figure 13. The imputed interest on book acquisitions (not the value of the acquisitions themselves) would be included in fixed costs. The fixed cost curve will "move up" over time with additional book acquisitions. If we allow for a compound interest principle—interest being earned on interest—this will also cause the fixed cost curve to move up.

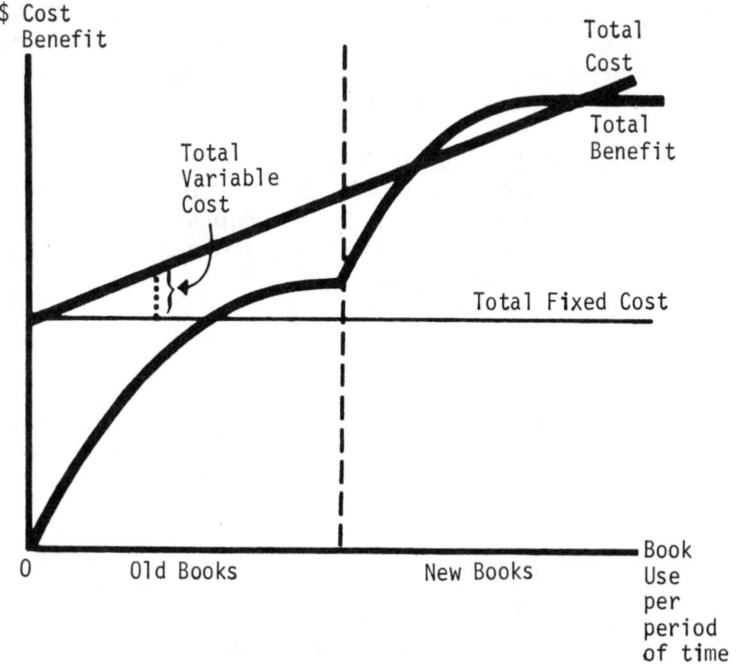

Figure 13. Cost and benefit of book use: acquisition cost included in fixed cost.

Once drawn, the cost and benefit curves become the basis for discussing the optimal scale of library operations. Optimality in a strict sense exists when marginal costs equal marginal benefits. "Marginal" refers to the costs and benefits associated with one more book use. These values are measured by the slopes of the total cost and total benefit curves at each point along these curves (for different amounts of book use). When the total cost curve is a straight line, as in Figure 13, this tells us that (1) marginal costs of book use are constant; and (2) they are the same as the average circulation cost of book use. The rationale of optimality is that marginal costs measure potential benefits from transferring inputs elsewhere. When marginal costs exceed the benefits from book use, the university is better off by shifting funds to other university programs (assuming that they too are attempting to optimize).

If we work with a straight line total cost curve throughout the diagram, the library's policy of satisfying all book requests can be shown to be consistent with optimal behavior. For so long as the extra ("marginal") benefits from book use exceed the circulation costs entailed, it pays to expand "output." Assuming that this is the case, this "best" output will be the same as maximum amount of book use (the terminus of the benefit curve).[13] A similar conclusion follows if the total cost curve lies above the total benefit curve at <u>every</u> possible amount of book use (not shown by the diagram). While "losses" are being incurred, so long as benefits exceed circulation costs, the losses are less than they otherwise would be (by not circulating the books).

It is likely, then, that libraries behave rationally in meeting all current book requests. It is their "long run" behavior—their "capital budgeting"—that is more questionable, however. For acquisitions may be responsible for pushing the total cost curve above the benefit curve resulting in a net "loss." Library behavior in this sense is uneconomic.[14]

C. Optimality of Library Operations Over Time

The "dynamics" of optimality are suggested in <u>Figure 14</u> measuring time on the horizontal axis. It portrays the "typical" library as steadily moving away

---

[13] Circulation costs per book use would be represented by a horizontal line below the total benefit curve. Its vertical distance from the horizontal axis would be equal to the total variable cost distances, each divided by the related amount of book use, measured on the horizontal axis.

[14] It is hoped that this will not fan anti-economist flames and lead to cries of "down with economic values" and "up with human values." Losses mean that some output of greater "human" value is being sacrificed elsewhere.

from optimality. The hypothetical shape of the total benefit curve reflects the dialectic of aging books versus new acquisitions. Books acquired in one period are used in succeeding periods. But at the same time old books are being used less frequently. Given a "steady state" situation with the same amount of acquisitions in each period, and with "obsolete" books regularly being replaced with new books, and neglecting the loss rate, the benefit curve should flatten out over time.[15]

On the other hand, total costs will be growing at an exponential rate because of imputed interest costs on acquisitions. Stable book use combined with a growing library means a growing disparity between benefits and cost over time.[16]

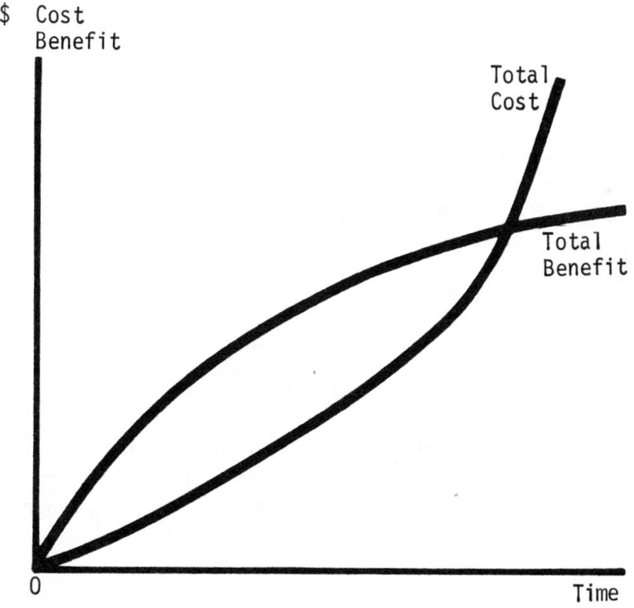

Figure 14. Behavior of cost and benefit over time.

---

15 In our analysis, the university population is considered to be a stable one, thus removing a major determinant of growth in book use and benefits.

16 On data with respect to growth trends in costs, see Wm. J. Baumol and Matityahu Marcus, Economics of Academic Libraries, American Council on Education, Washington, D. C., 1973, p. 72.

These propositions can be stated more rigorously. Assume that acquisitions have been made for a series of "n" years. Assume that in the current year a fixed proportion of these acquisitions circulate a certain number of times (yielding a given number of book uses in that year for the "n" year acquisitions), then in every period of time book uses will be stable. Stated algebraically:

$$U_t = a_0 AQ_{t-n} + a_1 AQ_{t-n+1} \ldots + a_{n-1} AQ_{t-1} + a_n AQ_t$$

where

U = number of book transactions

AQ = book acquisitions

t = current time period

n = number of periods (e.g., t-n where t=0, n=10, would indicate acquisitions 10 years earlier)

a_i = number of circulations for each year's acquisitions; with the "i" subscript indicating that the number can vary depending on the year of acquisition

We assume that each year's acquisitions are the same in value. Then, the expression simplifies to:

$$U_t = \sum_{i=o}^{n} a_i AQ_t$$

Given the constancy of the a's, the steady state value of U_t will also be constant. This can be translated into stable values of book benefits on the basis of an assumed relationship between book benefits and book use. The linkage between the two is the utility from book use (which is assumed to decline with book use). If the relationship between the total utility from book use and numbers of book use is described by the following power function[17]

$$SAT = aU^b$$

where

SAT = total utility

a and b = coefficients with b restricted to values less than 1

---

[17] For a discussion of total utility in terms of a power function, see D. E. James and C. D. Throsby, Introduction to Quantitative Methods in Economics, Sydney, Australia, 1973, pp. 92-93.

then

$$TB = c\,SAT = c(aU^b)$$ where c is a scalar transforming total utility into dollar benefits

So long as U retains the same value, so does TB. The time rate of change in TB—dTB/dtTB—will thus be zero.[18]

The likelihood is greater for a positive growth rate in total costs (dC/dtC), the second curve in Figure 14. Behind this positive growth rate will be the growth in fixed costs.

$$C_t = cU_t + F_t$$

where

C = total costs

c = average variable cost per transaction

F = total fixed costs

Total costs are the sum of variable costs and fixed costs. Variable costs are equal to average variable costs per book use (c) times the number of book uses. Fixed costs in the alternative version include the imputed interest on book acquisitions. We assume variable costs to be fixed over time on the basis of a constant volume of book use and a constant circulation cost per book use. (Such assumptions can of course be modified.) The total cost curve takes an exponential form because of compound interest. Assuming continuous reinvestment of interest earnings, the interest foregone on the investment in the library and its books rises over time at an exponential rate. Applying the formula for continuous compounding, the appropriate equation is

$$C_t = r(INV_{t-n} + AQ_{t-n})e^{rt}$$

where

r = the imputed interest rate

INV_{t-n} = initial dollar investment in the library

AQ_{t-n} = the initial acquisitions outlay

e = the number 2.71828

[18] The "TB" equation above is the key to the problems involved in estimating a "genuine" cost-benefit model. One would have to be able to estimate all three parameters, a, b, c, in one way or another—no easy task!

We multiply initial investment outlays by the imputed interest rate $(r[INV_{t-n}+AQ_{t-n}])$ in order to determine initial fixed costs (here restricted to imputed interest costs). Their rate of accumulation is then determined by e^{rt}. The time rate of change in C—(dC/dt)—is equal to rC. The rate of growth in C (percentage change) is $dC/dtC = rC/C = r$. Thus the imputed interest rate defines the rate of growth in total costs.

This rate of growth applies to successive investments in book and library plant. The path of total costs for each investment is typified by the total cost curve of Figure 14. A series of investments would then be represented by a series of curves, whose cumulative effect could be shown by a single curve. Successive investments do not change the rate of growth which still is equal to r, but make the overall cost curve steeper and reduce the time before intersection with total benefits.

D. Benefits from Book Use

1. Measuring Benefits

The benefit side of the economic model is more difficult to measure than the cost side. The "theory" of measuring benefits can be discussed, however.

We should think of a university as in the business of augmenting the value of human capital. We define the latter as the present value of future "labor" income. It does this directly by the teaching process and indirectly via research.[19] Many inputs go into the production of human capital, but they surely include the student body, student study time, the faculty, the curriculum and the faculty's research output. We consider library book use as an additional input although the other inputs are in part its output. The effect of book use on the augmented value of human capital measures the benefits from the library.

How would one go about estimating the library's contribution? Several possible approaches deserve exploration. On a cross-sectional basis, production functions (the relationship between human capital and the various inputs) could be estimated for a series of universities. We would estimate the capitalized value of future earnings by graduates of these universities and

---

19 One author would treat "increments in the stock of knowledge" as a separate university output and add also "entertainment services consumed currently and privately by students." Donald V. T. Bear, "The University as a Multi-Product Firm," Keith C. Lumsden, ed., Efficiency in Universities: The La Paz Papers, New York, 1974, p. 80.

regress these values against the values of the various inputs listed, including book use. As a second approach, in a given institution, departmental contributions to human capital could be related to book use, also disaggregated by discipline, plus other variables. On the simplest level of analysis, the production function would be a linear relationship. In such a case the benefit curve would be a straight line. A more complex production function would be nonlinear and for given amounts of the other inputs would (in theory) show diminishing benefits as book use increased.[20]

Such production functions assume that the value of human capital is influenced only by the amount and quality of inputs provided. Of course, the demand for educational outputs cannot be neglected. Such a demand variable (possibly measured by the excess demand for graduates of the various disciplines) should be added as an extra explanatory variable.

One cannot be too sanguine about isolating the effect of book use because of its close identity with the other explanatory variables. It may be too that book use fails to isolate many intangibles associated with the library. In the place of book use as the "library" variable in cross-sectional studies, one could substitute the size of the university collection. A composite variable might try to measure the book collection, study accommodations and reference services. Conceivably, the entire library budget could be tried as a proxy variable.

2. The Question of Substitutability

Left unanswered is the question of the relationship between benefit and the mode of book use—books on shelf versus borrowed books.

Is an interlibrary loan the equivalent of a book on the shelf? If faculty committees on the library ever speak as one voice it is in protest! The question of substitutability is illustreated in Figure 15. On the vertical axis we show books "on the shelf." On the horizontal axis we measure "books borrowed." The horizontal lines are "indifference" or "preference" curves. Every point on each of these curves measures the same amount of utility. Since the curves are horizontal, this means that more borrowed books in combination with a fixed amount of books on the shelf will not increase utility: they are not substitutes! Only with more books on the shelf will total utility

---

[20] For some introductory material on production functions, see Thomas F. Dernburg and Duncan M. McDougall, Macroeconomics, 5th ed., New York, 1976, pp. 255-6. For their application to the production of economic literature, see Lovell, op. cit.

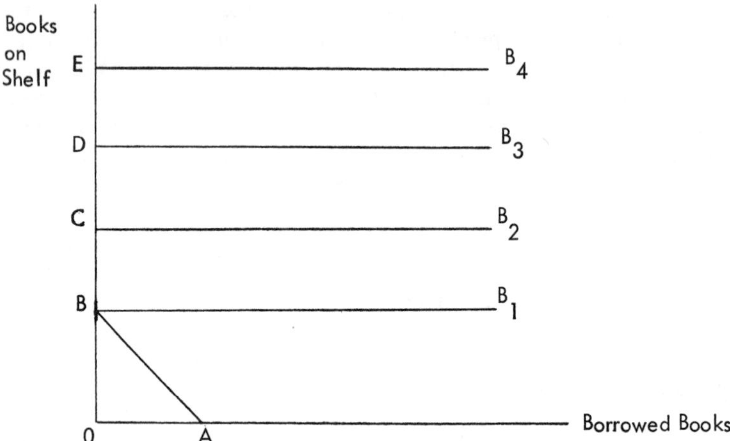

Figure 15. Nonsubstitutability of borrowed books for books on the shelf.

increase—the higher the indifference curve, the greater the utility. Given a certain book budget, it is possible to buy a certain number of books or borrow a larger number. One budget line has been drawn to intersect the lowest horizontal line on the vertical axis. This is called a "corner solution" indicating that given a certain budget benefits will be maximized solely by the purchase of books.

E. The Economies of Increasing Book Use

The costs of actual book use have been estimated in Chapter IV. To summarize, treating book acquisitions as a variable cost (based on fiscal 1974-75 data), the following costs of new book use were computed for the Hillman Library (Table 93). Adding variable (items a and b) and fixed (item c) costs together, the cost per new transaction ($71.49) and per new item ($127.24) greatly exceeded those for old transactions ($7.68) and items ($12.64) (sum of lines b and c). When old and new items are combined, the mean cost per transaction is $11.84 and per item $20.05.

Treating books as an investment (based on fiscal 1974-75 data), the costs shown in Table 94 were computed for the Hillman Library. These costs now apply to both old and new book transactions and items. They are to be compared with mean costs above (acquisitions treated as a variable cost) of $11.84 and $20.05, respectively.

Table 93

		Dollar Cost	
		Per Transaction	Per Book Item
a.	Acquisition of New Items (including processing)	$63.81	$114.60
b.	Circulation (assumed to be the same for old and new items)	1.94	3.46
c.	Fixed Costs	5.74	9.18
d.	TOTAL	$71.49	$127.24

Table 94

		Dollar Cost	
		Per Transaction	Per Book Item
a.	Circulation	$ 1.94	$ 3.46
b.	Fixed Costs	14.07	25.09
c.	TOTAL	$ 16.01	$ 28.55

The horizontal axis of Figures 12 and 13 above (section B.) suggests hypothetical costs for alternative levels of book use. These have been projected below on the basis of actual costs. For "one average book use" the figures shown are the "per book item" figures above. For two book uses these figures are divided by two, for three book uses they are divided by three, and so on. Table 95 assumes that average book use is the same for old and new books.

F. Measuring Cost-Benefit Over Time

In section C. the dynamics of optimality were discussed in general terms. The crucial test was stated to be the growth rate in book use in comparison with some imputed interest rate on book investment.

Table 95
Hypothetical Costs for Alternative Levels of Book Use

Number of Average Book Uses (New and Old)	Book Acquisitions Treated as a:	
	Variable Cost	Fixed Investment
1	$ 20.05	$ 28.55
2	10.03	14.28
3	6.68	9.52
4	5.01	7.14
5	4.01	5.71
6	3.34	4.76
7	2.86	4.08
8	2.51	3.57
9	2.23	3.17
10	2.00	2.86

The present study's use data enable us to trace the decay rate in book use as acquisitions age. Such type of analysis is necessary in order to understand the growth rate in book use since the total rate of book use is affected by variations in the amount of yearly acquisitions. Simply calculating the percentage change in total book use is thus not sufficient. Other departures from the "ceteribus paribus" of the mathematical assumptions will also affect the statistical comparability among years. An attempt has been made to allow for one of these factors—changes in the student population.

1. Description of Data in Matrices A and AA

Matrices A and AA (Tables 96 and 97) are the basic data matrices for the construction of the remaining matrices. Matrix A relates book transactions in a given year to acquisitions of the same or previous year. The column headings are year of acquisition while the rows show transactions by year. Thus, by reading down column 1 (for 1969), it is possible to see how many transactions occurred in succeeding years for books purchased in 1969. The element A_{31} (third row, first column), for example, represents the transactions in 1972 for items purchased in 1969. A similar interpretation holds for the other elements.

Matrix AA is similar in its construction to Matrix A, relating the number of items circulated, instead of transactions, to acquisitions. Thus, element AA_{31}, for example, shows the number of items circulated in 1972 for items purchased in 1969. In Matrices A' and AA' (Tables 98 and 99) the data were standardized for student enrollment,[21] that is, the figures were calculated as if student enrollment had remained constant over the observation period.

Table 96
Matrix A: Matrix of Number of Transactions

Year of Trans-action	YEAR OF ACQUISITION							Total Trans. for a given year	Yearly Percentage change
	1969	1970	1971	1972	1973	1974	1975		
1969	17,390							17,390	
1970	31,609	20,243						51,852	198.2%
1971	27,372	28,355	17,431					73,158	41.1%
1972	22,398	22,099	26,225	17,757				88,479	20.9%
1973	17,050	16,757	18,837	22,146	15,908			95,698	8.2%
1974	15,353	14,924	17,045	24,442	26,942	16,906		115,612	20.8%
1975	12,647	12,028	13,765	19,544	20,449	23,780	15,812	118,025	21.1%
Total trans. for each yr's acquisitions	143,819	114,406	93,303	88,889	63,299	40,686	15,812	560,214	
Total Acq.	36,869	35,997	27,311	30,199	28,438	35,097	30,894		

Table 97
Matrix AA: Matrix of Number of Items

Year of Item circula-tion	YEAR OF ACQUISITION							Total items circulated in given yr	Yearly Percentage change
	1969	1970	1971	1972	1973	1974	1975		
1969	9,704							9,704	
1970	13,174	9,873						23,047	137.5%
1971	11,805	12,008	8,687					32,500	41.0%
1972	10,568	10,230	10,675	9,245				40,718	25.3%
1973	8,704	8,523	8,790	12,255	8,413			46,685	14.7%
1974	8,030	7,758	8,073	11,221	11,357	8,664		55,103	18.0%
1975	6,881	6,559	6,816	9,399	9,378	10,630	8,528	58,191	5.6%
Total items circulated by yr. of acq.	68,866	54,951	43,041	42,120	29,148	19,294	8,528	265,948	
Total Acq.	36,869	35,997	27,311	30,199	28,438	35,097	30,894		

---

[21] The standardized tables do not include 1975.

Table 98
Matrix A': Matrix of Number of Transactions
(Data Standardized for Student Enrollment)

Year of Trans-action	YEAR OF ACQUISITION							Total trans. for a given year	Yearly percen-tage change
	1969	1970	1971	1972	1973	1974	1975		
1969	17,390							17,390	
1970	28,480	18,239						46,719	168.7%
1971	23,458	24,300	14,938					62,696	34.2%
1972	19,043	18,828	22,344	15,129				75,344	20.2%
1973	14,271	14,026	15,767	22,721	13,315			80,100	6.3%
1974	12,697	12,342	14,096	20,214	22,281	13,981		95,611	19.4%
1975									
Total trans. for each yr's acquisitions	115,339	87,735	67,145	58,064	35,596	13,981			
Total Acq.	36,869	35,997	27,311	30,199	28,438	35,097	30,894		

Table 99
Matrix AA': Matrix of Number of Items

Year of Item circulation	YEAR OF ACQUISITION							Total items circulated in a given year	Yearly percen-tage change
	1969	1970	1971	1972	1973	1974	1975		
1969	9,704							9,704	
1970	11,760	8,896						20,676	113.0%
1971	10,117	10,291	7,445					27,853	34.7%
1972	9,004	8,716	9,095	7,877				34,692	24.6%
1973	7,285	7,134	7,357	10,257	7,042			39,075	12.6%
1974	6,641	6,416	6,676	10,107	9,392	7,165		46,397	18.7%
1975									
Total items circulated by yr. of acq.	54,531	41,453	30,573	28,241	16,434	7,165			
Total acq.	36,869	35,997	27,311	30,199	28,438	35,097	30,894		

2. Matrices B and BB

Matrix B (Table 100) is a matrix of coefficients, representing the ratio of the number of transactions in a given year to the number of books purchased in a specific year. The number of books acquired in each year is given in the bottom row of Matrix A. Again, columns are associated with year of acquisition and rows with year of transactions. For example, element B_{32} (.788) represents the ratio of transactions in 1971 to total acquisitions in 1970.

Matrix BB (Table 101) is again similar in construction to Matrix B, except that it presents the ratios of items circulated in a given year to the number of books acquired in a specific year.

Table 100
Matrix B: Matrix of Transaction Coefficients

Year of Transactions		YEAR of ACQUISITION						
		'69	'70	'71	'72	'73	'74	'75
TR69 ÷ ACQ	'69	.472						
TR70 ÷ ACQ	'70	.857	.562					
TR71 ÷ ACQ	'71	.742	.788	.638				
TR72 ÷ ACQ	'72	.608	.614	.960	.588			
TR73 ÷ ACQ	'73	.462	.466	.690	.899	.559		
TR74 ÷ ACQ	'74	.416	.415	.624	.809	.947	.482	
TR75 ÷ ACQ	'75	.343	.334	.504	.647	.719	.678	.512

Table 101
Matrix BB: Matrix of Item Coefficients

Year of Item Circulation		YEAR of ACQUISITION						
		'69	'70	'71	'72	'73	'74	'75
IT 69 ÷ ACQ	'69	.263						
IT 70 ÷ ACQ	'70	.357	.274					
IT 71 ÷ ACQ	'71	.320	.334	.318				
IT 72 ÷ ACQ	'72	.287	.284	.391	.306			
IT 73 ÷ ACQ	'73	.236	.238	.322	.406	.296		
IT 74 ÷ ACQ	'74	.218	.216	.296	.372	.399	.247	
IT 75 ÷ ACQ	'75	.187	.182	.250	.311	.330	.303	.276

Alternatively, the matrix can be viewed as a series of diagonals—the longest diagonal measuring ratios of first-year use to each year's acquisitions, the second longest diagonal measuring ratios of second-year use to each year's acquisitions, and so on.

In Matrices B' and BB' (Tables 102 and 103) the data were again standardized for student enrollment.

Table 102
Matrix B': Matrix of Transaction Coefficients
(Standardized Data)

Year of Transactions		YEAR of ACQUISITION '69	'70	'71	'72	'73	'74
TR69 ÷ ACQ	'69	.472					
TR70 ÷ ACQ	'70	.772	.507				
TR71 ÷ ACQ	'71	.636	.675	.547			
TR72 ÷ ACQ	'72	.518	.523	.818	.501		
TR73 ÷ ACQ	'73	.387	.390	.577	.752	.468	
TR74 ÷ ACQ	'74	.344	.343	.516	.669	.783	.398

Table 103
Matrix BB': Matrix of Item Coefficients
(Standardized Data)

Year of Item Circulation		YEAR of ACQUISITION '69	'70	'71	'72	'73	'74
IT69 ÷ ACQ	'69	.263					
IT70 ÷ ACQ	'70	.322	.247				
IT71 ÷ ACQ	'71	.274	.286	.273			
IT72 ÷ ACQ	'72	.244	.242	.333	.261		
IT73 ÷ ACQ	'73	.198	.198	.269	.340	.248	
IT74 ÷ ACQ	'74	.18	.178	.244	.335	.330	.204

3. Matrices C and CC

Matrix C (Table 104) is a matrix of coefficients that cumulates the yearly column coefficients of Matrix B. For example: $C_{21} = B_{11} + B_{21}$ and $C_{31} = B_{11} + B_{21} + B_{31}$. Matrix CC (Table 105) has a similar interpretation for items.

Table 104
Matrix C: Cumulative Matrix of Coefficients

Year of Transactions		YEAR of ACQUISITION '69	'70	'71	'72	'73	'74	'75
Cumulative Totals	'69	.472						
	'70	1.329	.562					
	'71	2.071	1.35	.638				
	'72	2.679	1.964	1.598	.588			
	'73	3.141	2.43	2.288	1.487	.559		
	'74	3.557	2.845	2.912	2.296	1.506	.482	
	'75	3.9	3.179	3.416	2.943	2.225	1.16	.512

Table 105
Matrix CC: Cumulative Matrix of Coefficients

Year of Item Circulation		YEAR of ACQUISITION '69	'70	'71	'72	'73	'74	'75
Cumulative Totals	'69	.263						
	'70	.620	.274					
	'71	.940	.608	.318				
	'72	1.227	.892	.709	.306			
	'73	1.463	1.13	1.031	.712	.296		
	'74	1.681	1.346	1.327	1.084	.695	.247	
	'75	1.868	1.528	1.572	1.395	1.025	.55	.276

Matrices C' and CC' (Tables 106 and 107) contain standardized data.

Table 106
Matrix C': Cumulative Matrix of Coefficients
(Standardized Data)

Year of Transactions		YEAR of ACQUISITION '69	'70	'71	'72	'73	'74	'75
Cumulative Totals	'69	.472						
	'70	1.244	.507					
	'71	1.88	1.182	.547				
	'72	2.398	1.705	1.365	.501			
	'73	2.785	2.095	1.942	1.253	.468		
	'74	3.129	2.438	2.458	1.922	1.251	.398	

Table 107
Matrix CC': Cumulative Matrix of Item Coefficients
(Standardized Data)

Year of Item Circulation		YEAR of ACQUISITION '69	'70	'71	'72	'73	'74	'75
Cumulative Totals	'69	.263						
	'70	.585	.247					
	'71	.859	.533	.273				
	'72	1.103	.775	.606	.261			
	'73	1.301	.973	.875	.601	.248		
	'74	1.481	1.151	1.119	.936	.578	.204	

4. Matrices D and DD

Matrix D (Table 108) analyzes percentage changes in year-to-year transactions based on a given year's acquisitions. Thus, element D_{31} represents a negative change (-18.1% decrease) in transactions from year 1971 to 1972 for books purchased in 1969. Similarly, item D_{43} represents the change (-28.2% decrease) in transactions from 1972 to 1973, for books purchased in 1971. Changes are computed by subtracting transactions in year _t_ from transactions in year _t - 1_ and then dividing by year _t - 1_. A similar interpretation is given to Matrix DD (Table 109) for items.

Matrices D' and DD' (Tables 110 and 111) standardize the data for student enrollment.

Table 108
Matrix D: Matrix of Percent Changes in Number of Transactions

Transaction Period	YEAR of ACQUISITION						
	'69	'70	'71	'72	'73	'74	'75
'69 - '70	81.8						
'70 - '71	-13.4	40.0					
'71 - '72	-18.1	-22.0	50.5				
'72 - '73	-23.9	-24.2	-28.2	52.9			
'73 - '74	-10.0	-10.9	- 9.5	-10.0	69.4		
'74 - '75	-17.6	-19.4	-19.2	-20.0	-24.0	40.7	

Table 109
Matrix DD: Matrix of Percent Changes in Number of Items Circulated

Circulation Period	YEAR of ACQUISITION						
	'69	'70	'71	'72	'73	'74	'75
'69 - '70	35.8						
'70 - '71	-10.4	21.6					
'71 - '72	-10.4	-14.8	23.0				
'72 - '73	-17.5	-16.7	-17.7	22.6			
'73 - '74	- 7.7	- 9.0	- 8.2	- 8.4	35.0		
'74 - '75	-14.3	-15.5	-15.6	-16.2	-17.4	22.7	

Table 110
Matrix D': Matrix of Percentage Changes of Transactions (Standardized Data)

Transaction Period	YEAR of ACQUISITION						
	'69	'70	'71	'72	'73	'74	'75
'69 - '70	63.8						
'70 - '71	-17.6	33.2					
'71 - '72	-18.7	-22.5	49.6				
'72 - '73	-25.2	-25.5	-29.4	50.2			
'73 - '74	.0 -11.0	-12.0	-10.6	-11.0	67.3		

Table 111
Matrix DD': Matrix of Percent Changes in Number of Items Circulated (Standardized Data)

Circulation Period	YEAR of ACQUISITION					
		'70	'71	'72	'73	'74
'69 - '70	22.3					
'70 - '71	-14.8	15.7				
'71 - '72	-11.0	-15.3	22.2			
'72 - '73	-19.0	-18.2	-19.1	30.2		
'73 - '74	- 8.8	-10.0	- 9.3	- 1.5	33.4	

5. Analysis of Results

Matrices B, C and D (and BB, CC and DD) are different ways of looking at the same data in order to analyze whether any distinct patterns of use emerge. Though the number of observations in each of the matrices is necessarily limited, one can hypothesize about similarities in patterns of use.

Analyzing the longest diagonal in Matrix B (transaction coefficients), one looks for similarities in the number of transactions in the first year of a book's use. The coefficients are seen to vary from .472 to .638 and all coefficients fall within two standard deviations of the mean of the diagonal (mean = .545; std. dev. = .06). For Matrix BB (items), the values on the longest diagonal vary from .247 to .318, also within two standard deviations of the mean of the diagonal (mean = .284; std. dev. = .03). For the second longest diagonal in Matrices B and BB, one is evaluating similarities in the second year of a book's use. For Matrix B, the coefficients vary from a low of .678 to a high of .960, which are again within two standard deviations of the mean of the diagonal (mean = .86; std. dev. = .107). For Matrix BB, the coefficients of the second longest diagonal vary from .334 to .406, all within two standard deviations of the mean (mean = .365; std. dev. = .04).

These comparative values along the first and second diagonals suggest that the use of material rises in the second year after acquisition. In succeeding years use declines as demonstrated by lower values along succeeding diagonals.[22]

---

[22] Similar conclusions follow, of course, if we look down the matrix columns. The advantage of looking along the diagonals is that similar values along a given diagonal suggest the uniform patterns of use for different years' acquisitions.

Matrix C enables us to estimate the total number of times each year's acquisitions were used after a given number of years. Thus, looking at the third diagonal, for example, the average use by the time of the third year ranged from 1.96 to 2.29. If we go down the 1969 column, giving us the longest experience for a single year, by 1974 acquisitions had been used an average of 3.5 times.

Such average use is the result both of a given item circulating in successive years and its multiple use in a given year. Comparison of the C and CC matrices indicates the average turnover (multiple use) of a given item over the period considered. Thus, comparing the final values in the 1969 columns, each item on the average circulated in a given year .29 times beyond the initial circulation ($\frac{3.9 - 1.87}{7} = .29$).

The percentage change in book use is shown in Matrices D and DD. What is brought out is the peak percentage increase in the second year after a book's acquisition, followed by percentage decreases (negative percentages). The total percentage change in transactions is shown in the final column of Table 96, Matrix A. One notes that in many years the percentage change is positive, indicating the offsetting effect of new acquisitions' use versus the decay in old acquisitions. If more years' experience were included beyond the present seven-year subset, the negative effect of previous years' acquisitions would overwhelm the effect of more recent years' acquisitions. Thus, when we compare total library transactions (reflecting the library's entire book collection) we secure the transaction totals 222,467, 211,346 and 208,348 respectively (see Tables 76 and 77 in Chapter IV). The analysis of use patterns for a series of yearly acquisitions helps us understand such decline in terms of the declining rates of use for earlier acquisitions.

The similarities of the diagonals in the Matrices B, BB, C, CC, D and DD result in overall use patterns that are very similar regardless of the year of acquisition. These similarities are best seen by graphing the use pattern of each year's acquisitions. Figure 16 does this for the coefficients of Matrix B (Table 100). One clear pattern is that book use peaks in the year immediately after the year of purchase and declines after that. Another pattern (somewhat less clear because of limited observations) is that the rate of decline appears to slow down after three to five years of book use. While the data are insufficient to project beyond the fifth year of use, one could hypothesize that use will continue to decline at a steady rate. Certainly this is consistent with earlier findings in Chapter II with circulations of a given year's acquisitions reaching asymptotic values of 60% after six or seven years.

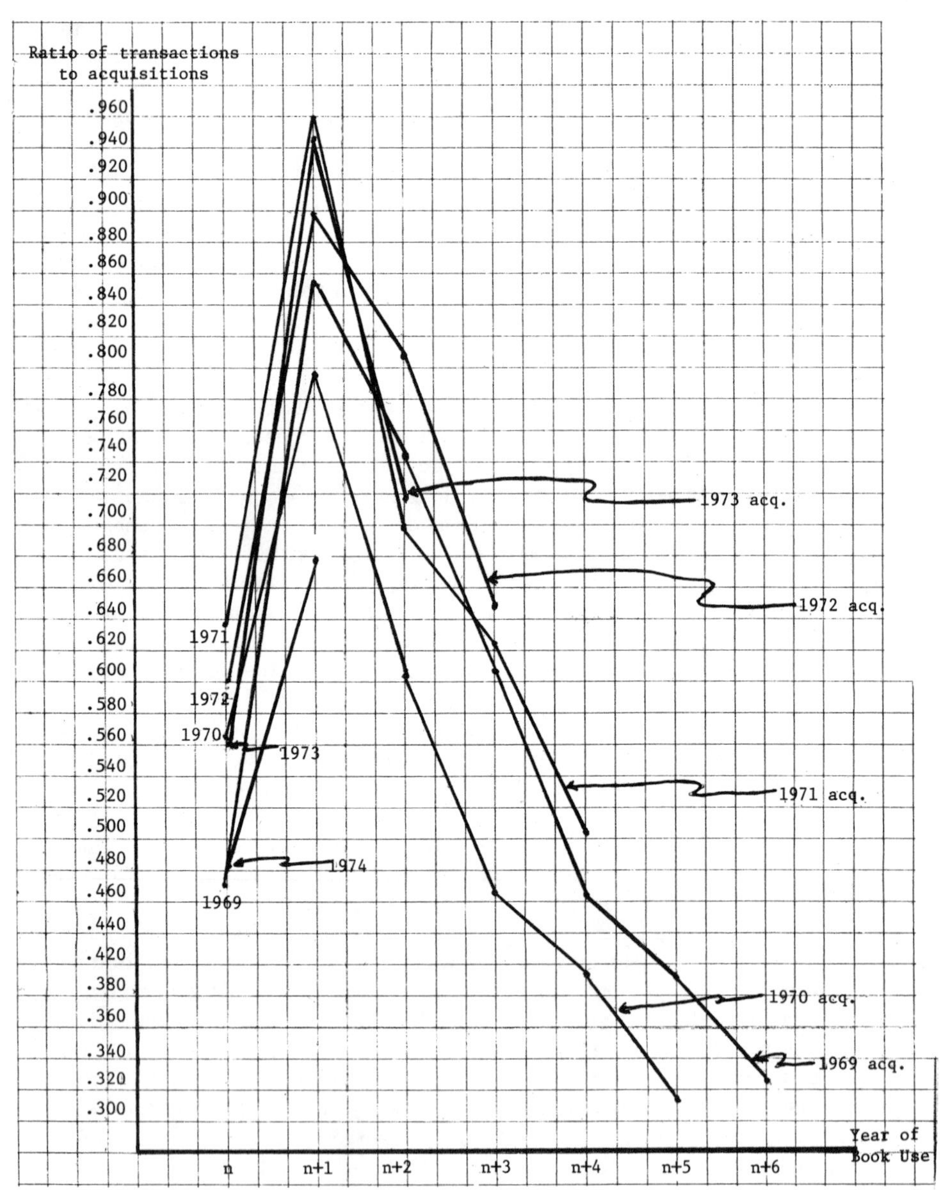

Figure 16. Yearly ratios of book transactions to acquisitions for different years' acquisitions.

(Source: Table 100)

6. Standardizing the Data for Student Enrollment

On the basis of the number of student credit hours, data in all the above matrices were standardized by reducing transactions by the appropriate index.[23] There were no significant differences in the results. Since student enrollments have been rising, the use figures shown in Tables 98 and 99 are downward revisions of the figures in Tables 96 and 97. The values in the other matrices are similarly adjusted downwards.

7. Similar analysis of aging was done for transactions for seven important LC Classes—B (Philosophy, Psychology, Religion), D (History: Oriental and Old World), E (History: American, General), H (History: American), L (Education), P (Language and Literature), and T (Technology). The expected divergencies from the "average" for the entire LC collection are in evidence.[24] Comparisons based on the transaction coefficients (Matrices B and C) are given in Table 112. In Table 112 (a) the diagonals of the LC classes are analyzed. The first diagonal shows ratios of first-year use of acquisitions, the second diagonal shows ratios of second-year use. What this table demonstrates is the same upsurge in use in the second year discussed earlier for the total collection. What the standard deviation statistic shows is the extent of individual departures from mean values. If we examine the second diagonal, for example, considerable diversity is suggested for different second-year values for LC Class L, with B and D being more homogeneous.

The high coefficient values for L are confirmed in the second part (b) of the table, which compares cumulative values of the coefficients. Other categories with above average transaction coefficients are E and H. Those

---

[23] The index was constructed utilizing FY 1969 total student credit hours as the base. The deflation factors for all other fiscal years were determined by dividing the base year credit hours by the current year credit hours and mutliplying this factor times the original data set. The data for credit hours was obtained from the "University of Pittsburgh Statistical Highlights, 1975-76."

	Deflation Factor
(1) Total student credit hours in FY '69 = 675,247........	1. (base)
(2) 1970 factor = 675,247 ÷ 748,788 ('70 SC hrs)	.901
(3) 1971 factor = 675,748 ÷ 788,156 ('71 SC hrs)	.857
(4) 1972 factor = 675,748 ÷ 793,557 ('72 SC hrs)	.852
(5) 1973 factor = 675,748 ÷ 807,259 ('73 SC hrs)	.837
(6) 1974 factor = 675,748 ÷ 816,636 ('74 SC hrs)	.827

[24] The detailed tables are omitted from this book.

noticeably below the "all" average are the Classes T and D. Earlier years' values for the coefficients exceed later years' values because of the progressive shortening of the time period covered. The exception is the acquisition year 1971. The cumulative values for all classes except T exceed those for 1970 because of the high second-year values of the coefficients.

Table 112
Comparison of Transaction Coefficients, LC Subclasses and Total Collection

(a) Matrix B: Transaction Coefficients

Class	1st DIAGONAL			2nd DIAGONAL				
	Range of Values	Mean	Std.Dev.	Range of Values	Mean	Std. Dev.		
B	.495 - .736	0.569	.085	.7 - 1.2	1	.18		
D	.295 - .379	0.335	.034	.353 - .615	0.504	.093		
E	.574 - .865	0.770	.094	.943 - 1.3	1.2	.163		
H	.582 - .732	0.653	.057	.836 - 1.3	1.0	.183		
L	.96 - 1.7	1.3	.32	1.4 - 2.6	2.1	.458		
P	.357 - .656	0.5	.3	.509 - .930	0.752	.137		
T	.166 - .673	0.389	.195	.247 - 1.0	0.575	.284		
ALL	.472 - .638	0.545	.06	.678 - .960	0.855	.107		

(b) Matrix C: Cumulative Coefficients

Class	YEAR OF ACQUISITION							Asymptotic value of items circulated
	1969	1970	1971	1972	1973	1974	1975	
B	4.983	3.785	4.243	4.203	2.335	1.219	.500	68.3525
D	2.782	1.848	2.034	1.745	1.193	.655	.295	53.5649
E	5.096	3.684	4.346	3.661	2.976	1.744	.574	78.2002
H	4.71	3.348	4.086	3.234	2.927	1.551	.692	62.0130
L	8.356	7.785	9.393	7.672	5.75	2.424	1.002	83.5651
P	3.563	3.11	3.236	2.496	1.865	.866	.429	61.5159
T	1.624	1.643	1.05	2.513	2.542	1.106	.673	38.3639
ALL	3.9	3.179	3.416	2.943	2.225	1.16	.512	60.4907

The final column of Table 112 (b) presents the asymptotic values for items circulated. Consistent with its high coefficient values, Class L has the highest asymptote—83.56%—indicating that in the limit this percentage of acquisitions in this category will circulate at least once.

8. The analysis in all of subsection F. points to diminishing use of books after the second year. While no precise estimates have been made of their respective influence, the long-run aging effects would seem to swamp the second-year effects, pointing to declining average use of the overall collection and individual LC classes. If this impression is correct, then no matter what the opportunity cost of book investment is (so long as the market rate is a positive percent), the maintenance of a library's acquisition program on a steady keel suggests an equally steady departure from an optimal library investment in books. For benefits, assuming their dollar value has a definable relation to book use, will fall progressively below their cost.[25]

25 "Optimality" refers to equality of marginal benefits and marginal costs.

Chapter VI

ALTERNATIVES TO LOCAL ACQUISITIONS

Allen Kent, James G. Williams and Jacob Cohen

A. The Move Towards Resource Sharing[1]

The data in this study, if confirmed in other environments, can be extremely important in making purchase and/or resource sharing decisions. In the purchase decision, the most critical area is not when a clear buy/no-buy judgment can be made. Rather in the grey area, when there is uncertainty, can data such as these be helpful, particularly when there is consideration of the subject-area/client data which may differentiate behavior and needs in different disciplines. It is evident that resource sharing alternatives to local purchases must be explored in certain instances. One of the consequences of this exploration could be decisions to acquire fewer materials locally, and to depend, for access, on resource sharing networks, or on sources for securing authorized royalty-paid journal articles (e.g., Institute for Scientific Information (ISI), University Microfilms, National Technical Information Service (NTIS)).

Resource sharing denotes a mode of library operation whereby all or part of the library functions are shared in common among several libraries. The basic functions may be classified as acquisitions, processing, storage and delivery of service. There is no single system currently in operation in which all of these functions are shared, although networks which might become "full service" (all functions to be shared) are coalescing in connection with several developing national systems. The dominant aspects of resource sharing to date have been in the areas of processing and delivery of service. There have also been significant activities in the areas of centralized storage and acquisitions. In addition, several commercial organizations offer bibliographic access, via national computer time-sharing systems, to the journal and document literature of many disciplines.

---

[1] See also Chapter II of this report for a discussion of "Weeding" and "Storage."

But a move towards a philosophy of cooperative access to shared resources is not an easy one. It raises many issues, some of which are set out below in the form of a dialectic. It may seem unfair to list the issues emerging from the literature and the debate concerning resource sharing in the extreme terms of thesis-antithesis. And yet, it appears instructive to bring these to light, even if they may seem like strawmen in some cases. It may permit those who read this document to develop a focus which may aid in reconciling conflicting points of view. This procedure may also help to identify and acknowledge other positions yet unstated (or inadvertently omitted)—positions which may be even more important than any identified here.

THESIS	ANTITHESIS
1. Increased emphasis on library resource sharing is inevitable, given continuing inflation, increasing rate of publication, and stable (or decreasing) budgets.	1. The library should enjoy a larger share of the university budget to support local collections development, lest scholarly pursuits and independent study be inhibited.
2. Given <u>any</u> budget level, the goal of self-sufficiency is no longer feasible.	2. Self-sufficiency was never the goal, rather the goal was selective acquisitions in a relatively autonomous mode of operation.
3. To support the development of research collections, even selective acquisitions can result in local holdings much of which may never have been used and are unlikely to be used in the future.	3. Past use is not an adequate guide to future needs; there might even be justification for the availability of specialized collections that are used only once in a hundred years. Selection criteria based on use will lead to research which is based on repetition of what is written in heavily-used materials. Important research or bibliographic compilations may sometimes not be undertaken if a sufficient percentage of the materials is not accessible locally.
4. User requests (often ephemeral) must be evaluated on <u>some</u> basis, either by predicting use or by other criteria which would consider the quality of the demand.	4. User demand should be the primary criterion for establishing acquisitions policy. Many of our problems result from the supply systems in libraries having been divorced from users and user-programs in the university.

THESIS (continued)	ANTITHESIS (continued)
5. Resource sharing arrangement will permit adequate access to lesser-used materials.	5. If all libraries turn to resource sharing, none will have books to lend.
6. The concept of mutual benefits is essential to the success of any resource sharing activity. An extensive form of coalition decision-making for collections development must be adopted.	6. If resource sharing proves unworkable, the library will be even further behind.
7. The resource sharing activities organized in at least one field, Medicine, (by the National Library of Medicine) are operational and successful; they pervade the health science library activity in dealing with several library systems, acquisition, cataloging, reference and availability.	7. The major defects with resource sharing proposals are that the technology and organizational structures are not presently available to provide a level of service comparable with that available today with existing methods.
8. Resource sharing addresses the difficult problem of predicting which materials will be needed for future research. Attempting to solve this problem alone leads to considerable expenditures for materials to increase the probability that desired items will be available in the local collection.	8. The cost of obtaining access to materials may sometimes equal or exceed the cost of purchasing the same materials for the local collection.
9. Resource sharing is being presented as a methodology to provide access to an increased volume of material while utilizing a stationary (or decreasing) acquisition budget.	9. Resource sharing is being touted as a way of reducing costs. Yet there is no way that resource sharing can reduce costs.
10. Some faculty requests lead to support of esoteric interests without regard to a balance among competing programmatic demands and overall university priorities. The esoteric needs can be addressed in a less costly way in a resource sharing context.	10. Most faculty can predict future needs better than some librarians.

THESIS (continued)

11. Local needs for most of the important publications will require local purchases, avoiding debilitating price increases, even in resource sharing arrangements. Marginal publication programs, many of which were developed promiscuously by publishers during the period of rapid expansion of library budgets, will drop out of existence as they price themselves out of the market, with little negative effect on scholarship.

12. The plans of national resource sharing systems are based on the philosophy of absorbing the demand that would otherwise lead to excessive borrowing from individual libraries and increased fees for loans from other sources.

13. The success of library cooperation is at the mercy of people's intentions; not technological capabilities. No system of supply of materials is of any value which is not tailored so carefully that the library patrons' objectives can be achieved; it is the patrons and their objectives which, in the last analysis, define the goal which the supply mechanisms must achieve.

ANTITHESIS (continued)

11. Resource sharing will affect the economics of publishing by increasing unit pricing as library orders decline. A substantial part of the prospective savings from resource sharing will evaporate.

12. The university library may become more and more a lender (rather than a borrower) of materials, causing resource sharing to be a drain rather than a source of additional materials.

13. Faculty lack of enthusiasm for, or opposition to, sharing activities is based upon genuine concern for the dangers of weakening the research collections.

One serious worry, not reflected above, is that libraries embarking on resource sharing may develop the mechanisms for resource sharing without complementary and supporting developments elsewhere; and that a theoretically ideal system might be realized which would stand unused. For reassurance on this point, one can turn to numerous instances of satisfactory resource sharing efforts over a number of years. Some examples on the national level are: (1) National Bibliographic Control; (2) Composite National Data Base of Serials; (3) National Lending Library for Journals; (4) Machine-Readable

Catalog for Book-Form Materials; (5) Ohio College Library Center; and (6) BALLOTS.

These national efforts are expected to coalesce into the required foundation for resource sharing activities. The philosophy of each of these developments, moreover, is to resolve the "net lending" problems of individual libraries and local and regional consortia: that is, to relieve the burden of those libraries loaning more than they borrow. A number of regional library networks are also in existence, or are developing, to provide the mechanisms for resolving problems of clusters of institutions engaged in resource sharing activities. Examples of these are: Western Interstate Bibliographic Network; Southeastern Library Network; Southwestern Library Interstate Cooperative Endeavor. These activities are being supported by agencies such as the Council on Library Resources with the understanding that their operating systems will be compatible with the national systems. The regional efforts are expected to provide the structure to support local resource sharing activities and to develop the mechanisms for delivering needed materials to cooperating libraries.

Thus, the first consideration of a library contemplating resource sharing is also the final consideration: to seek consensus that further attention to resource sharing is necessary. This should be an urgent priority, since the coalescence of national activities strongly suggests that without an alternative strategy, a library should not proceed counter to these developments, lest it find itself unequipped to deal with a future that may present crises for its library services. A course should be charted quickly, albeit deliberately, since external developments may otherwise leave no option.

B. The Goals of Resource Sharing

The goals of resource sharing are to provide a positive net effect: (1) on the library user in terms of access to more materials or services; and/or (2) on the library budget in terms of providing level services at less cost, increased service at level cost, or much more service at less cost than current arrangements. These goals should be realized without harm to the missions of participating libraries, although their methods of operation invariably must be adjusted. Similarly, the goals will undoubtedly require changes in the habits of some users.

There are several requirements that must be met if a full service resource sharing system is to be developed. These requirements include:

- multilateral decision making
- reciprocal services

Once these requirements are met, system alternatives present themselves which need to be understood and negotiated. One such alternative relates to choice of resource sharing partners. Should they have similar or dissimilar clienteles? Other choices are with regard to size of clienteles, size of budgets, and size of holdings. Should they be similar, dissimilar, or mixes? Also, there is a question as to budget assumptions to be made for each of the partners: anticipation of more? same? less?

There are, of course, other alternatives to be considered: full service or limited function. In the latter case, one or more functions or operations may be chosen (e.g., shared cataloging, lending). For a full service system the mix of partners will dictate a "star" system (one library with most of the resources), a "distributed" system (each library with equal, but different, resources) or an "hierarchical" system (access requests referred to next higher level in the system when the "lower" level resources do not yield results).

C. Classification of Resource Sharing

Although there is no operational example of a resource sharing network which exhibits all possible library functions for all types of materials, there are now in existence so many cooperative resource sharing activities and/or networks that it becomes possible and instructive to classify them among a number of different dimensions, such as:

(1) Functions Performed

- acquisitions
- processing
- storage
- reference
- delivery

(2) Type of Library (e.g., public, school, college, special)

(3) Subject Matter (e.g., medicine, chemistry, social sciences)

(4) Type of Material (e.g., bibliographic databases, journals, books)

(5) Form of Material (e.g., print, nonprint)

(6) Nature of Cooperative Effort (formal versus informal)

(7) Means of Financing

(8) Degree of Automation

(9) Tax Status (profit versus nonprofit)

Another dimension of interest is distribution of resources. Three resource distribution types have been identified:

- Equally distributed networks:

  all participants holding equal (but different) quantities of material to be utilized only by participants

- Star networks:

  one participant holding substantially all the resources, to be utilized by other participants

- Hierarchical networks:

  unsatisfied needs are passed along to the next greater resource center.

Resource sharing networks must operate under a number of constraints, such as:

(1) Delivery time for remotely accessed materials generally exceeds that for locally held materials;

(2) Materials loaned are not available for local access;

(3) Browsing among collections is inhibited;

(4) If all libraries depend on the holdings of others, there will be no resources to share;

(5) The sharing of resources may lead to institution of fees by copyright holders;

(6) An unfavorable "balance of trade" implies that non-local patrons are being subsidized.

These constraints are present to some degree even when no formal resource sharing arrangements are undertaken. However, they are made explicit and thus translated into design parameters for developing networks. Overcoming such constraints entails both technical solutions and behavioral adjustments. The latter apply primarily to veteran library users who are accustomed to relying chiefly on local resources.

D. Unanswered Questions

In spite of the strong case that can be made for the sharing of resources, it must be admitted that the economics of participation in resource sharing network is as yet poorly understood, with the exception of a few unit functions such as shared cataloging or tradeoffs regarding purchase versus interlibrary loan of journals. Some of the unanswered questions are:

(1) Will it work in an operational environment?

(2) Is it economically feasible?

(3) What effect will it have on the policies, practices and services of participating libraries?

(4) What is the optimum size and composition of a library network?

(5) Can low use materials be identified in advance of purchase?

(6) Can past use serve as a predictor of future use?

(7) Should factors other than use (that is, potential use) be considered in collection building?

(8) Should quality of use be a factor in assessing effectiveness of an acquisitions program?

(9) Are interlibrary loan costs greater than the cost of the materials themselves?

(10) Should the cost of locally acquiring and storing little used materials be shared by all local libraries, or only by those who wish to maintain these materials in readiness for potential future use?

(11) How should a resource sharing system be configured in terms of three alternative network models: star, distributed, hierarchical?

(12) How can the benefits of each configuration be anticipated or forecast before a design decision is made?

The cost-benefit framework developed earlier might illumine some of the essential questions.

E. Minimizing Book Cost by Resource Sharing

Measuring Cost-Effectiveness via Resource Sharing Models

The hypothesis is that it may cost less to provide book use by substituting interlibrary resource sharing for books in the library. In terms of Figures 12 and 13 (Chapter V), we could draw a total cost curve beginning at the origin of the diagram steeper than the original total cost curve which began at the level of fixed costs. The greater steepness is due to the additional variable costs such as photocopying and mailing costs assumed to be absorbed by the requesting library. But the absence of substantial fixed costs makes it difficult for interlibrary borrowing to be more expensive than books on the shelf.[2]

The borrowing library in these circumstances enjoys a "free ride" at the expense of the lending library. But this is a tenuous basis for long-run resource sharing. The rationale of a consortium is its ability to reduce acquisition costs for a given level of service for all libraries or improve the level of service for given budgets.

The required reduction in book purchases in order that costs stay constant can be calculated from the cost equations "before" and "after" resource sharing.

Before resource sharing, the cost equation is:

$$C = cU + F$$

After resource sharing, the cost equation is:

$$C_s = c_s U + F_s - rg\Delta X_s$$

Where the new symbols are:

c_s = circulation costs per book use per period of time after resource sharing (including interlibrary borrowing costs, such as photocopying and postage)

F_s = fixed costs per period of time after resource sharing (including costs of lending to other libraries and network costs)

g = the dollar acquisition cost per book (including processing costs) expressed in dollars of present value

ΔX_s = the total reduction in book purchases after resource sharing (cumulative total)

Since $[g\Delta X_s]$ represents the present value of books no longer purchased as a result of library resource sharing, the imputed interest saving on these books is calculated by multiplying $g\Delta X_s$ by the imputed interest rate, r.

---

2 Membership in library consortia as a condition for interlibrary loan should be regarded as a fixed cost of interlibrary lending. The total cost curve for interlibrary lending then begins at some positive intercept value.

The change in costs associated with resource sharing is arrived at by subtracting the first equation from the second:

$$\Delta C = c_s U + F_s - rg\Delta X_s - (cU + F)$$

We wish to determine the breakeven amount of acquisitions (over the life of resource sharing) holding uses (U) constant. This means determining the amount of acquisitions for which the change in total costs will be zero. Setting ΔC equal to zero and solving for ΔX_s,

$$rg\Delta X_s = c_s U + F_s - cU - F$$

$$\Delta X_s = \frac{c_s U + F_s - cU - F}{rg}$$

From this equation, the breakeven amount of acquisitions will be smaller, the larger are the values of r, g, and the smaller are c_s and F_s in relation to c and F.

For example, we can assume the following hypothetical values:

C_s = \$3.00

F_s = \$1,000,000

g = \$30.00

c = \$2.50

U = \$20,000

F = \$800,000

yielding:

ΔX_0 = 70,000 volumes

Using hypothetical values, this is the minimum reduction in book acquisitions for resource sharing to pay for itself.

For resource sharing to succeed, the entire consortium should achieve this necessary minimum reduction. Individual members of the consortium at the same time may be achieving savings (cost reductions on balance) with other members experiencing losses. In such a situation, the benefiting members would have to subsidize the losing members in order to preserve the coalition.

Chapter VII

THE PATH AHEAD

Allen Kent, K. Leon Montgomery and James G. Williams

A. The Implications of the Present Study

The intent of this study has been to develop measures for determining the extent to which library materials are used, and the full cost of such use. It was our expectation that much of the material purchased for research libraries was little or never used, and that when costs are assigned to uses, the cost of book use will be unexpectedly high. These expectations have been substantially supported by the study.

The question arises, then, as to whether—and how—these results might influence decision-making.

1. Implications for the University of Pittsburgh

For the University of Pittsburgh there are both short- and long-range implications. From a university perspective the administration must be permitted to understand the impact of its investment in the University libraries. In the short-term, the results of this study indicate that a continued tracking of the use of library materials within libraries at the University is necessary. It is not clear whether a book and monograph usage rate of 56% - 60% is good or bad in a university environment. It is clear that this usage rate must be continuously monitored to detect whether or not this rate changes, positively or negatively. The extension of book and monograph use measurement to other school and departmental libraries is also necessary. In support of this extension it will be necessary to extend the automated circulation system to all school and departmental libraries.

Similarly, journal usage must also continue to be monitored. The study indicates that journal usage varies widely among the science and engineering libraries. Now that a mechanism exists for tracking journal usage, these librarians have a tool for tracking changes as they are made. Journal use studies will be needed in the other campus libraries. In addition, the library administrators will be able to judge the book/journal collection balance because of the data on the journal collection and its usage, as well as data on the book and monograph collection and its usage.

One of the areas clearly requiring more work is the understanding of the relationships between library users and non-users and the library collection. This study only began this process. For example, the relationships between a department faculty and students and the library collection they might use is not well understood. If the University chooses to add or delete a department, the implications for library expenditures and for the library collection need to be better understood.

Perhaps one of the more interesting implications of this study involves the relationship of faculty library committees and individual faculty suggestions to library collection development and use. This study suggests, and current procedures permit, the tracking of faculty library committee acquisition requests. It would be most interesting to see whether or not items acquired as a result of faculty library committee requests were used at all, or were used more than those acquired by other means. Similarly, it is important that individual faculty requests be tracked over a number of years to see whether or not these are good predictors of use.

The cost of book use has been investigated with depth and detail in this study. The use of similar techniques to determine costs must be continued on a periodic basis. As procedural changes are made and as resource sharing activities are developed, it is necessary to estimate the cost impact of these changes.

The study has suggested that use varies with the LC classification, as does the cost risk associated with each classification. The likelihood of use probably varies with time as the University makes programmatic decisions with regard to schools, departments, degrees, and number of students. For example, the library requirements are different to support a Ph. D. degree program than those to support a B. S. degree program. Further development and testing of these models in the context of different programs would be advisable.

2. Implications for the Library and Information Science Field

One of the principal results of this study shows that only 56% to 60% of the books and monographs added to the collection in any one year ever circulate. Similar results are being confirmed in a few other library environments. Further studies are needed to confirm whether in fact these results are widespread. Although the project reported here had essentially the total population of external patron circulations, sampling methodologies have been studied and tested; these should also prove useful to other libraries.

If we assume that these results are confirmed, there are a number of important questions and implications. The first question is: Why? The answer or answers to this question are likely to influence librarianship and libraries in dramatic ways. If, for example, it can be shown that the card catalog does not allow reasonable access to the book collection, then new approaches to bibliographic access would be in order. If, for example, it can be shown that more refined acquisition policies and procedures are needed, then more sophisticated collection development techniques must be developed and tested.

Further, the study shows that for books and monographs added to the collection during a one-year period, approximately forty percent are never used; fourteen percent are used only once; eight percent are used twice; six percent are used three times; and so on. (See Table 3 in Chapter II.) These data indicate that should a library find it fiscally attractive to acquire only those items that will be used twice, then fifty-four percent would not be acquired. The problem, of course, is that the techniques for predicting which books and monographs are likely to circulate 0, 1, or 2 times do not currently exist.

It seems safe to say that there is a portion of the collection that reasonably should be shared among several libraries. The principal questions are how to identify those books and monographs before acquisition and to identify the cost-effective equilibrium points where access rather than ownership makes sense.

The effectiveness of the card catalog as a tool for guiding potential users to the collection must be re-examined in the light of the 56% - 60% utilization rate of the book collection. With the closing of card catalogs in several libraries, including the Library of Congress, there is a major opportunity to review the purposes that it serves. In addition, machine-readable catalogs permit many new services not commonly associated with or possible with card catalogs. For example, the removal of or labelling of the catalog cards for books moved to storage is a clumsy and costly process at best. Machine processes will facilitate these changes.

One of the interesting questions that arises concerns the effectiveness of blanket order programs in terms of use. The results of this study suggest that the books acquired via a blanket order plan be tracked and compared with books acquired via other means.

Often research libraries have been measured in terms of size of collection. Public libraries have often been measured in terms of number of book uses. This study suggests that a complementary measure is use of collection. Book acquisition, processing, and storage have significant costs compared to book use costs. However, both types of costs are important. This suggests that a combination of collection size and use are necessary to measure library effectiveness.

The Jordan-Clapp formula[1] has been thought of as a model for allocation of library resources. This study suggests a re-examination of this formula.

Considering the rapid drop-off in use of journals with age, fewer journals should be permanently bound. This would not only reduce costs, but would reduce frustration caused by needed materials being in the bindery as many temporary bindings can be accomplished in-house.

Also, confronted with use data on journals, alternatives to local completeness may be considered, particularly those involving "de-acquisition" (removal to lower cost storage facilities) and resource sharing arrangements with other institutions.

3. Implications for Publishers

The results of the current study also have implications for publishers. Decisions which may be made to reduce the number of publications purchased may lead to a reduction of print runs and further price increases for the smaller number of copies which must then carry the burden of basic publication costs.[2] This, of course, could lead to a price increase spiral. Recommendations have been made that publishers take on the business of "leasing" their publications, instead of outright sale. The few publishers that have been consulted believe this to be an unprofitable approach. Should this turn out to be the case, the implication—other than ceasing publication of some materials—would be to package products in different, less costly, forms; or to change the nature of the products substantially. Several discussions of such alternatives (on-demand publishing and photocopying of manuscripts) have been reported recently in the literature.[3,4]

---

[1] Verner Clapp and Robert Jordan, Quantitative Criteria for Adequacy of Academic Library Collections, Washington, D. C.: Council on Library Resources, 1965.

[2] See transcript of CONTU (Commission on Technical Uses of New Copyrighted Works) meeting No. 15, July 15, 1977, PB No. 271,336, pp. 135-141, for a discussion of this point between Dan Lacy and Eugene Palmour.

[3] Malcolm G. Scully, "An On-Demand Publishing System Weighed for Some Scholarly Works," Chronicle of Higher Education, January 23, 1978, p. 9.

[4] William T. Knox, Letter to the Editor, Science, January 13, 1978.

4. Implications for Further Research

In considering resource sharing alternatives to local holdings, many patrons express uncertainties—uncertainties which are not relieved by rhetoric alone. Substantial evidence must be offered. A number of potentially fruitful research projects have already been mentioned.

In a study being designed at the University of Pittsburgh, it is proposed to develop computer simulations of alternative resource sharing network configurations, which would take into account the full range of functions that are entailed in "full service" network operations. The parameters of local library environments would be introduced into the simulation, which would permit equilibrium (break-even) points to be identified to aid decision processes for assessing local purchasing versus remote accessing.

Two aspects of the methodology of the proposed study may be of sufficiently general interest to warrant mention here:

a. <u>Taxonomy of Resource Sharing Networks</u>: Resource sharing networks currently in operation or in planning can be analyzed in terms of three factors: (1) Type of network; (2) Type of source material; and (3) Operations (functions) performed. If these three factors are displayed in three dimensions (see <u>Figure 17</u>), it is possible to depict a taxonomy in terms of specific operations performed by specific network types for given types of source materials.

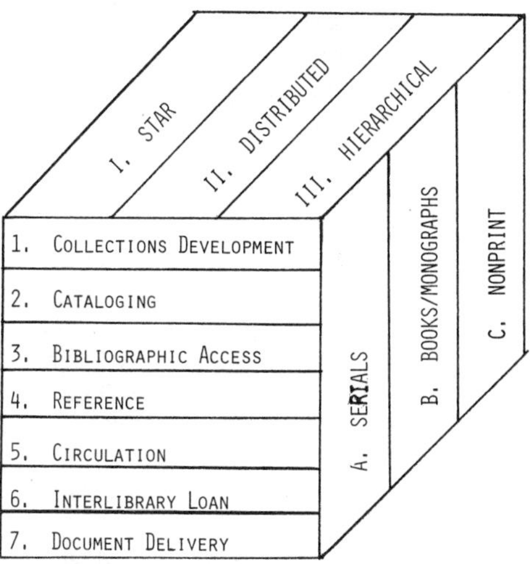

Figure 17. Three-dimension characterization of networks in terms of operations (functions) and types of materials.

Thus, a star network (I) which offers bibliographic access (3) to books and monographs (B) would be characterized symbolically as I. 3. B. For example, the Research Libraries Group (R. L. G.) would be characterized as II. 3. A, since it is working towards a distributed network (II) for three libraries (Yale, Columbia, New York Public - Science Technical Division) with initial emphasis on bibliographic access (3) and on serials (A). The concept of a national periodicals bank (III. 7. A) is being proposed as an hierarchical network (III) for serials (A), with primary emphasis on delivery (7). The experimental Western Pennsylvania Buhl Network (WEBNET) is developing as a distributed network for books and monographs, but with all types of operations represented (II. 1-7. B).

If one were to characterize the hundreds of resource sharing or cooperative activities in the nation, one would find a morass of types of networks, operations, and materials involved, most with no clear interrelationships apparent, and no clear way of integrating networks which undoubtedly will be needed for long run cost-beneficial services.

Therefore, it is hoped that the new study will provide a taxonomy for network activities which will serve as the basis for the development and application of measures for evaluation. This will be done by developing a model which will identify the common core of parameters of networks, independent of network type, operations, and types of materials.

b. A Model of Resource Sharing Networks: First a "meta" model of resource sharing would be prepared which would be used to generate submodels which would deal with more specific aspects of resource sharing. Then simulation of these would be developed which could be "exercised" to permit computation of equilibrium (break-even) points among the many variables, allowing for preferences of users, intermediaries, and systems designers.

During the course of the research, exemplar networks currently in existence would be characterized in terms of the meta model and submodels.

The meta model would be implemented as a parameter-driven computer program that would in turn generate a computer program that could simulate the desired resource sharing configuration. The meta model must incorporate the necessary functions for building any desired model of a library resource sharing network. These functions must incorporate the simulation requirements of the end-use model. The essential factor will be to identify those functions that must be included in the meta model, the variables that should be included, and the relationships among the variables.

It appears then that there is promise for the use of simulation techniques which can assess the consequences of alternative network configurations, employing use and cost data. This should contribute to the development of performance criteria which would address cost-benefit objectives, both locally and nationally.

Finally, as the effects become evident of royalty payments for use of copyrighted materials, these costs can be introduced into the simulations and the effect on equilibrium points may be understood.

APPENDIX

Roger Flynn

This Appendix, which was prepared by Roger Flynn, supplements the material in Chapter III of the report, "Use of Journals." It has been arranged in three separate parts, the contents of which are as follows:

		Page
Part 1:	TECHNICAL DATA—JOURNALS STUDY	209
	Methodology	209
	Usage Statistics	216
	Usage by Title	229
	Usage by Age	240
	Usage by Alert Method	242
	Uses per Person	243
	Predicting Usage in the Physics Library	244
	Usage by Department	245
Part 2:	APPLYING THE METHODOLOGY TO JOURNAL USE STUDIES ELSEWHERE	247
	Introduction	247
	Sampling the Patron Characteristics	247
	Processing the Data	251
	A Problem	253
	Usage of Particular Journals	253
	Usage per Person	257
	Projecting the Percent of the Collection Used a Given Number of Times	258
	Conclusion	264
Part 3:	THE MANAGEMENT AND "MARKETING" OF THE JOURNAL COLLECTION	265
	A Management Model	265
	"Peeling the Onion"	268

Part 1

TECHNICAL DATA—JOURNALS STUDY

I. METHODOLOGY

A. The Questionnaire

Two different observation forms were developed for our study (Figures 18 and 19).

The Shortened Form

As can be seen from a comparison of the two forms, the second form was shortened by the elimination of the following fields:

author's last name, 2 initials
multiple or single authorship
page number
range of dates
range of volumes
follow-up interview
questionnaire

The "author's name" and "multiple or single authorship" were dropped because the concentration of the study was on the user. The "page number," which could be used to identify the exact article being consulted, was also dropped as it became apparent that we would concentrate on journal title and volume. The "range of dates" and "range of volumes" (for journals that could not be identified exactly, as when the user reshelved the journal as the observer was approaching) proved to be of little use. The "follow-up interview" and "questionnaire" referred to a parallel study, in which one of the observers later contacted the user to see how useful the perusal of the article had been. (This latter study applied only to the Physics Library.)

Format of the Form

The form was divided vertically down the middle. Data were recorded on the left-hand side at the time of the interview, in a speedy fashion, so that the intrusion on the user's time was kept to one or two minutes. Then, these data were recoded on the right-hand side at a later time, using code dictionaries that provided standard terms. This coded section was then used to keypunch the data onto cards, for later submission to the processing program.

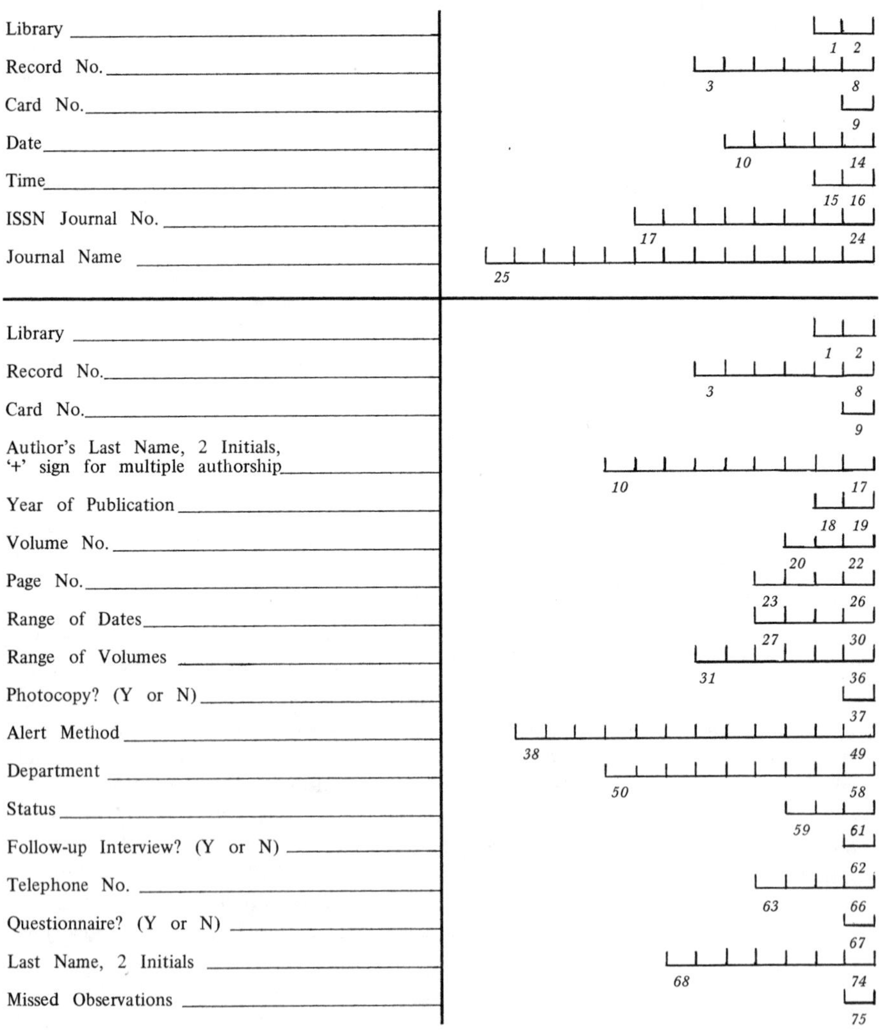

JOURNAL OBSERVATION RECORD

Field	Columns
Library	1–2
Record No.	3–8
Card No.	9
Date	10–14
Time	15–16
ISSN Journal No.	17–24
Journal Name	25

Field	Columns
Library	1–2
Record No.	3–8
Card No.	9
Author's Last Name, 2 Initials, '+' sign for multiple authorship	10–17
Year of Publication	18–19
Volume No.	20–22
Page No.	23–26
Range of Dates	27–30
Range of Volumes	31–36
Photocopy? (Y or N)	37
Alert Method	38–49
Department	50–58
Status	59–61
Follow-up Interview? (Y or N)	62
Telephone No.	63–66
Questionnaire? (Y or N)	67
Last Name, 2 Initials	68–74
Missed Observations	75

Figure 18. Questionnaire used in the Physics Library.

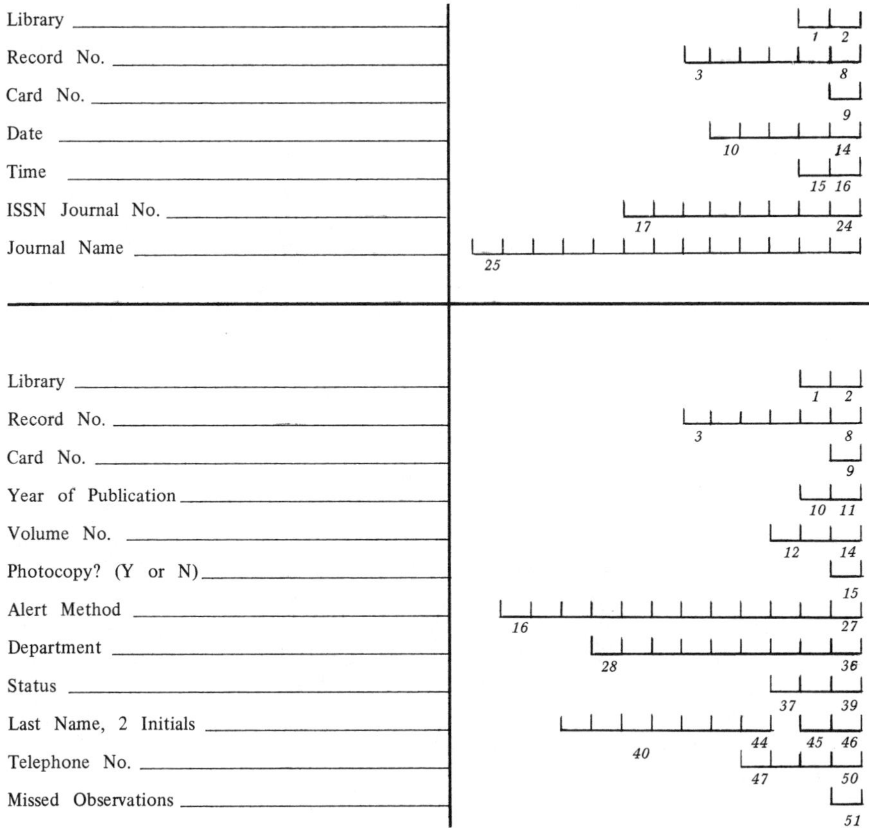

JOURNAL OBSERVATION RECORD

Library ________ (1–2)
Record No. ________ (3–8)
Card No. ________ (9)
Date ________ (10–14)
Time ________ (15–16)
ISSN Journal No. ________ (17–24)
Journal Name ________ (25–)

Library ________ (1–2)
Record No. ________ (3–8)
Card No. ________ (9)
Year of Publication ________ (10–11)
Volume No. ________ (12–14)
Photocopy? (Y or N) ________ (15)
Alert Method ________ (16–27)
Department ________ (28–36)
Status ________ (37–39)
Last Name, 2 Initials ________ (40–44, 45–46)
Telephone No. ________ (47–50)
Missed Observations ________ (51)

Figure 19. Questionnaire used in remaining five libraries (Langley Life Sciences, Engineering, Chemistry, Computer Science and Mathematics).

While repetitious input procedures are not always desirable, they served a purpose in this case, for at least three reasons: (1) the initial recording of the data in quick, non-standard fashion kept the user's resistance to a minimum, ensuring a greater return of information; (2) the later recoding of the data by the observer, in a quiet study with the code dictionaries on hand, reduced the initial number of errors; and (3) once data were coded, the keypuncher did not need to understand the system in order to perform the keypunching task. And, because the volume of forms was light, one of the clerical staff could be employed in spare time to process them. A fast turnaround was not necessary, so that batches of between 50 and 200 cases were handled in anywhere from a day to a week. These cases were then added to the data base by the computer programs (described later in this Appendix).

Two Cards

Two cards were used for each case. This is indicated by the horizontal division of the form. Both cards contained the library code, record number, and card number. The library code was used to file the original forms, in case reference had to be made to them in correcting errors. The record number was a unique number assigned to each case—the "key." The card number was used to identify "Card 1" and "Card 2" of each case, and was checked during the data validation run in order to detect any cards that were out of place.

The Remaining Fields

On the first card, we recorded the "date and time of the interview." This was used to track the number of uses in each sampling hour. The "ISSN number" and the "name of the journal" were recorded in capturing the title. The ISSN number was the code used by the computer programs. However, the full alphabetic version of the name was used by the observer in checking for errors, since this was more convenient. When a particular journal did not have an ISSN number, it was assigned a numeric code. Thus, two dictionaries were maintained for the journal titles, one with the ISSN numbers, the other with our own numbers.

The second card included the "year of publication" and "volume number" for exact identification of the journal used. The question about "photocopying" was asked at the time of the interview. Very often, the response to this question was "unknown" because the person had just begun to read, and was still uncertain as to the worth of the article. At other times, the user had read far enough to make a definite "yes" or "no" judgment.

The "alert method" was the means by which the user had been directed to the article. In the Physics Library, the following list of responses was used: card catalog, browsing, personal communication, index/abstract, conferences, book reviews, bibliography, publisher advertisements, class assignment, journal reference, other, and unknown. Some of these categories of responses proved not to be useful, so that they were revised in the study of the remaining five libraries. The categories retained were: browsing, personal communication, index/abstract, class assignment, previous reference, other, and unknown.

The "department" of the user was supplied by the user, using the official list of departments within the University. The "status" of the user was defined as: undergraduate, graduate, post-doctoral students; faculty, staff, visitors; other, and unknown.

B. The Computer Programs

The processing of the data collected for the study involved two major steps:

(1) validation of the data;

(2) statistical processing of the data.

The validation program was written in FORTRAN by a member of the research team; the statistical routines used were those provided by the SPSS (Statistical Package for the Social Sciences).

Some notes on each of these follow:

1. The Validation Program

The purpose of this program was twofold:

- to check the incoming data for errors; and
- to translate the alphabetical codes recorded by the observer-keypuncher into numerical codes for processing by SPSS.

Some of the errors that were checked were:

- record numbers of the two cards constituting a single case not equal
- card in the wrong order
- library code not found in the dictionary of libraries (this would indicate incorrect coding)
- illegal value for date and time of interview (e.g., value for day is not between 1 and 31)
- the check-digit in the ISSN number incorrect
- codes for alert method, department, or status not found in respective dictionaries
- illegal value in photocopy field (not Y, N, or U for "yes," "no," or "unknown")

If any of the above errors occurred, the case was rejected, and a message identifying the record number, its physical placement in the deck, and the type of error, was output. In all cases, the person inputting the data was one of the observers, who would then check the cards. Obvious keypunching errors were corrected immediately (e.g., misspellings); errors that were not immediately obvious were corrected by referring to the original data collection form.

The errors in the original inputting of cards ranged from 2% to 10%. However, with the corrections, it is believed that we kept the erroneous data in the database to under 1%.

It was in order to facilitate this correction process that alphabetic codes were chosen for recording the original data. However, the computational programs of SPSS work better with numeric data, so the codes of the "good data" were translated from the alphabetic to the numeric, e.g., undergraduate was recorded as "UND" in the alphabetic code, then translated to "1" by the validation program.

These translations were accomplished by dictionary look-ups for most of the fields: "library," "alert," "department" and "journal number." These dictionaries were stored on disk. Other fields were translated within the program itself, e.g., "photocopy" which had only three values: N = 1, Y = 2, U = 3.

The program itself was also stored on disk and triggered by the submission of a pre-arranged small deck of cards. Thus, the data collector needed only to know how to read cards into the card-reader and how to get printout from the printer.

Cards that were corrected were simply resubmitted, and the data on them was added in incremental fashion to the file of good data, which was also stored on disk. This good data file was then submitted automatically to an SPSS program, which was also stored on disk. The resulting data file was stored in a form facilitating easy access by any other SPSS run. Thus, the entire process of capturing, validating and storing the data are flowcharted in Figure 20.

The deck handled by the data collector consisted of only six cards. Both the validation program and the SPSS program, and two control decks for these programs, were stored on the disk.

2. The SPSS Programs

The "frequency" and "cross-tabulation" routines of SPSS were heavily used, with only occasional use of "correlation" and "regression" routines. However, the full range of SPSS routines can be used. The routines for "frequency" and "cross-tabulation" are not difficult to write, so that an installation not having SPSS or some other statistical package available could compose its own processing programs.

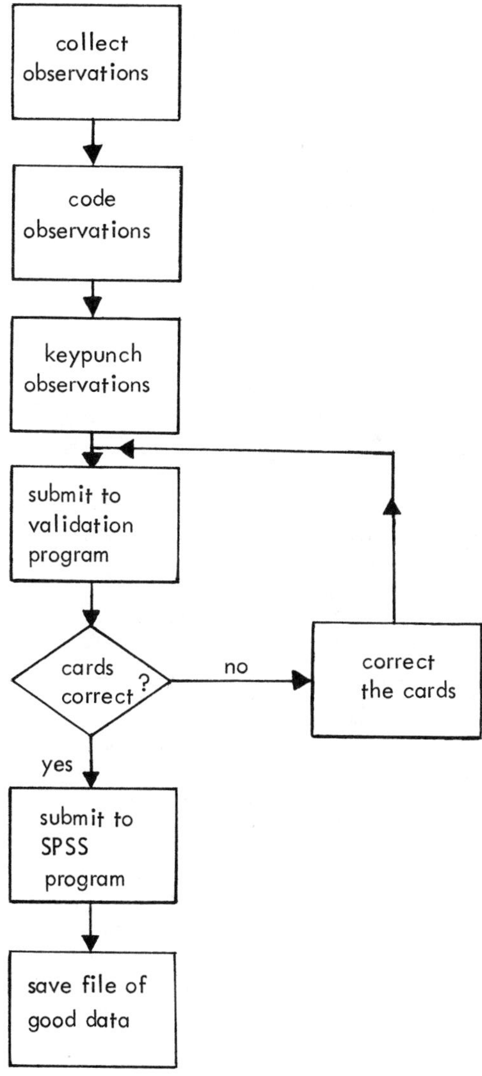

Figure 20.

As in the validation program, the control information for the SPSS programs was stored on disk, so that the data collector had to manipulate only a few cards in order to obtain processed data. The processed data were later analyzed by other members of the research team.

All computer programs were run on the Digital Equipment Corporation DECsystem 10, so that control information is that appropriate to this system.

II. USAGE STATISTICS

In the main part of the report, we included the rounded figures for projecting sample usage into trimester and yearly usage. Here we provide detail about the methods.

A. The Multiplying Factor

We developed a "multiplying factor" to project the sample usage into yearly usage. The trimester multiplying factor is based on the percentage of time sampled. For example, if we sample 30 hours per trimester, and the library is open 600 hours per trimester, the trimester multiplying factor is 20.

The trimester multiplying factors we used are given in Table 113; the resulting usage projections are given in Tables 114 and 115.

Table 113
Multiplying Factor

LIBRARY	Hours Open Weekly	Week * 15 = hrs. open per trimester	Adjustment if necessary	Hours Sampled	Trimester Multiplying Factor
Physics	60.00	900	no adjustment	60	15
Langley (Life Sci.)	79.75	1196.25	no adjustment	39	30.67
Engineering	68.75	1031.25	2062.5 (2 trim.)	81	25.5
Chemistry	66.50	997.5	no adjustment	39	25.6
Computer Science	66.50	997.5	no adjustment	39	25.6
Mathematics	54.50	817.5	no adjustment	39	21.0

Note: The Engineering Library was the only library with a different number of hours in each trimester sampled (39 and 42); thus, we adjusted the Engineering totals to two trimesters before dividing by the number of sampling hours.

Table 114
Projected Trimester Usage

LIBRARY	Sample Usage	No. of Trimesters in sample	Normalized Trimester Usage	Trimester Multiplying Factor	Projected Trimester Usage
Physics	439	2	219.5	15	3293
Langley (Life Sci.)	211	1	211	30.67	6471
Engineering	172	2	86	25.5	2193
Chemistry	160	1	160	25.6	4096
Computer Science	24	1	24	25.6	614
Mathematics	30	1	30	21	630
TOTAL	1036				5297

Table 115
Projected Yearly Usage

LIBRARY	Trimester Usage	Trimester * 3	Rounded to nearest 50
Physics	3293	9879	9900
Langley (Life Sci.)	6471	19413	19400
Engineering	2193	6579	6600
Chemistry	4096	12288	12300
Computer Science	614	1842	1850
Mathematics	630	1890	1900
TOTAL	17297	51891	51950

B. Frequency of Use by Title

The frequencies of usage of the titles in the various collections are given in two forms: first we list the relative frequencies in non-cumulative form; then we list the cumulated frequencies. These numbers may be of interest to researchers who wish to categorize the data differently than we have done in the main report.

In listing the frequencies,

- "times used" means the number of times a particular title was used in the sample; this is referred to as the "category of usage."

- "Number of titles" is the number of titles that showed that "category of usage."
- "% of collection" is calculated on the total number of titles in the collection.
- "Sample uses" is the number of uses supplied by that "category of usage."
- "% usage" is the percent of the sample usage supplied by that category of usage.
- "Projected yearly usage" is computed by multiplying sample usage times the multiplying factor.

The non-cumulative frequencies for each library are given in Tables 116 - 121.

Table 116
Physics Library
298 Titles in Collection; Multiplying Factor = 22.5

Times used	Number of Titles	% of Collection	Sample Uses	% of Usage	Projected yearly usage
40	1	0.33	40	9.1	900
29	1	0.33	29	6.6	653
25	1	0.33	25	5.7	562
20	1	0.33	20	4.6	450
17	1	0.33	17	3.9	383
15	1	0.33	15	3.4	337
13	1	0.33	13	3.0	293
12	1	0.33	12	2.7	270
11	1	0.33	11	2.5	247
10	2	0.7	20	4.6	450
8	1	0.33	8	1.8	180
7	2	0.7	14	3.2	315
6	3	1.0	18	4.1	405
5	9	3.0	45	10.25	1013
4	8	2.7	32	7.3	720
3	13	4.4	39	8.9	877
2	18	6.0	36	8.2	810
1	45	15.1	45	10.25	1013
Subtotal	110	36.9	439	100.0	9878
0	188	63.1	0	0	0
Total	298	100.0	439	100.0	9878

Table 117
Langley (Life Sciences) Library
914 Titles in Collection; Multiplying Factor = 92

Times used	Number of Titles	% of Collection	Sample Uses	% of Usage	Projected yearly usage
13	1	0.1	13	6.2	1196
8	1	0.1	8	3.8	736
6	1	0.1	6	2.8	552
5	2	0.2	10	4.7	920
4	7	0.8	28	13.3	2576
3	10	1.1	30	14.2	2760
2	29	3.2	58	27.5	5336
1	58	6.3	58	27.5	5336
Subtotal	109	11.9	211	100.0	19412
0	805	88.1	0	0	0
Total	914	100.0	211	100.0	19412

Table 118
Engineering Library
1,643 Titles in Collection; Multiplying Factor = 38.25

Times used	Number of Titles	% of Collection	Sample Uses	% of Usage	Projected yearly usage
10	1	0.06	10	5.8	383
7	1	0.06	7	4.1	268
4	2	0.1	8	4.7	306
3	7	0.4	21	12.2	803
2	26	1.6	52	30.2	1989
1	74	4.5	74	43.0	2830
Subtotal	111	6.8	172	100.0	6579
0	1532	93.2	0	0	0
Total	1643	100.0	172	100.0	6579

Table 119
Chemistry Library
433 Titles in the Collection; Multiplying Factor = 76.8

Times used	Number of Titles	% of Collection	Sample Uses	% of Usage	Projected yearly usage
27	1	0.2	27	16.9	2074
13	1	0.2	13	8.1	998
10	1	0.2	10	6.3	768
6	3	0.7	18	11.3	1382
5	1	0.2	5	3.1	384
4	3	0.7	12	7.5	922
3	5	1.2	15	9.4	1152
2	12	2.8	24	15.0	1843
1	36	8.3	36	22.5	2765
Subtotal	63	14.5	160	100.0	12288
0	370	85.5	0	0	0
Total	433	100.0	160	100.0	12288

Table 120
Computer Science Library
198 Titles in the Collection; Multiplying Factor = 76.8

Times used	Number of Titles	% of Collection	Sample Uses	% of Usage	Projected yearly usage
5	1	0.5	5	20.8	384
3	1	0.5	3	12.5	230
2	1	0.5	2	8.3	154
1	14	7.1	14	58.3	1075
subtotal	17	8.6	24	100.0	1843
0	181	91.4	0	0	0
Total	198	100.0	24	100.0	1843

Table 121
Mathematics Library
265 Titles in the Collection; Multiplying Factor = 63

Times used	Number of Titles	% of Collection	Sample Uses	% of Usage	Projected yearly usage
4	1	0.4	4	13.3	252
3	1	0.4	3	10.0	189
2	3	1.1	6	20.0	378
1	17	6.4	17	56.7	1071
Subtotal	22	8.3	30	100.0	1890
0	243	91.7	0	0	0
Total	265	100.0	30	100.0	1890

C. Projected Yearly Percentages

Using logarithmic probability paper, the figures on sample usage can be projected into figures on yearly usage. The method is as follows: [1]

(1) Plot the sample with percent of collection along the X-axis, number of uses supplied by each title in that group along the Y-axis.

(2) In plotting the percent of collection, use cumulative percentages; each point on the X-axis thus represents the percent of the collection which is used either exactly that number of uses or a fewer number of uses. For example, we might have 80% of the titles in the collection being used 50 or less times.

(3) Multiply the points on this line by the yearly multiplication factor, increasing the values along the Y-axis. That is, raise the points representing number of uses, not the points representing percent of the collection. These points are simply redrawn at a greater height in the vertical direction.

(4) Draw this new line through the points resulting from step 3; this line is parallel to the line depicting sample usage; however, it depicts yearly usage.

(5) Read the percent of the collection accounting for a given number of uses (or less) from this new line.

The cumulative frequencies for each library are shown in Table 122 and Figures 21 - 26.

---

[1] The method was brought to the attention of the investigator by Donald W. King, and is explained fully in the work by Aitchison and Brown, The Lognormal Distribution, Cambridge University Press, 1973, pp. 31ff.

Table 122
Cumulative Frequencies

Times used	Number of Titles	% of Collection	Sample Uses	% of Usage	Projected yearly usage
PHYSICS LIBRARY					
10+	11	3.7	202	46.0	4545
8+	12	4.0	210	47.8	4725
7+	14	4.7	224	51.0	5040
6+	17	5.7	242	55.1	5445
5+	26	8.7	287	65.4	6458
4+	34	11.4	319	72.7	7178
3+	47	15.8	358	81.5	8055
2+	65	21.8	394	89.7	8865
1+	110	36.9	439	100.0	9878
LANGLEY (Life Sciences) LIBRARY					
5+	5	0.5	37	17.5	3404
4+	12	1.3	65	30.8	5980
3+	22	2.4	95	45.0	8740
2+	51	5.6	153	72.5	14076
1+	109	11.9	211	100.0	19412
ENGINEERING LIBRARY					
10+	1	0.1	10	5.8	383
7+	2	0.1	17	9.9	651
4+	4	0.3	25	14.5	957
3+	11	0.7	46	26.7	1760
2+	37	2.3	98	57.0	3749
1+	111	6.8	172	100.0	6579
CHEMISTRY LIBRARY					
27+	1	0.2	27	16.9	2074
13+	2	0.4	40	25.0	3072
10+	3	0.6	50	31.3	3840
6+	6	1.3	68	42.5	5222
5+	7	1.5	73	45.6	5606
4+	10	2.2	85	53.1	6528
3+	15	3.4	100	62.5	7680
2+	27	6.2	124	77.5	9523
1+	63	14.5	160	100.0	12288
COMPUTER SCIENCE LIBRARY					
5+	1	0.5	5	20.8	384
3+	2	1.0	8	33.3	614
2+	3	1.5	10	41.7	768
1+	17	8.6	24	100.0	1843
MATHEMATICS LIBRARY					
4+	1	0.4	4	13.3	252
3+	2	0.8	7	23.3	441
2+	5	1.9	13	43.3	819
1+	22	8.3	30	100.0	1890

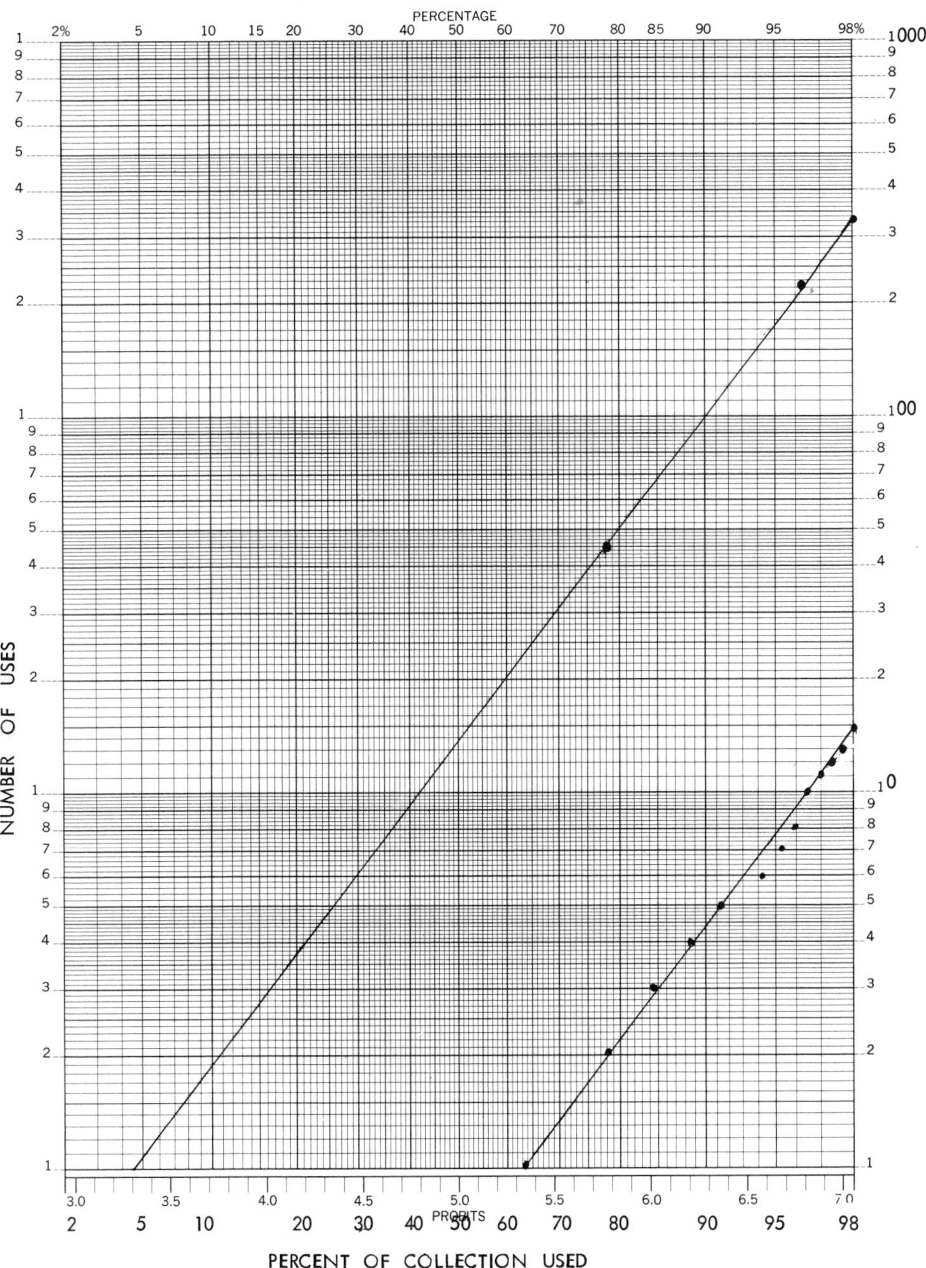

Figure 21. Physics — 298 Titles — 439 Uses
*22.5 110 Titles Used

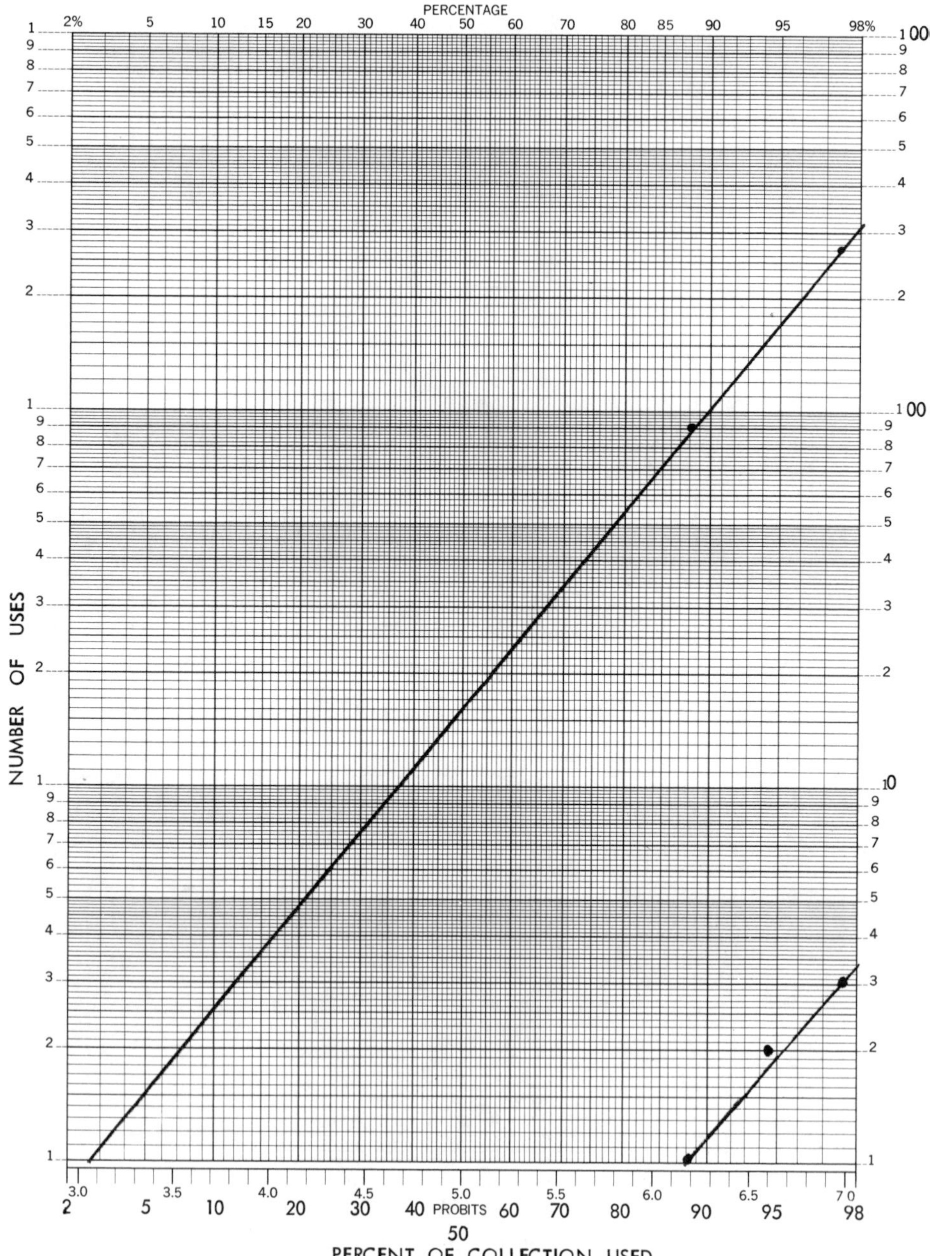

Figure 22. Langley (Life Sciences) — 914 Titles — 211 Uses
*92 109 Titles Used

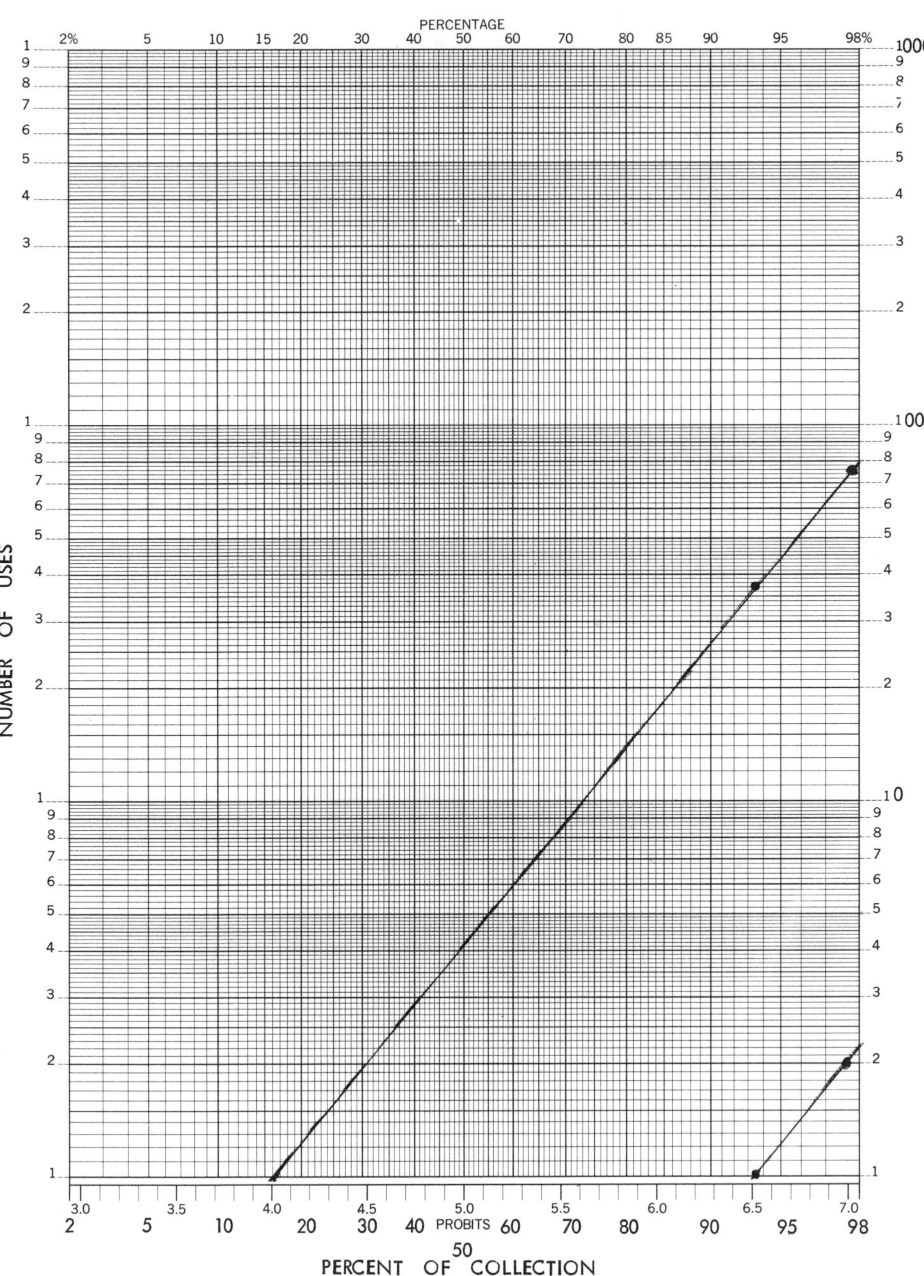

Figure 23. Engineering — 1,643 Titles — 172 Uses
*38.25 111 Titles Used

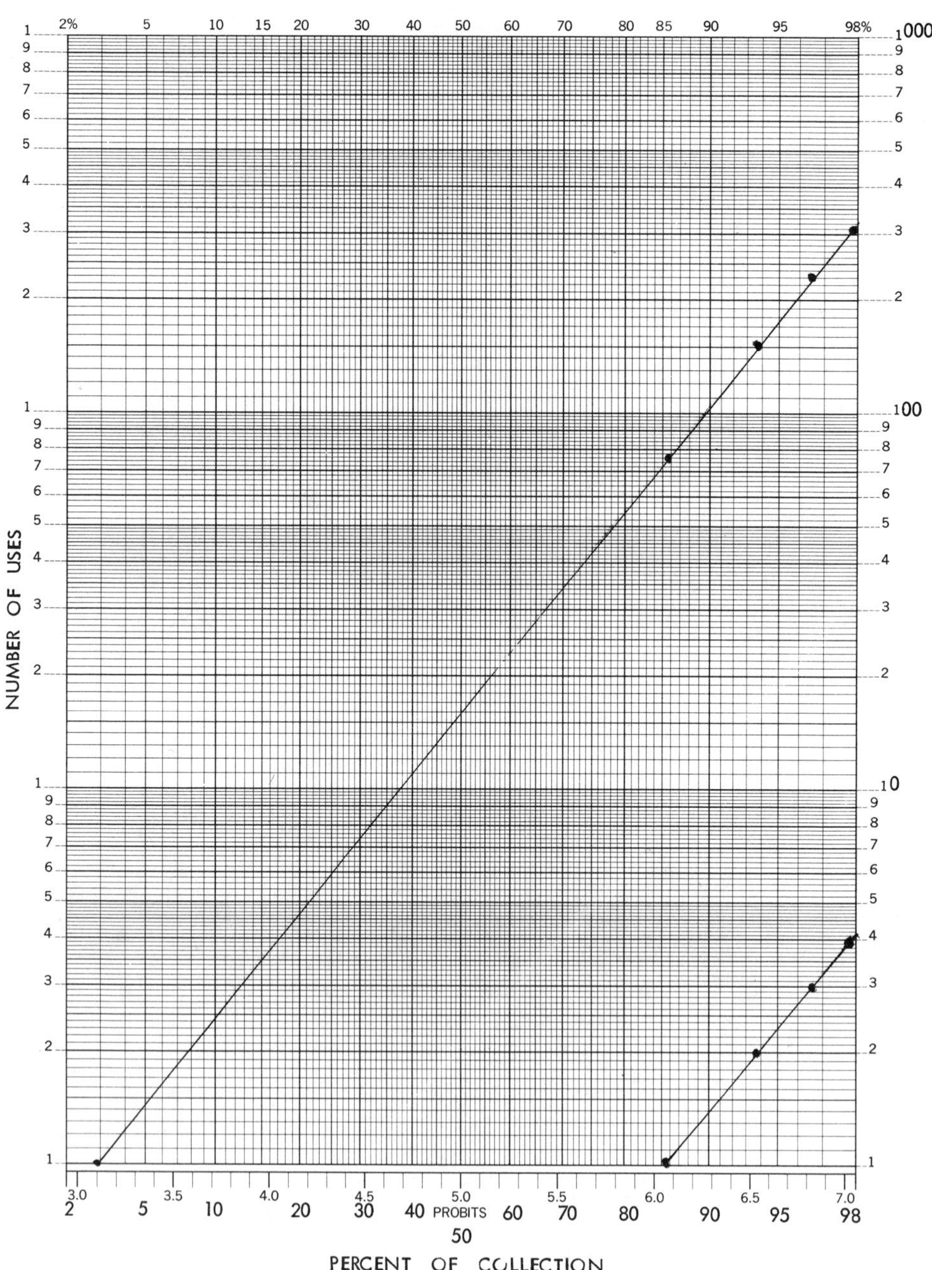

Figure 24. Chemistry — 433 Titles — 160 Uses
*76.8 63 Titles Used

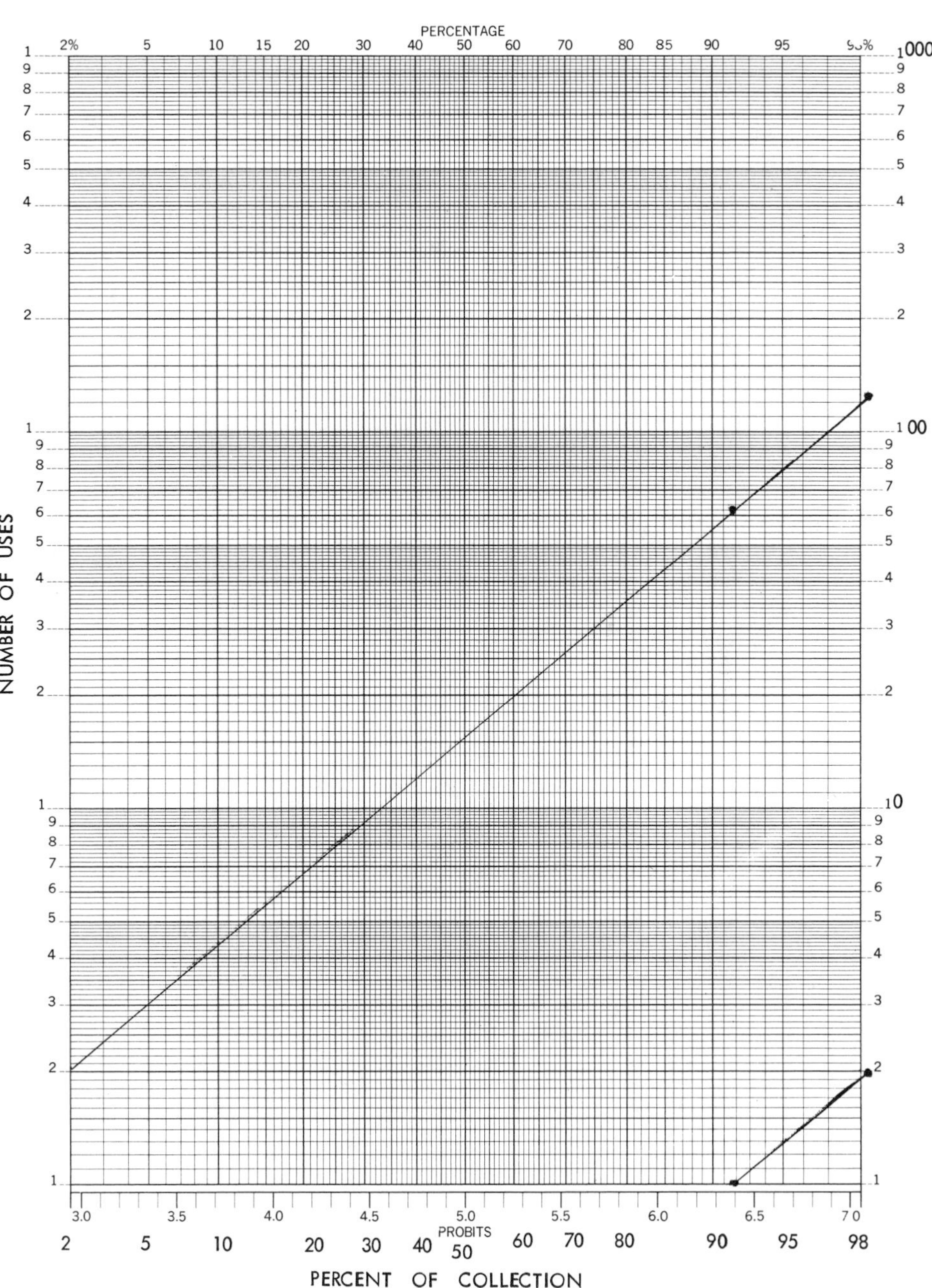

Figure 25. Computer Science — 198 Titles — 24 Uses
*76.8 17 Titles Used

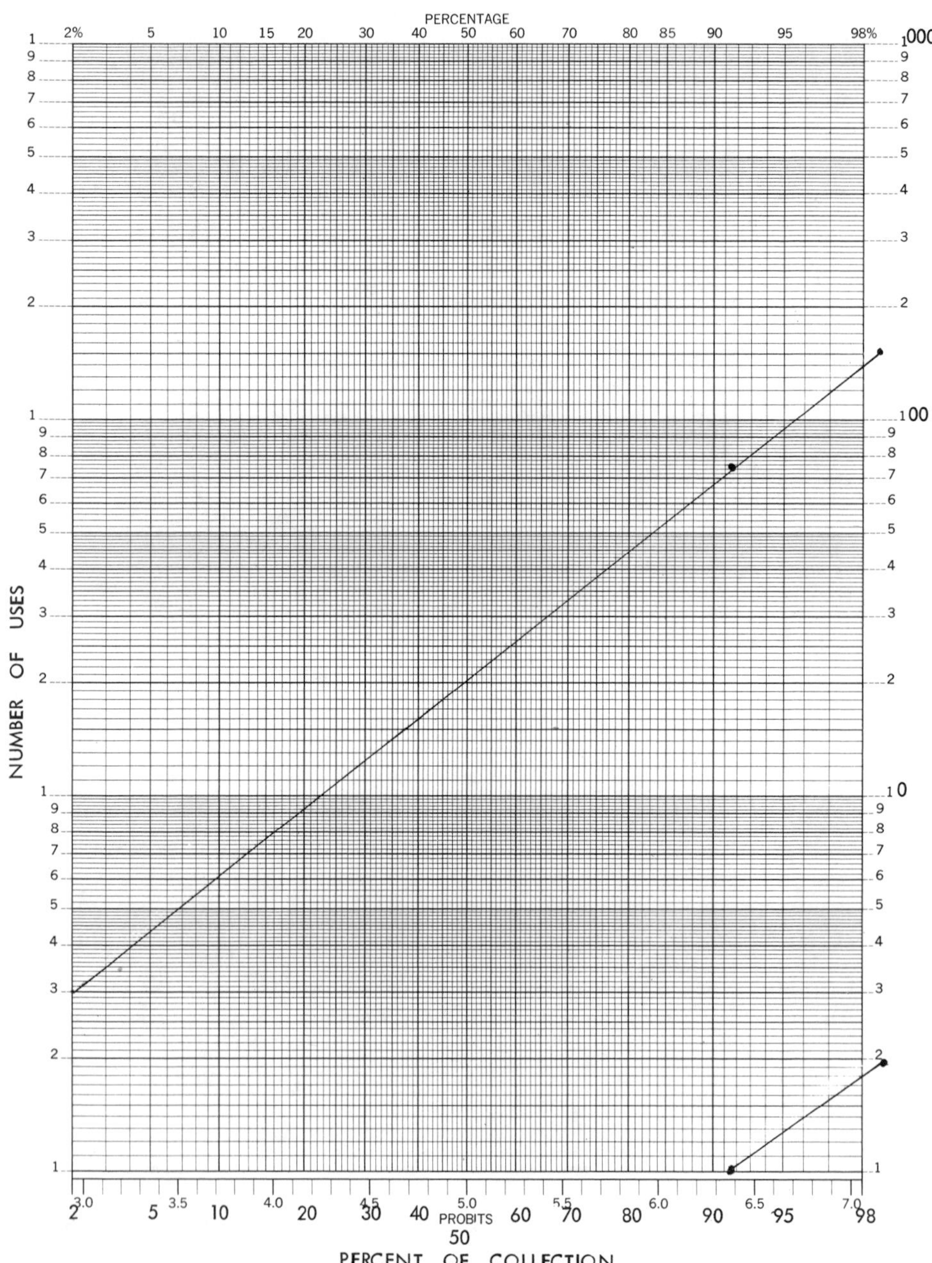

Figure 26. Mathematics — 265 Titles — 30 Uses
*63 22 Titles Used

III. USAGE BY TITLE

One item of interest is the titles of the journals that were used during our sampling period. These are listed below, by library:[2] T = total in category; C = cumulative totals for each library.

A. Physics Library

More than 10 Uses — T = 12 journals, 229 uses; C = 12 journals, 229 uses

1. Physical Review (A, B, C, D) — 49
2. Physical Review Letters — 29
3. Nature — 25
4. Journal of Chemical Physics — 20
5. Journal of Physics (A, B, C, D, E) — 18
6. New Scientist — 17
7. Chemical Physical Letters — 15
8. Science — 13
9. Nuclear Physics — 12
10. Physics Letters — 11
11. Reviews of Modern Physics — 10
12. Sky and Telescope — 10

5 - 9 Uses — T = 12 journals, 68 uses; C = 24 journals, 297 uses

1. Journal of Mathematical Physics — 8
2. American Journal of Physics — 7
3. Annals of Physics — 6
4. Aviation Week and Space Technology — 6
5. Journal of Applied Physics — 6
6. Bulletin of the Atomic Scientists — 5
7. Foundations of Physics — 5
8. Nuclear Instruments and Methods — 5
9. Optics Communications — 5
10. Scientific American — 5
11. Surface Science — 5
12. Applied Physics — 5

---

[2] The original listing of journal titles used in calculating the tables differed from the above list, which resulted from corrections to the original list made by the librarians. This would affect the calculations involving percent of collection used, but not by a great amount. It did not seem cost-effective to recalculate the various tables involved.

Physics Library (continued)

4 Uses — T = 6 journals, 24 uses; C = 30 journals, 321 uses

1. Applied Physics Letters
2. Astronomy and Astrophysics
3. Astrophysical Journal
4. Atomic Data
5. Physica Status Solidii
6. Solid State Communications

3 Uses — T = 12 journals, 36 uses; C = 42 Journals, 357 uses

1. Advances in Physics
2. Applied Optics
3. Contemporary Physics
4. Icarus
5. Physica
6. Review of Scientific Instruments
7. Soviet Physics, "Doklady"
8. Soviet Physics, Jetp
9. Zeitschrift für Physik
10. Geophysical Journal
11. Physics Reports
12. Mercury

2 Uses — T = 17 journals, 34 uses; C = 59 journals, 391 uses

1. American Physical Society, Bulletin
2. Astronomical Journal
3. Astronomical Society of the Pacific, Publications
4. Bell System Technical Journal
5. Critical Reviews in Solid State Science
6. Current Papers in Physics
7. International Journal of Theoretical Physics
8. Optical Society of America, Journal
9. Physics in Canada
10. Physics of Fluids
11. Physics Today[3]
12. Soviet Physics, Technical Physics
13. Space Science Reviews
14. Journal of Physics and Chemistry of Solids
15. Academie des Sciences, Comptes Rendus
16. Nuovo Cimiento
17. Spectrochimica Acta

---

3 Physics Today is not kept on journal shelves. Patrons must ask for it, so our observation methods would not catch all uses.

Physics Library (continued)

1 Use	T = 44 journals	44 uses
	C = 103 journals	435 uses

1. Acta Physica Austriaca
2. American Scientist
3. Annalen der Physik Leipsig
4. Applied Spectroscopy
5. Astrophysical Letters
6. Astrophysics and Space Science
7. Atomic Energy Review
8. Australian Journal of Physics
9. Beitrage zur Physik der Atmosphare
10. Communications in Mathematical Physics
11. Fortschrifte der Physik
12. General Relativity and Gravitation
13. Helvetica Physica Acta
14. IEEE Transactions on Nuclear Science
15. Infrared Physics
16. Institue Henri Poincaré, Annales Section A, Physique
17. International Journal of Magnetism
18. Journal of College Science Teaching
19. Journal of Computational Physics
20. Journal of Geophysical Research
21. Journal of Magnetic Resonance
22. Journal of Research, National Bureau of Standards, Section .. ISSN 00224340
23. Lettere al Nuovo Cimiento
24. Naval Research Review
25. Nuclear Data, A
26. Nuclear Science and Engineering
27. Optica Acta
28. Particle Accelerators
29. Particles and Nuclei
30. Philips Technical Review
31. Philosophical Magazine
32. Physics Teacher
33. Physik der Kondensierten Meterie
34. Progress of Theoretical Physics
35. Royal Astronomical Society, Monthly Notices
36. Royal Astronomical Society, Quarterly Journal
37. Soviet Journal of Quantum Electronics
38. Soviet Physics, Solid State
39. Soviet Physics, USPEKHI
40. Zeitschrift für Angewandt Mathematik und Physik
41. Nuclear Physics, B
42. Astrophysical Journal, Supplement Series
43. Case Studies in Atomic Physics
44. Physics Abstracts

B. Langley Library (Life Sciences, including Psychology)

4 or More Uses — T = 12 journals, 66 uses; C = 12 journals, 66 uses

1. Science — 13
2. Plant Physiology — 8
3. Biochimica et Biophysica Acta — 6
4. Developmental Biology — 5
5. National Academy of Sciences Proceedings — 5
6. Nature — 5
7. Journal of Consulting and Clinical Psychology — 4
8. Journal of Molecular Biology — 4
9. Virology — 4
10. Journal of Abnormal Psychology — 4
11. American Psychologist — 4
12. Psychological Review — 4

3 Uses — T = 10 journals, 30 uses; C = 22 journals, 96 uses

1. Canadian Journal of Botany
2. Journal of Personality and Social Psychology
3. Journal of Biological Chemistry
4. Journal of Applied Psychology
5. American Journal of Psychotherapy
6. Journal of Psychedelic Drugs
7. Experimental Cell Research
8. Ecology
9. Journal of Bacteriology
10. Journal of Theoretical Biology

2 Uses — T = 29 journals, 58 uses; C = 51 journals, 154 uses

1. Cognitive Psychology
2. Marine Biology
3. Journal of Experimental Psychology
4. Quarterly Review of Biology
5. Molecular and General Genetics
6. Brain Research
7. American Journal of Psychology
8. Family Process
9. Journal of Consulting Psychology
10. Journal of Clinical Psychology
11. American Journal of Orthopsychiatry
12. American Journal of Psychiatry
13. Psychiatry
14. Drug Forum
15. Journal of Educational Psychology

Langley Library (Life Sciences) **(continued)**

2 Uses (continued)

16. Psychology Today
17. Antimicrobial Agents and Chemotherapy
18. Biochemical and Biophysical Research Communications
19. Behaviour
20. Physiology and Behavior
21. Biochemistry
22. Royal Society of London, Proceedings
23. Cell
24. Folia Primatologica
25. Federation Proceedings, Federation of American Society for Experimental Biology
26. Journal of Cell Biology
27. Scientific American
28. Child Development
29. Journal of Behavioral Analysis

1 Use

T = 53 journals 53 uses
C = 104 journals 207 uses

1. Journal of Applied Behavioral Analysis
2. Seminars in Psychiatry
3. Genetics
4. Science Forum
5. Contemporary Psychology
6. Memory and Cognition
7. Journal of Nervous and Mental Disease
8. Journal of Behavior Therapy and Experimental Psychiatry
9. Journal of Sex Research
10. Journal of Applied Social Psychology
11. Academie des Sciences Comptes Rendus, Part D
12. Biological Reviews
13. Animal Behaviour
14. Journal of Cell Science
15. Journal of Embryology and Experimental Morphology
16. Evolution
17. Infection and Immunity
18. Journal of Cellular and Comparative Physiology
19. Psychophysiology
20. Development, Growth and Differentiation
21. Journal of Experimental Biology
22. Paleontological Journal
23. Journal of Clinical Investigation
24. Endocrinology
25. Journal of Endocrinology

Langley Library (Life Sciences) (continued)

1 Use (continued)

26. Acta Endocrinologica
27. Behavior Therapy
28. American Naturalist
29. Journal of Experimental Zoology
30. Journal of Personality Assessment
31. Journal of Molecular Evolution
32. Journal of Mathematical Psychology
33. Developmental Psychology
34. Zoologica Scripta
35. Comparative Biochemistry and Physiology
36. Cell and Tissue Research
37. Annals of Human Genetics
38. Journal of Autism and Childhood Schizophrenia
39. Behavioral Science
40. Journal of General Psychology
41. Merrill-Palmer Quarterly
42. Organizational Behavior and Human Performance
43. International Journal of Psychoanalysis
44. Freshwater Biology
45. Planta
46. Canadian Journal of Biochemistry
47. Acta Zoologica
48. Zeitschrift für Zoologische Systematik und Evolutionsforschung
49. Quaternary Research
50. Plant Physiology
51. Soil Science Society of American Journal
52. Zeitschrift für Vergleichende Physiologie
53. The Soviet Journal of Psychology

C. Engineering Library

3 or More Uses

T = 13 journals 52 uses
C = 13 journals 52 uses

1. Civil Engineering — 10
2. Aviation Week and Space Technology — 7
3. Photochemistry and Photobiology — 4
4. Journal of Construction Division of ASCE — 4
5. Management Science — 3
6. Engineering News Record — 3
7. Water Pollution Control — 3
8. Datamation — 3
9. Electronics — 3

Engineering Library (continued)

3 or More Uses (continued)

10. Journal of Fluid Mechanics — 3
11. IEEE Transactions on Magnetics — 3
12. AIME Transactions (Mining) — 3
13. Metallurgical Transactions AIME (A, B) — 3

2 Uses

T = 25 journals 50 uses
C = 38 journals 102 uses

1. Acta Metallurgica
2. Combustion and Flame
3. Engineering Economist
4. Power
5. Geotechnique
6. Public Works
7. Combined Index to ASCE Publications (Index)
8. Mechanical Engineering
9. Physics of Metals and Metallography
10. IEEE Transactions, Power Apparatus and Systems
11. Science
12. IEEE Transactions (subdivision unknown)
13. Industry Week
14. Chemical Engineering
15. Journal of Mathematical Analysis and Application
16. International Journal of Environmental Studies
17. Transactions of the Japan Institute of Metals
18. American Institute of Chemical Engineers, Journal
19. Journal of the Air Pollution Control Association
20. Human Factors
21. Chemical Engineering Science
22. Scripta Metallurgica
23. Transportation Journal
24. Ironmaking Proceedings
25. AIME Transactions (Petroleum)

1 Use

T = 65 journals 65 uses
C = 103 journals 167 uses

1. Power Technology
2. Research Management
3. Communications of the ACM
4. Navy Civil Engineer
5. Polymer News
6. Mathematical Reviews (Index)
7. Mining Engineering
8. ASHRAE Journal

Engineering Library (continued)

1 Use (continued)

9. Computer Aided Design
10. Computers and People
11. Technical Communication
12. Journal of Applied Polymer Science
13. IEEE Proceedings (subdivision unknown)
14. Mathematics of Computation
15. Canadian Mining Journal
16. Journal of Applied Physics
17. Canadian Journal of Chemical Engineering
18. Metallurgical Reviews
19. Journal of Metals
20. Technology Review
21. Metal Finishing
22. Journal of Materials Science
23. Theory of Probability and its Application
24. Iron and Steel Institute, Journal
25. Nuclear Engineering International
26. Water Services
27. Physics of Fluids
28. Petroleum Engineer
29. Transportation: Current Literature
30. AIAA Journal (American Institute of Aeronautics and Astronautics)
31. IEEE Transactions on Communications and Electronics
32. International Chemical Engineering
33. Journal of the ACM
34. Institute of Electrical Engineers, London—Proceedings
35. Oil and Gas Journal
36. American Waterworks Association Journal
37. Journal of Environmental Engineering
38. International Journal of Heat and Mass Transfer
39. Chartered Mechanical Engineer
40. Electronic Engineering
41. Australian Institute of Metals Journal
42. Pipeline and Gas Journal
43. Welding Journal
44. Industrial and Engineering Chemistry (subdivision unknown)
45. Rail Engineering International
46. Journal of Optimization Theory and Applications
47. IEEE Transactions on Automatic Control
48. New Scientist
49. Water Resources Bulletin
50. Engineering Fracture Mechanics

Engineering Library (continued)

1 Use (continued)

51. Coal Age
52. Hydrocarbon Processing
53. Hewlett-Packard Journal
54. Journal of Computers and Structures
55. Metallurgical Transactions
56. International Journal of Engineering Science
57. Sewage and Industrial Wastes
58. Surveying and Mapping
59. NASA Technical Briefs
60. QST
61. Automotive Engineering
62. Iron and Steel International
63. Energy Policy
64. Photogrammetric Engineering and Remote Sensing
65. Journal of Biomedical Engineering

D. Chemistry Library

5 or More Uses

T = 7 journals 74 uses
C = 7 journals 74 uses

1. Journal of the ACS — 27
2. Tetrahedron Letters — 13
3. Analytical Chemistry — 10
4. Journal of the Chemical Society — 7
5. Synthesis — 6
6. Journal of Organic Chemistry — 6
7. Inorganic Chemistry — 5

4 Uses

T = 3 journals 12 uses
C = 10 journals 86 uses

1. Angewandte Chemie
2. Journal of Chemical Physics
3. Journal of Less Common Metals

3 Uses

T = 5 journals 15 uses
C = 15 journals 101 uses

1. Journal of Physical Chemistry
2. Scientific American
3. Helvetica Chimica Acta
4. Journal of Catalysis
5. Chemical Reviews

Chemistry Library (continued)

2 Uses

T = 12 journals 24 uses
C = 27 journals 125 uses

1. Nature
2. Journal of Inorganic and Nuclear Chemistry
3. Accounts of Chemical Research
4. Journal of Gas Chromatography
5. Spectrochimica Acta
6. Canadian Journal of Chemistry
7. Journal of Chromatography
8. Journal of Biological Chemistry
9. Journal of Molecular Spectroscopy
10. Current Contents
11. Biochemistry
12. Berichte der Deutschen Chemische Gesellschaft

1 Use

T = 32 journals 32 uses
C = 59 journals 157 uses

1. Journal of Medicinal Chemistry
2. Chemistry Letters
3. Review of Scientific Instruments
4. Inorganic and Nuclear Chemistry Letters
5. Journal of Solid State Chemistry
6. Berichte der Bunsen Gesellschaft für Physicalische Chem.
7. Biopolymers
8. Physical Review Letters
9. Chemical Society Reviews
10. Analyst
11. Analytica Chemica Acta
12. Acta Chemica Scandinavica
13. Critical Reviews in Analytical Chemistry
14. Journal of Organic Chemistry of the USSR
15. Organic Mass Spectroscopy
16. Journal of Molecular Structure
17. Science
18. Journal of Applied Physics
19. Chemical Physics Letters
20. Chemical and Pharmaceutical Bulletin
21. Chemical Communication
22. Journal of Chemical Education
23. Chemical Physics
24. Journal of Organometallic Chemistry
25. Journal of Electroanalytical Chemistry
26. Bulletin of the Chemical Society of Japan
27. Zeitschrift für Naturforschung
28. Chemical Society Journal, Dalton Transactions

Chemistry Library (continued)

1 Use (continued)

29. Chemical Society of London Journal
30. The Physics and Chemistry of Solids
31. Journal of Coordination Chemistry
32. Pure and Applied Chemistry

E. Computer Science Library

2 or More Uses

T = 3 journals 10 uses
C = 3 journals 10 uses

1. Communications of the ACM — 5
2. Byte, Journal of Small Systems — 3
3. Creative Computing — 2

1 Use

T = 14 journals 14 uses
C = 17 journals 24 uses

1. Pattern Recognition
2. Data Processing Digest
3. Computer World
4. Current Papers on Computers and Control
5. BIT
6. Computer Decisions
7. Computing Surveys of ACM
8. ACM Proceedings on Microprogramming
9. Computers and People
10. Computer Journal
11. International Journal of Computer Mathematics
12. Operating Systems Review
13. Computers and Graphics
14. Infosystems

F. Mathematics Library

2 or More Uses

T = 6 journals 15 uses
C = 6 journals 15 uses

1. American Mathematical Society — 4
2. Mathematische Zeitschrifte — 3
3. Journal of Algebra — 2
4. General Topology and its Applications — 2
5. Fundamenta Mathematicae — 2
6. Soviet Mathematics — 2

Mathematics Library (continued)

<u>1 Use</u>

T = 15 journals 15 uses
C = 21 journals 30 uses

1. Studies in Applied Mathematics
2. American Mathematical Monthly
3. Dissertationes Mathematicae
4. Mathematical Notes of the USSR Academy
5. Pacific Journal of Mathematics
6. Advances in Mathematics
7. Mathematische Nachrichten
8. The College Mathematics Journal
9. Notices of the American Mathematical Society
10. Acta Scientarum Mathematicarum
11. Bulletin of the London Mathematical Society
12. Russian Mathematical Survey
13. American Mathematical Society Bulletin
14. Mathematische Annalen
15. Siam Journal of Applied Mathematics

IV. USAGE BY AGE

The complete breakdown of usage by age is given in <u>Table 123</u> (all figures are percentages except for "number of sample uses"). The cumulative figures are given in <u>Table 124</u>. While the Physics and Chemistry Libraries seemed to reach further back in time (oldest use: 56 years and 42 years, respectively), the Mathematics Library showed use of older journals more consistently (20% over 15 years old, and 10% over 20 years old). That the Computer Science Library had no uses over 15 years old probably reflects the fact that it serves a new field, so that it holds very few journals published more than 20 years ago.

We can attempt to break out the statistics for the current year only by estimating the number of journals that were 12 months or less old during the sample time. This involves a formula for amortizing the uses of various years. The formulas vary according to the time of the sample. The sample periods for each library were as follows:

Library	Sampling Period
Physics	Fall '75 - Winter '76
Langley (Life Sciences)	Fall '76
Engineering	Fall '76 - Winter '77
Chemistry	Winter '77
Computer Science	Winter '77
Mathematics	Winter '77

For the studies occurring only in the Fall, we used the formula:
current year = current year + .083 * previous year.

For the studies occurring only in the Winter, we use:
current year = current year + .75 of previous year.

For the studies occurring in both Fall and Winter, we use:
current year = final year + .90 * previous year + .04 * two years ago.

The results of the breakdown are given in Table 125. Thus, the Physics Library has the heaviest usage of the "most current" material. With the exception of the Computer Science Library, which had but a slight sample usage, all other departmental libraries had well below 50% usage of the most immediate journals.

Table 123
Usage by Age

LIBRARY:	Physics	Life Science	Engineering	Chemistry	Comp.Sci.	Math.
USES	419	211	172	160	24	30
0- 1	67.8	34.1	41.3	36.9	54.2	23.3
2- 5	15.0	32.2	32.6	28.8	29.2	33.3
6-10	8.1	18.0	13.4	16.3	4.2	6.7
11-15	3.3	7.1	6.4	11.3	8.3	16.7
16-20	1.9	4.3	2.3	1.3	4.2	10.0
21-25	2.1	1.9	2.3	0.6	0.0	6.7
26+	1.7	2.4	1.7	5.0	0.0	3.3
Oldest use						
Year	1920	1940	1942	1935	1958	1951
Age (yrs)*	56	36	35	42	19	26

* The age in years is computed by subtracting the year of the oldest use from the year in which the sample was taken. This is 1976 for some libraries, 1977 for others.

Table 124
Usage by Age—Cumulative

LIBRARY	Physics	Life Science	Engineering	Chemistry	Comp.Sci.	Math.
0- 1	67.8	34.1	41.3	36.9	54.2	23.3
2- 5	82.8	66.3	73.9	65.7	83.4	56.6
6-10	90.9	84.3	87.3	82.0	87.6	63.3
11-15	94.2	91.4	93.7	93.3	95.9	80.0
16-20	96.1	95.7	96.0	94.6	100.0	90.0
21-25	98.2	97.6	98.3	95.2	100.0	96.7
26+	100.0	100.0	100.0	100.0	100.0	100.0

Table 125
Estimated Current Use

LIBRARY	Physics	Life Sci.	Engineering	Chemistry	Comp.Sci.	Math.
current uses	45 (1976)	49 (1976)	19 (1977)	44 (1977)	8 (1977)	4 (1977)
previous year	239 (1975)	23 (1975)	52 (1976)	15 (1976)	5 (1976)	3 (1976)
two past years	23 (1974)	n.a.	27 (1975)	n.a.	n.a.	n.a.
estimated current uses	261	51	66	55	12	6
total sample uses	419	211	172	160	24	30
% current use	62.3	24.2	38.4	34.4	50.0	20.0

V. USAGE BY ALERT METHOD

The complete breakdown for each category of alert method is given in Table 126.

Table 126
Alert Method

LIBRARY:	Physics	Life Sci.	Engineering	Chemistry	Comp.Sci.	Math.
USES	439	211	172	160	24	30
Browse %	65.6	20.9	38.4	27.5	41.7	26.7
Personal communication	6.2	3.3	5.8	10.0	8.3	3.3
Index/ Abstract	4.8	32.7	21.5	10.6	20.8	26.7
Class Assignment	2.1	5.2	10.5	6.9	12.5	0.0
Previous reference	17.1	33.2	16.9	40.6	16.7	43.3
Other	2.1	1.4	2.3	2.5	0.0	0.0
Unknown	2.3	3.3	4.7	1.9	0.0	0.0

VI. USES PER PERSON

In normalizing the statistics by "uses per person," the composition of the various departments was as given in Table 127.

Table 127
Uses per Person

Status	Number	%	Sample Uses	Trimester Multiplier	Projected trimester use	%	Uses per Person
PHYSICS LIBRARY							
Faculty	41	24.1	101	15 ÷ 2	758	26.0	18.5
Undergrad.	48	28.2	7	15 ÷ 2	52	1.9	1.1
Graduate	81	47.7	268	15 ÷ 2	2010	71.2	24.8
Total	170	100.0	376	15 ÷ 2	2820	100.0	16.6
LANGLEY LIBRARY (Life Sciences, incl. Psychology)							
Faculty	85	4.2	10	30.67	307	5.1	3.6
Undergrad.	1717	84.3	42	30.67	1288	21.2	0.75
Graduate	234	11.5	146	30.67	4478	73.7	19.1
Total	2036	100.0	198	30.67	6073	100.0	3.0
ENGINEERING LIBRARY							
Faculty	112	3.5	15	25.5÷2	192	9.0	1.7
Undergrad.	2320	72.7	70	25.5÷2	893	41.9	0.38
Graduate	759	23.8	82	25.5÷2	1046	49.1	1.37
Total	3191	100.0	167	25.5÷2	2130	100.0	0.67
CHEMISTRY LIBRARY							
Faculty	35	5.8	27	25.6	691	18.1	19.7
Undergrad.	412	68.8	19	25.6	486	12.7	1.2
Graduate	152	25.4	103	25.6	2637	69.2	17.3
Total	599	100.0	149	25.6	3814	100.0	6.4
COMPUTER SCIENCE LIBRARY							
Faculty	12	5.4	0	25.6	0	0.0	0.0
Undergrad.	171	76.7	8	25.6	205	36.4	1.2
Graduate	40	17.9	14	25.6	358	63.6	9.0
Total	223	100.0	22	25.6	563	100.0	2.5
MATHEMATICS LIBRARY							
Faculty	41	11.2	11	21.0	231	36.7	5.6
Undergrad.	260	70.8	0	21.0	0	0.0	0.0
Graduate	66	18.0	19	21.0	399	63.3	6.0
Total	367	100.0	30	21.0	630	100.0	1.7

VII. PREDICTING USAGE IN THE PHYSICS LIBRARY

A comparison of the distributions in the Physics Library between the "total population" and the "population of graduate students" indicates why we consider the graduate student population to be a good predictor of the usage in the general population.

In regard to "usage in general" and "usage by title," the top 11 journals accounted for 46% of the usage in the general population. The same 11 journals accounted for 46.5% of the usage in the graduate student subset of the population.

In regard to the "alert method" used to access the journals, the comparison is:

Alert Method	% in General Population	% in Graduate Student Usage
Browsing	65.6	63.5
Personal Communication	6.2	7.1
Index/Abstract	4.8	5.8
Book Reviews	0.2	0.4
Bibliography	8.4	10.8
Class Assignment	2.1	3.7
Journal Reference	8.4	6.2
Other	2.1	1.7
Unknown	2.3	0.8

If we compare the ranks on "alert method," we see that the two groups differ in just one pair of items, which have their relative positions reversed:

Rank, General Population	Rank, Graduate Students
1. Browsing	1. Browsing
2. Bibliography	2. Bibliography
3. Journal Reference	3. Personal Communication
4. Personal Communication	4. Journal Reference
5. Index/Abstract	5. Index/Abstract
6. Class Assignment	6. Class Assignment
7. Book Review	7. Book Review

Note: To compare these statistics for the Physics Library with the "alert method" statistics in the other five libraries, simply combine "bibliography," "journal reference" and "book review" into "previous reference."

Table 128
Comparison of Graduate Students
to Total Population—Physics Library

USER	Current (75-76)	70's (73-74)	60's	50's	40's	30's	20's
Total pop.	64.7	15.5	10.5	3.6	0.5	0.5	0.2
Graduate students	64.7	13.3	11.2	5.4	0.8	0.4	0.4

In regard to "usage by age" the usage of current journals (0 - 1 years old) was 64.7% in the general population and 64.7% among graduate students. Even a more detailed breakdown by decade preserves the relationship (Table 128).

The graduate students comprise about one-half of the Physics user population. They account for close to 75% of the usage. In a restricted "mini-study" of the library, a scheme involving only these graduate students might be a sufficient indicator of the usage. Of course, if the usage patterns change (e.g., more undergraduates enter the picture in Physics), this relation between the graduate students and the total population would change. The tracking should always be geared to identifying the changes in user patterns, for these are the information-pregnant events.

VIII. USAGE BY DEPARTMENT

With the "unknown" category eliminated, the raw data figures on "usage by department" are as given in Table 129.

Table 129
Usage by Department

LIBRARY	USER							
	Physics	Life Sci.	Engineering	Chemistry	Comp.Sci.	Math.	Other.	Total
Physics	308	1	4	52	0	3	27	395
Langley	0	152	2	0	0	0	50	204
Engineering	0	3	141	3	1	4	15	167
Chemistry	0	2	1	149	0	0	6	158
Comp.Sci.	0	0	5	3	9	1	4	22
Math.	0	0	0	0	0	30	0	30
Total	308	158	153	207	10	38	102	976

The diagonal figures (first figure in column 1, descending to last figure in column 6) represent the usage of each library by its "own" user group. If we eliminate the diagonal, the row totals give the service "provided" to others; the column totals (without the diagonal) represent service "demanded" from others. Thus, while the Physics Library supplied 87 uses to "others" during the sample period (22% of its total sample usage), the Physics users made no demands on the remaining five libraries in the study. As can be seen from comparing the column totals (without diagonal), there is only one instance of a heavy demand, in terms of absolute usage, by users of one department of another department's library: Chemistry department users using the Physics Library 52 times.

If the above figures are to be used in forming percentages, it must be remembered that the Physics and Engineering data are based on two-semester samples, while the other four libraries are based on one-semester samples. Thus, the usage for Physics and Engineering should be halved in order to get comparable figures.

These raw data are included so that readers may make categorizations and comparisons other than those made in our main report.

Part 2

APPLYING THE METHODOLOGY TO JOURNAL USE STUDIES ELSEWHERE

I. INTRODUCTION

The methodology for sampling may be varied according to the purpose of that methodology. For example, if the library is interested in an analysis of the characteristics of the user population, an extended observation form (see sample form in Part 1 of this Appendix) should be used, supplemented by a human observer. If a library wishes to track only journal titles, a simpler method—for instance, a list of titles to be checked off while reshelving journals—is appropriate. We will discuss each of these methodologies in turn.

II. SAMPLING THE PATRON CHARACTERISTICS

a. General Characteristics of Patrons

The characteristics of the major users of a given library are easily ascertained. For example, we have found that as few as 100 uses are sufficient to ascertain:

- the status of users
- the departments of major users
- the primary alert methods
- the age of the journals used
- the photocopying habits of the user population

Some of the most popular journal titles will also be identified in such a limited sampling period. However, we recommend a longer period of sampling for greater precision in the identification of journal titles.

b. Hours Sampled

The number of hours sampled will depend on the library in question. A heavily used library will require fewer sampling hours in order to achieve 100 uses. For example, Langley Library (Life Sciences), with over 5 uses per hour, could feasibly be sampled in a 20-hour period. We actually used 39 sampling hours in our study of this library, which time period accounted for 211 sample uses.

Libraries with lower use-per-hour factors might require more hours of sampling in order to discern the user characteristics. However, in 39 hours of sampling the Mathematics Library, which gave us a total of only 30 uses (less than one per hour), we were still able to discern that:

- graduate students were the primary users, followed by faculty; undergraduate usage was virtually nil
- the members of the Mathematics department were the primary users of the Mathematics journal collection
- journals were primarily accessed through a previous reference (almost 3 to 1 over browsing)
- the age of the journals used was fairly old, with only 56% being under 6 years old and 80% being under 16 years old. This was in stark contrast to the other five libraries, which had over 90% of the material accessed being under 16 years old. Thus, the Mathematics Library seems to be forced to keep more material on hand than the other libraries
- the majority of accesses did <u>not</u> result in photocopying of the article (70% were not photocopied)

The picture generated by these 30 uses in the Mathematics Library is quite lucid and the amount of time spent interviewing the user was negligible. Since it took only one to two minutes for each interview, the maximum amount of time invested was about one hour. Of course, since the observer was not the librarian, we actually invested a full 39 hours in the taking of these observations, mostly idle time.

c. The Librarian-Observer — A Definite Advantage

If a librarian were to observe his or her own library's operation, the investment of time would not be as great, since the observation form could be filled in for patrons only when they come to the library, utilizing the remainder of the time for normal duties.

Because of the facility with which the librarians can take their own observations, more hours could be sampled per term than we sampled. In order to simplify the operation, a shortened observation form is suggested, for example:

Journal Observation Form

PART 1 — To be filled in by librarian and user

Journal Title ____________________

Volume Number ____________________

Year Published ____________________

Status of User ____________________

Department of User ____________________

Alert Method ____________________

Photocopy (Yes or No)? ____________________

PART 2 — To be filled in by librarian only

Date of Interview ______________ (month, day, year)

Time of Interview ______________ (hour of day, with midnight = 0 thru 11 pm = 23 hours)

Unique Record No. ______________ (to be assigned to each observation for unique identification)

The first seven items can be filled in in the user's presence very quickly, with the remaining items being filled in by the librarian later. The entire process should take less than two or three minutes.

d. Choosing the Observation Hours

The hours of observation may vary from library to library. Because of the constraints of our research period, we sometimes did the entire sample within one school trimester. However, a librarian who is on the premises should be able to spread the sampling over a wider period of time. Furthermore, the librarian is in a position to identify high-use periods, in which many samples can be garnered in a short period of time.

One possible method of sampling would be:

(1) Set aside an entire morning, afternoon, or evening session as a "sampling period" and have the librarian collect samples throughout this period, as convenient.

(2) Have at least one morning, one afternoon, and one evening session per term.

(3) If the terms are somewhat equally heavy in usage, sample in each term.

(4) This method would give at least 9 or 10 hours of sampling per term, or 30 hours over a year's time.

(5) The sampling period can be selected randomly (using a list of random numbers) but should probably be restricted to the period from one week or so after the term begins (so that studying is under way) to about one week before the end of term (since the final week may not be typical in terms of usage). However, each librarian should make these judgments according to local usage patterns.

(6) More extensive studies can be made by simply increasing the number of sample periods.

The above method has the one disadvantage of clustering the sampling hours into morning, afternoon and evening sessions. While we do not see this as being particularly harmful, a more random approach can be taken by assigning individual "sampling hours" spread over the term's duration.

The first method—utilizing blocks of time for sampling—is somewhat easier to handle administratively; however, it does not give an even distribution of hours sampled. The second method gives an even distribution of hours, but is somewhat more demanding on the librarian who must keep track of which hours are "sampling hours."

In either case, a better sampling will be achieved if more hours are sampled. Thus, if a librarian could designate three mornings, afternoons and evenings (three of each) as "sampling times," (s)he could get about 30 hours of sampling per term, or 90 hours per year. This would give as many as 150 term uses, or 450 yearly uses, in a heavily used library. Yet, if the library is open five days a week, fifteen weeks per term, it would represent only three days out of seventy-five devoted to sampling—less than 5% of the time devoted to getting to know the user. This does not seem excessive. Furthermore, since the sampling is done "in between other duties," the actual investment of time might be on the order of fifteen minutes per sampling hour, so that a period of thirty hours of sampling might result in as little as seven to ten hours of actual time devoted to the sampling process. Given these figures on time invested, it would seem feasible that the librarian could devote such periods to a task as worthwhile as obtaining objective data on the user population.

Furthermore, if the librarian feels that these sampling methods tend to miss some of the major users (for example, the researcher who works heavily at rather sporadic intervals), (s)he can readily include this researcher's data in the sample by observing and interviewing that particular researcher whenever (s)he shows up. With this combination of random sampling and biased sampling, the picture of actual usage patterns should become even clearer.

III. PROCESSING THE DATA

While we have made heavy use of automation in processing the data for our study, this is not a strict necessity. At five or six uses per hour, a ten-hour sample consists of only 50 - 60 observation forms. These can be tallied by hand. One tally sheet can be devised for each data field; for example, the "status" tally sheet might be divided as follows:

STATUS

Graduate & Post-doctoral	Undergraduate	Faculty	Staff	Visitor	Other	Unknown

At the end of the sampling period, the tallies for each field are simply entered into the tally sheet and a running total is kept from one period to the next.

These tallies can then be converted into relative percentages by simple division (e.g., 32 graduate students out of 50 users = 64%). While more esoteric statistics are possible, the relative percentages of each type of user, alert method, etc., have proven highly useful in our study. These descriptive statistics are the foundation upon which predictive statistics and simulations can be built.

In order to study the interaction of two variables, we simply construct a matrix. For example, an abbreviated matrix for status times photocopy might be:

		STATUS		
		Graduate	Undergraduate	Faculty
Photo?	Yes			
	No			

We first enter the raw tallies, then convert these raw tallies to relative frequencies (percentages), for example:

STATUS

Photo?		Graduate	Undergraduate	Faculty
	Yes			
	No			

which would indicate that the graduate students do proportionately more photocopying than the rest of the users.

The purpose of starting with raw tallies, e.g.:

	Graduate	Undergraduate	Faculty	Total
Yes	45	10	7	62
No	5	10	13	28
Total	50	20	20	90

is that we can use various totals in order to compute the relative percentages. For example, if we are interested in computing the relative proportion of photocopying "within" each user group, we use the column totals. Thus, the graduate students have:

Yes 45/50 = 95%
No 5/50 = 5%

The completed matrix of relative frequencies for this analysis is the matrix given immediately above.

However, if we ask the question, "Among those who photocopy ("Yes" row), what is the proportion of users doing the photocopying?," we use the row totals:

	Graduate	Undergraduate	Faculty	Total
Yes	45/62 = 72.6%	10/62 = 16.1%	7/62 = 11.3%	62/62 = 100%
No	5/62 = 8.1%	10/62 = 16.1%	13/62 = 21.0%	28/28 = 100%

In this case, the <u>row</u> percentages must sum to 100%, while the <u>column</u> percentages will normally not sum to 100%.

One further cut at the data can be made by using the grand total (90 in this example) as the denominator of each fraction. This gives the percentages relative to the entire population. However, in general, we have not found these percentages to be as useful as the row and column percentages.

Further analysis can be performed on these matrices by methods such as the chi-square method, which are described in most statistics textbooks.

IV. A PROBLEM

One problem exists in creating the matrices when hand tallying: either the matrix must exist from the beginning—that is, we must anticipate the question—or the original raw data must be preserved. There is no way to tell from the summary data on "status":

Graduate	Undergraduate	Faculty	Total
50	20	20	90

what proportion of the graduates did photocopy and which proportion did not photocopy.

Since it is difficult to anticipate all questions, we recommend that the raw data be preserved, at least until the time at which enough data have been examined to enable one to anticipate most questions that might arise.

As the number of questions on interactions between two or more variables increases, the job of hand tallying becomes more difficult. At this point some automation techniques should be considered. For example, the data can be keypunched onto hollerith cards, and these cards can then be submitted to a statistical package, such as "SPSS" (Statistical Package for the Social Sciences). If an installation does not have such a statistical package, a satisfactory job can be done with two computer programs—one that calculates the relative frequencies, and one that calculates the cross-tabulations (matrices). These are not difficult programs to write, so that the job could typically be handled by the local data processing personnel.

V. USAGE OF PARTICULAR JOURNALS

So far, we have concentrated on the usage characteristics that are most easily obtained: status of user, department of user, alert method, amount of photocopying, and cross-tabulations among these variables.

We now turn to the usage of particular journals. The questions most frequently asked by us were:

- Which journals are used?
- Which journals are not used?
- What is the age of the journals that are used?

The last question—the age of the journal used—is the most easily answered. As we have indicated above, the relative proportion of new (say under 6 years old) to old (6 years and over) journals being accessed can be indicated with as few as 100 observations.

a. Age of Journals Used

This age factor is important when considering storage of the older journals: should it be primary storage? secondary storage? should they be stored at all?

While age itself is a factor, it is also meaningful to consider the age of the journals used by different user groups. For example, do Mathematics users use "older" material more than Physics users? While our study indicated that in all disciplines there is more use of new materials than of old, we did discover that various disciplines seem to use the older materials more often than the newer materials. In fact, we did find that the users in the Physics department accessed the more recent publications much more than the users in the Mathematics and Chemistry departments. Of course, if a particular library has a strictly disciplinary clientele, this interaction effect of department might not be significant. However, interactions between the age of the journal and the alert method used to access that journal (e.g., "Are older journals accessed because of class assignments?"), or between age and status (e.g., "Do the graduate students access more older material than the faculty?"), or age and photocopying (e.g., "Are more older journals photocopied?") should prove enlightening.

The more difficult question to answer is the question most pertinent to evaluating our acquisitions policies: "Which journals are used, and which are not used?" This is the next question to be addressed.

b. Titles of Journals Used

The easiest prediction to make is that a great number of titles in the journal collection will either not be used at all or will receive little usage. It is somewhat more difficult to predict <u>all</u> of the titles that will not be used. However, we advocate an evolutionary policy whereby a certain number of the unused titles might be considered for subscription cancellation, with the other titles remaining in the collection. If this periodic review occurred once or twice a year, a portion of the unused titles could be weeded out over a period of a few years. The handling of the weeding in this periodic, evolutionary fashion should forestall great outcries from faculty and students at once-and-for-all drastic reductions in the size of the collection. Furthermore, the consideration of a limited number of titles for cancellation would allow the librarian to forewarn the library's clientele of the proposed reductions and consider any objections that might be raised to the proposed cuts. The sampling of the user population, as described above, should serve to identify the clientele needing notification. In the absence of objections to any proposed cuts, the librarian can feel reinforced in the decision to drop the subscriptions in question.

c. Sampling the Titles

The sample of the journal titles actually being accessed can be carried out in conjunction with the above sample of users. In a 30-hour sampling period, with about 150 uses, we can safely predict that one-third to one-half of the journal titles will be in the "zero-use" category. These titles can then be examined individually on a "keep/drop" basis. However, an examination of one-third to one-half of the collection is a lengthy process. And, if we project yearly usage, many of the sample's "zero-use" items would see some usage over a year's time. Thus, in making the economically crucial decisions about keeping and dropping journal subscriptions, it might be wise to employ a longer sampling period.

An abbreviated form could be used for tracking titles only. At specified periods during the year, the person(s) who are responsible for reshelving journals that have been used can be instructed to either: (1) check off the titles used on a pre-printed list of titles; or, if this is too cumbersome, (2) jot down the titles for later processing against the title list. As before, the hours sampled can be assigned randomly. We simply emphasize here that a longer sampling period is justified when making the decision to continue or discontinue a subscription.

Of course, this abbreviated method does not allow us to attach these titles to any specific user population. Yet, it would seem that the shorter sampling period mentioned above should suffice for a general picture of the user population.

In notifying the users of potential discontinuances, the librarian cannot be expected to contact the less frequent users. Furthermore, the impact of a discontinuance on an infrequent user should generally not be so great as the impact on a regular user.

d. Projecting Sample Usage into Yearly Usage

As the number of sample uses is usually quite small, we would like to be able to estimate the yearly usage from the sample usage. One method of doing this is to use a "Multiplying Factor" that is based on the percent of time sampled.

For example, if a sample was taken during 30 hours of a term, and the library was open for 1,000 hours during that term, we could use a multiplying factor of 1,000/30 or 33 1/3 to project "term usage." Furthermore, if there are three terms in a school year, we can then multiply the number of term uses by 3 in order to project the yearly usage. Thus, if our 30-hour sample showed 150 uses, we would project the term usage as:

$$150 \times 33\ 1/3 = 5{,}000 \text{ uses per term}$$

The yearly usage would be:

$$5{,}000 \text{ uses/term} \times 3 \text{ terms/year} = 15{,}000 \text{ uses/year}$$

e. Calculating Cost per Use

A crude calculation of the cost per use can be made from the subscription expenditures that the library has incurred. For example, if the subscription expenditure for the current year is $25,000, and the projected yearly usage is 15,000 uses, we have an average cost per use of:

$$\$25{,}000 / 15{,}000 \text{ uses} = \$1.67 \text{ per use}$$

This cost figure is an underestimate, since it does not take account of the fixed costs, such as storage space, personnel salaries, etc., nor the variable costs involved in processing the journals, such as binding the journals for storage, reshelving journals, etc. In our study these costs were generally about 20% - 25% of the total. Thus, the librarian can simply add about one-quarter to one-fifth of the subscription cost to the subscription cost to obtain a truer figure. Using the one-quarter additional cost rule, our cost per use would increase from $1.67 to $2.09 per use:

$$\$1.67 + \$0.42 = \$2.09$$

Whether this cost per use would be considered high or low depends on both local judgment and on the standard for university libraries, which has not yet been ascertained. In fact, such a standard will not be ascertained until more university libraries attempt to track their usage patterns.

f. Three Decisions[4]

Three types of decisions need to be made by the librarian:

(1) Decision to continue or discontinue a particular title
(2) Decision to acquire or not acquire a new title
(3) Decision about weeding particular volumes

Each of these decisions can be aided by a different type of distribution The first decision, to continue to discontinue a particular item, can look to the "history of the title." Has the title actually been used during the sample period? The second decision, to acquire or not acquire, can be considered with the help of the projected percent of collection used. This distribution presents the probability of a given title's being used heavily or not, abstracting from any other information about the individual title. The third question —weeding—can make use of the data on aging. How old are the volumes that the users of the journal collection are accessing?

VI. USAGE PER PERSON

Another statistic that has proven useful—and may be easy to come by—is the number of journal uses per person. The number of persons in the departments identified as major users can usually be ascertained from either that department or from the school's official statistics. Thus, a breakdown as to the number of faculty, graduate students and undergraduate students in the "potential user" population might be:

Faculty	23	
Graduate	98	
Undergraduate	432	Total: 553

We then ascertain the number of sample uses, broken down by status:

Faculty	20	
Graduate	120	
Undergraduate	150	Total: 150

and project these into term uses:

Faculty	667	
Graduate	4,000	
Undergraduate	333	Total: 5,000

---

4 The author is indebted to Donald W. King for pointing out the need to highlight these three different decisions, and the three distinct distributions, one applicable to each decision. Personal conversation.

Then divide the projected uses per term by the number of persons in that status group in order to get the index of uses per person per term:

Status Category	Projected Term Usage	No. Persons in Status Category	Uses per Person per Term
Faculty	667	23	29
Graduate	4,000	98	40.8
Undergraduate	333	432	0.77
Total:	5,000	553	9.04

So that we see that the faculty and graduate students are well above average users of the journal collection in this hypothetical library, with the undergraduate students barely using the collection.

This statistic of uses per person normalizes the usage data to take into account differences in the population size of various status groups. It can as easily be applied to a comparison of usage figures per department.

The choice of restricting the uses per person to a single term was made in order to avoid the fluctuations in enrollment that occur over an entire school year.

VII. PROJECTING THE PERCENT OF THE COLLECTION USED A GIVEN NUMBER OF TIMES

One question we have asked is: "How many of the journals will be accessed one time, two times, three times, etc., in a given year?" This question can be answered by projecting the sample usage figures into yearly usage figures.

For example, in our sample we may find that 95% of the collection was used less than 10 times per title; 75% of the collection was used less than 5 times per title; and 65% of the collection was not used at all.

We can plot these figures on logarithmic probability paper, then use the multiplying factor to draw a parallel line, which line will represent the yearly usage figures. As an example, we present the calculations for the Physics Library.

The sample for the Physics Library showed the following usage:

No. Uses (less than)	% of Collection
15	98%
13	97.7%
12	97.3%
11	97%
10	96.3%
8	96%
7	95.3%
6	94.3%
5	91.3%
4	88.6%
3	84.2%
2	78.2%
1	63.1%

Plotting these values on the logarithmic probability paper, we get the results shown in Figure 27. Note that the number of uses is plotted on the vertical or Y-axis, the percent of journals falling below that usage is plotted on the horizontal or X-axis.

We then attempt to draw a straight line through these points. The line will normally be an approximation, since not all sample points will conveniently fall on the straight line. This is shown in Figure 28.

We next project the sample number of uses into yearly number of uses by utilizing the multiplying factor. In our study of the Physics Library, the multiplying factor was 22.5, so that we increase each category of usage by this amount. Thus, 15 uses in the sample become 338 uses over a year's time. Ten sample uses become 225 yearly uses. One sample use becomes 22.5 or 23 yearly uses. The percent of collection falling below a certain number of uses remains the same; that is, in plotting the new points, we simply plot them directly above the old points. This is shown in Figure 29.

Having plotted two or three "projected points," we can now draw a line parallel to the original line. This parallel line represents the yearly usage figures, as in Figure 30.

We then read the yearly projections from this new line. For example, since the new line crosses the X-axis at about 4%, we can expect only 4% of the collection to go unused over a year's time. Or, looking at the figure of "2 uses or less," we see that 10% of the collection can be expected to have two or fewer uses during the course of the year.

These graphs, as well as a summarized explanation of their usage, are also discussed in Part 1 of this Appendix.

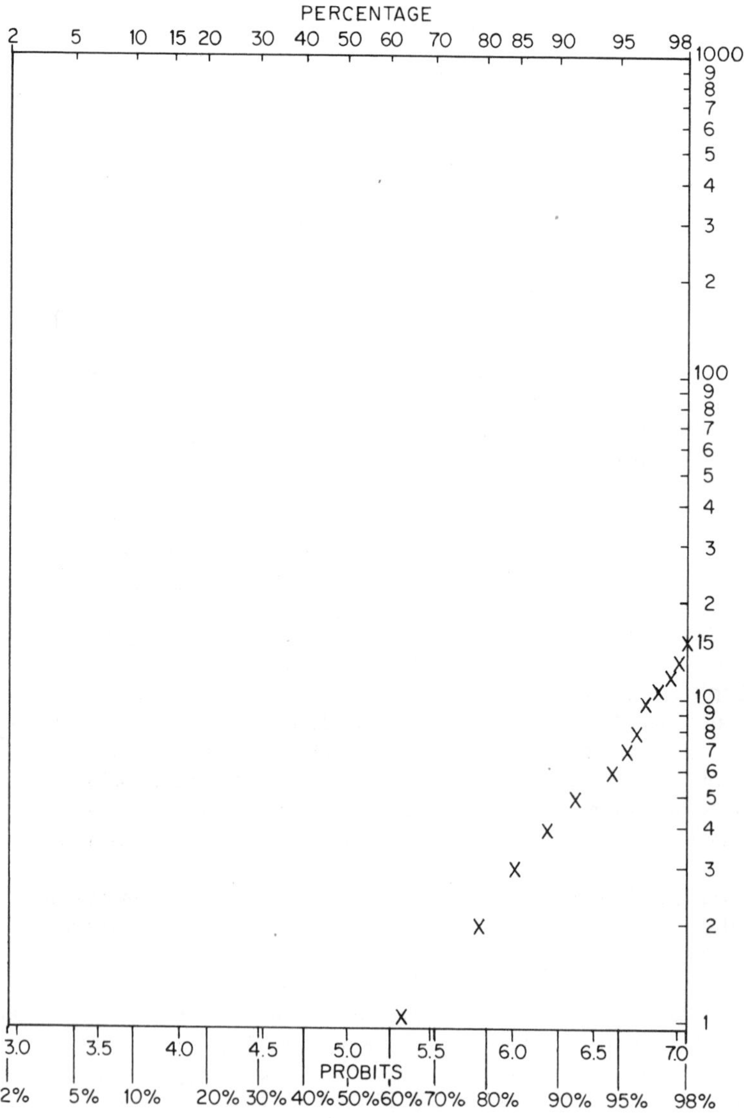

Figure 27.

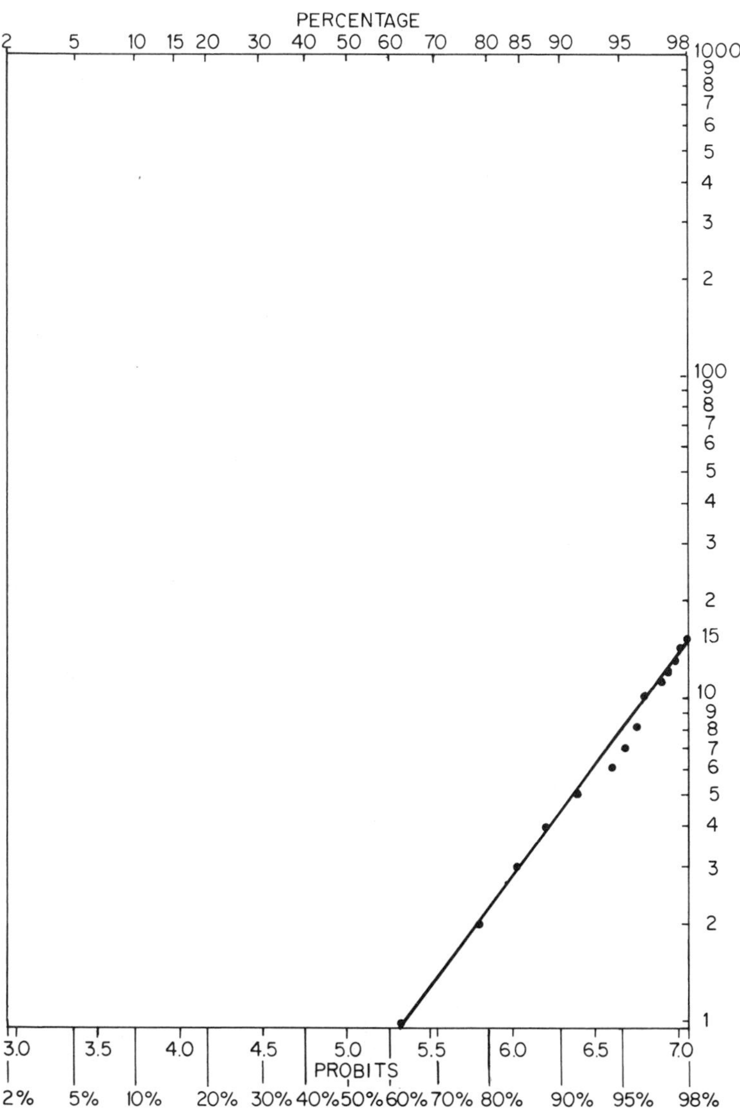
PERCENTAGE
2 5 10 15 20 30 40 50 60 70 80 85 90 95 98
1000 9 8 7 6 5 4 3 2
100 9 8 7 6 5 4 3 2
15
10 9 8 7 6 5 4 3 2
1
3.0 3.5 4.0 4.5 5.0 5.5 6.0 6.5 7.0
PROBITS
2% 5% 10% 20% 30% 40% 50% 60% 70% 80% 90% 95% 98%

Figure 28.

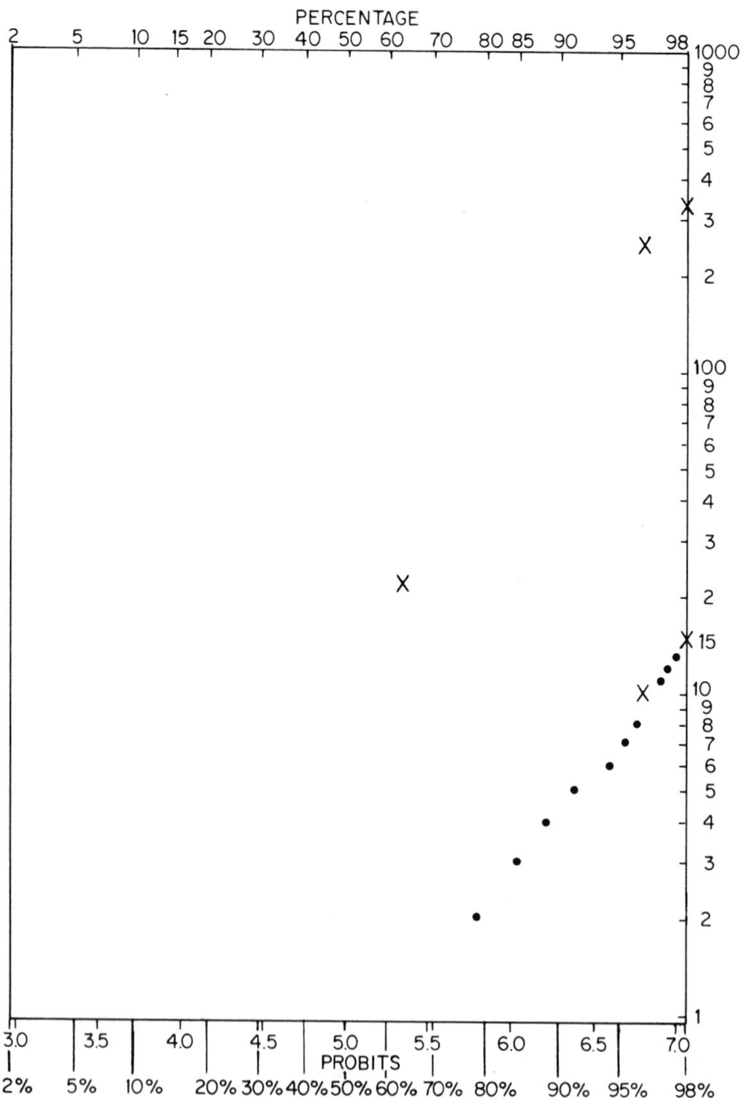
PERCENTAGE
2 5 10 15 20 30 40 50 60 70 80 85 90 95 98
1000 9 8 7 6 5 4 3 2 100 9 8 7 6 5 4 3 2 15 10 9 8 7 6 5 4 3 2 1
3.0 3.5 4.0 4.5 5.0 5.5 6.0 6.5 7.0
PROBITS
2% 5% 10% 20% 30% 40% 50% 60% 70% 80% 90% 95% 98%

Figure 29.

Physics
*22.5

298 Titles — 439 Uses
110 Titles Used

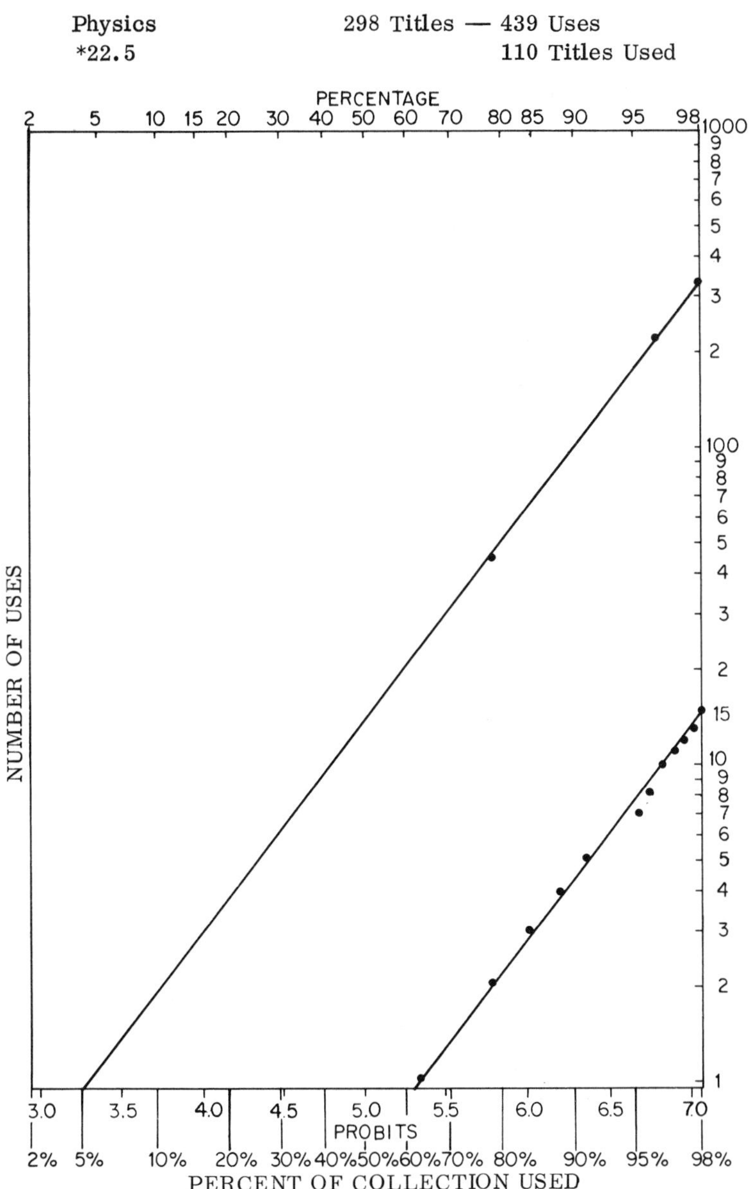

Figure 30.

VIII. CONCLUSION

The main point of this section of the Appendix is to show that with very little investment of time and effort, and no automation whatsoever, any library can track its own usage patterns, and then utilize these patterns to provide better service to its clientele. Service will be provided more economically, as unused items will be dropped, and it will be provided more personally, as knowing the major portion of the clientele will enable the librarian to notify them of proposed changes in operation, solicit their recommendations, etc.

With extended investment of time and money, and with good automation facilities, a more detailed study would be possible. However, this large an investment is not a necessary ingredient for the process described here.

Part 3

THE MANAGEMENT AND "MARKETING" OF THE JOURNAL COLLECTION

I. A MANAGEMENT MODEL

While we have implied that the low-use journals are likely candidates for having their subscriptions discontinued, this is not the only decision available to the librarian. Alternative courses of action could be taken to increase usage of the low-use journals.

In regard to usage and cost, there is a four-fold division:

(1) high use - low cost
(2) high use - high cost
(3) low use - high cost
(4) low use - low cost

The high-use, low-cost journals would almost certainly be candidates for retention. They are the most economical, and the high use-to-cost ratio (or low cost per use) makes the easy accessibility of a local holding attractive.

The low-use, high-cost journals are the least desirable. One pays a lot for very little benefit in actual use. Both the high-use, high-cost and the low-use, low-cost categories are enigmatic. In the first instance (high-use, high-cost), the question would be: "Can we reduce the cost by alternative means <u>without</u> a major hindrance in usage?" To answer this question, we might want to study the usage pattern by alert method, age of issues used, user, and user need for quick response in order to determine whether the item must be kept locally or not. For example, a journal accessed by previous reference, with a response need of more than a day, might be provided through resource sharing. A journal accessed primarily through browsing, with a need for immediate response, will find the usage hindered through resource sharing (e.g., a journal whose aim is current awareness does not lend itself to remote access). We therefore have a conflict in this case: the cost of keeping the journal indicates discontinuance at the local level, while the mode of access demands local availability. It is in these decisions that the librarian must exercise careful judgment, considering the "worth" of the usage in non-monetary terms (e.g., it is a prestige journal, or it spurs on significant research).

The low-use, low-cost journals are another enigma. They neither cost much to keep locally nor contribute much to the library's service. The high-use, low-cost journals can be described as "economical and fruitful." The high-use, high-cost journals are "fruitful but not economical"; the low-use, low-cost journals are "economical but not fruitful"; the low-use, high-cost journals are neither "economical nor fruitful."

Let us discuss the case of the non-fruitful journals. In deciding whether or not to keep the low-use, low-cost journals, the question to be asked is whether they are of value in terms other than the "number of uses." That is, whether they represent particularly important research; whether they are historically important; whether they are prestigious in the field; and so on. If so, perhaps they should be retained on the subscription list. But usage must be increased if an economic rationale for their retention is to be available.

There are a variety of ways in which this can be achieved—all well known to librarians; three possible approaches are:

(1) The librarian could personally promote the use of these journals;

(2) The librarian could encourage faculty to promote such use;

(3) Both (1) and (2) could be implemented; that is, both librarian and faculty could encourage use of the journals in question.

The librarian could take measures similar to those taken in the Physics Library: prominent displays, well publicized, at regular periods. These displays could be of the journal itself, or of prominent articles related to current interests of the users, as defined by the courses being offered or research in progress.

Or, if on consultation none of the faculty considers the journal to be important, the librarian might want to reconsider the evaluation. If this evaluation of "worth" still stands, then the librarian must so persuade the faculty. If not, the journal should probably be dropped. The most likely case would be that one or two faculty members consider the journal important; in this case, greater use of the journal must be achieved through inclusion in class assignments, and such methods.

The high-cost journals could be treated in similar fashion. For example, the non-economical but fruitful high-cost, high-usage journals could be made economical on a cost-per-use basis by increasing the number of uses. Even the low-use, high-cost journals could be made economical by increasing the usage, although the usage must be increased by an even greater proportion.

Considering the three variables of "use," "cost" and "value," we have eight possible outcomes (Table 130).

Table 130

USE	COST	VALUE	POSSIBLE DECISIONS
High	Low	Low	Keep the journal. Although the low value suggests that it should be dropped, the high usage indicates that it is seen as valuable by some, possibly as entertainment. It seems like a good buy.
High	High	Low	Possibly discontinue the subscription. High use indicates that people want it, but at what price? Would they subsidize it? Yet, discontinuance may cause hard feelings; can the cost here be subsidized by the lower cost per use of the more economical journals? This case requires further study: who uses the journal? why? will a less costly alternative suffice? does an alternative exist?
High	High	High	Keep the journal. This journal is used and is valuable and the cost should be subsidized. However, alternative means should also be explored. Study the use patterns: user, alert method, need for physical copy, desirable access time, age of issues consulted, and so on.
High	Low	High	A winner! Keep it. It is used, valuable and cheap—an endangered species.
Low	Low	Low	Consider dropping this journal. Nobody considers it to be worth anything, neither the user nor the expert judges; so the low cost is not really low if supporting "junk."
Low	High	Low	Drop this journal. Nobody likes it and the high cost cannot be justified.
Low	Low	High	Increase the usage. If it is judged valuable, promote it so that it becomes high-use, low-cost, as well as high-value.
Low	High	High	Increase the usage, which will put it in the subsidized category, but it is probably worth it.

The above classification enables the librarian to blend hard data with intuitive judgment. Decisions are not cut and dried; they are merely clearer, enabling the librarian to choose among alternatives. In only two cases (the high-use, high-value, low-cost item and the low-use, low-value, high-cost item) are the decisions obvious. In all other cases, the judgment can go either way, with the decisions taken reflecting the managerial style of the librarian, the interests of the faculty, and the influence of the users. It is the data that enable us to decide between alternatives that have now been delineated.

II. "PEELING THE ONION"

While we advocated complete tracking of titles in the first part of this report, an alternative method can be employed. A sample period of 40 - 50 hours could be set aside in order to identify high-use versus low-use journals. The high-use journals that are low-cost would be kept. High-use, high-cost journals would be subjected to further scrutiny in terms of the users and their habits of use.

The low-use, low-value journals would be discontinued. Low-use, high-value journals would be marketed more vigorously. The results of the marketing effort would be sampled to see whether any of the journals in question move into the "high-use" category as a result. If not, continue marketing; but if all marketing efforts by both librarian and faculty fail to increase usage, then the estimate of "value" must be reconsidered—valuable to whom? for what? It would seem that they are not valuable to the users; possibly they have a nice cover? a persuasive salesman? or a falsely-held good reputation?

This type of sampling reduces the number of journals that need to be "tracked." With successive cuts that result in keeping the good journals and weeding the unproductive ones, a smaller and smaller proportion of the collection needs to be tracked on a continuous basis, although periodic checks to see if the usage has changed are not only desirable, but necessary. However, by this time the situation should be under control: the librarian should be driving the journals, rather than the journals driving the librarian!

INDEX

Academic department, of users of journals, 59
Academic status, of users of journals, 59, 86
Acquisitions, books, 1969-1975, circulation, 17
Acquisitions, journals, cost analysis for six science libraries, 157
Age, of journals, definition, 64
  usage, 60, 77, 240, 242
Aging, of book collections, 13
Alert method, journals, definition, 64
  and age, 80
  and photocopying, 84
  and use, 60, 78, 242
    and user status, 93, 95
Alternative levels of book use, hypothetical costs, 174
Asymptotic regression analysis, of circulations, 9

Background of the study, 1-7
Baumol, Wm. J., 167
Bear, Donald V. T., 170
Bellassai, Marcia C., 74
Benefit, in terms of use, 44, 170
  measurement, 2
Bernhardt, Homer, 104
Books and monographs, circulation and in-house use, 9-55
    measure of output, 163
  cost, minimizing by resource sharing, 196
Bradford-Zipf distribution, of circulation, 38

Browsing, and book use, 10
  and journal use, 57, 78
Budgetary data, Hillman Library, 144
Bulick, Stephen, 9-55

Chemistry, journal usage, 58-104, 216
Circulation, 9-55
  external vs. in-house, 25
  frequency, 19
  unique items, 12
  use by LC class, 10
Clapp, Verner, 202
Class assignment, and journal use, 80
Cohen, Jacob, 105-159, 161-187, 189-198
Collection behavior, predicted, 53
Collection size vs. usage, 69
Collection use, cost data, 10
Computer programs, journal study, 213
Computer Science, journal usage, 58-104, 216
  subscription costs, 121
Core collection, 49
Cost of book use, inter-year comparisons, 115
  measuring, 105, 107
Cost, inter-year comparisons, 115
Cost of journal use, 76, 124, 256
  measurement, 116
Cost-benefit model of library operations, 161-187
  book use, 163
Cost center, cost analysis of book use, 132
  risk in ordering books, 136

Cost-effectiveness via resource sharing models, measurement, 196
Coursework, relationship of use, 43
Current collection, definition, 64
Current subscription titles, 75

Data collection, books and monographs, 11
Data gathering, journal usage, 60
Data reduction, journal usage, 63
De Gennaro, Richard, 3
Decisions, storage, 51
Decision-making, influence of the use study, 199
Decision model for book purchase, 126
 variables, 127
Department of user, definition, 64
Dernburg, Thomas F., 171
Dialectic on resource sharing, 190
Distributed network, 204
Drake, Miriam A., 45, 50, 88

Economical journals, 70
Economics of materials' use, 105-159
Economic model of library operations, 162
Economies of increasing book use, 172
Engineering, journal subscription costs and journal use, 119
 journal use, 58-104, 216
Excluded costs, 105
External versus in-house circulation, 25. See also Circulation.

Faculty, journal usage, 90
First-time use, predicting, 20
Fixed costs, 105
 cost benefit model, 164
Flynn, Roger, 9-55, 57-104, 207-268
Frase, Robert W., 90
Frequency of use, circulation, 9, 38
Fussler, Herman H., 3, 13, 26, 31, 48, 50
Future needs, forecasting, 2
Future use, predicting, 19

Galvin, T., 161
Gore, Daniel, 55
Graduate students, journal usage, 86

Hayes, Robert N., 161, 162
Hierarchical network, 204
Hillman Library, locus of the study, 5
Hypotheses of the study, 6

Imputed fixed cost, 108
Inflation, allowance, 115
In-house use, books and monographs, 6, 10
 sampling, 25
Interlibrary loan, 10, 31
Items vs. titles, 12

Jain, A. K., 48, 49
James, D. E., 168
Jordan, Robert, 202
Journal(s), definition, 65
 use, 57-104, 207-268
  and photocopying, 83
  and subscription costs, 116, 256
  titles most used, 59
Journal collection, management and marketing, 265-268

Kent, Allen, 1-7, 161, 189-205
Kern, James R., 126
King, Donald W., 74, 257

Knox, William T., 202
Kountz, John, 162

Lacy, Dan, 202
Language of books, use, 43
Library of Congress classes, use patterns, 45
 cost analysis, 128
 mean cost per transaction, 135
 risk in ordering books, 137
Library operations, cost benefit model, 161-187
Library quality vs. budget, 3
Life sciences, journal usage, 58-104, 216
 and subscription costs, 118
Local acquisitions, alternatives, 189-198
Log normal distribution, circulation, 38
Lovell, Michael C., 161
Lumsden, Keith C., 170

Marcus, Matityahu, 167
Marginal costs, cost benefit model, 166
Mathematics, journal usage, 58-104, 216
 and subscription costs, 122
McDougall, Duncan M., 171
McGrath, William E., 134
McKenzie, Richard B., 161
Mean acquisition cost/transaction, 127
Measuring cost-benefit over time, 173
Measuring benefits, 170
Missing observations, journal usage, 99
Model, cost benefit, for library operations, 161-187
 of resource sharing networks, 204
Monographs, circulation and in-house use, 9-55. See also Books.
Montgomery, K. Leon, 199-205
Morse, P. M., 13, 48

Neumann, Robert, 105
Nonpurchase of books, criteria, 42
Nonsubstitutability, cost benefit model, 172

Observation period, definition, 64
Obsolete books, cost benefit model, 167
Officer, Lawrence H., 161
Official list of titles in the collection, definition, 64
Older journals, use, 77
Olsen, H. A., 115
Optimality, 187
 of library operations over time, 166

Palmour, Vernon E., 74, 202
Patron characteristics, journals, 57, 86, 247
Permanent storage, of journals, and use, 81
Personal communication, and journal use, 80
Photocopying of journals, 57, 82
 definition, 64
Physics, journal usage, 58-104, 216
 and subscription costs, 117
Pierce, Thomas J., 134
Predicting usage, journals, 93, 244
Previous reference, definition, 64
 and journal use, 79
Projected uses, journals, definition, 64
 yearly, 66, 221
Psychology, journal usage, 58-104, 216
Publishers, implications of the use study, 202

Quandt, R. E., 38
Questionnaire, journal use study, 209

Replacement value of books, 106
Reserve book room item use, 31
Resource sharing, 189
  constraints, 195
  functions, 194
  goals, 193
Risk in ordering books, 134
Roderer, Nancy K., 74

Sabor, William N., 9-55
Sample uses, definition, 63, 65
  journals, 61, 65, 247, 255
  reliability, 44
Sampling algorithms, 10, 43
Samuelson, Paul A., 162
Scully, Malcolm G., 202
Shaw, W. M., 74
Shelf space availability, 52
Simon, Julian L., 3, 13, 26, 31, 48, 50
Simulation techniques, in assessing cost benefit, 205
Staff, definition, 92
  journal use, 91
Status of user, definition, 64
Stiefel, Leanna, 161
Storage, decisions, 51
Strasser, Alexander, 59
Student(s), enrollment, standardizing the data, 185
  journal use, 86
Subscription costs, measurement, 116
Substitutability, cost benefit model, 171
Summer months, journal usage, 100

Taxonomy of resource sharing networks, 203
Throsby, C.D., 168
Title, definition, 64
  vs. item, 12
  journal use, 229, 254

Transaction, cost, 107
  definition, 64
Trueswell, R. W., 13, 48, 49, 50
Tullock, Gordon, 161

Undergraduate students, journal usage, 88
Usage, economics, 105-159
Use of books. See also Circulation.
  change over time, 13
  and collection size, 69
  and cost, 107
  and coursework, 43
  cumulative, 16
  first time, 14
  frequency, 38
  by Library of Congress class, 45
  types, 42
  of unique items, 12
Use of journals, 57-104, 207-268
  by age, 77, 240, 254
  by alert method, 78, 242
  categories, 69
  definition, 61, 63
  by departments, 95, 245
  hourly, 65
  per person, 66, 91, 243, 257
  photocopying, 64
  projections, 72, 221, 244, 256
  by title, 67, 69, 229, 254
Use model, predictive ability, 22
User, definition, 64
Utility, of books, 164

Variable costs, 105
  cost-benefit model, 164

WEBNET, 7, 204
Weeding, 48
Wiederkehr, Robert R. V., 74
Williams, Alan, 162
Williams, James G., 189-205
Wolfe, J. N., 162

Zenk, Margaret L., 52